Created and Directed by Hans Höfer

INSIGHT GUIDES

Yemen

Project Editor: Joachim Chwaszcza
Advisor: Dr. Werner Daum
Photographs by Lyle Lawson and Joachim Chwaszcza
Editor: Dieter Vogel
Translated by Susan James and Barbara König

APA PUBLICATIONS

Yemen

Second Edition
© **1992 APA PUBLICATIONS (HK) LTD**
All Rights Reserved
Printed in Singapore by Höfer Press Pte. Ltd

ABOUT THIS BOOK

For many centuries Yemen has been a magnet for travellers from all over the world – but its gates remained resolutely locked. Isolated from the outside world by its rulers, the Zaidi Imams, and by the reserve and pride of its mountain tribes, the sovereign territory of Yemen kept foreigners at bay. After the revolution and a prolonged civil war, the North relied on its own strength for development.

The South, which a few years later threw off the yoke of the British empire, continued to keep its gates locked. Only selected groups were allowed to travel in South Yemen – and then only under strict official supervision. But suddenly, in May 1990, the situation changed with the long-awaited but nevertheless abrupt unification of the two halves of the country. One of the consequences of this spectacular development is that whole new areas of Yemen have now been opened up to tourism, presenting even the most seasoned of Yemen travellers with new and fascinating routes and destinations.

Two Into One

Apa Publications was quick to react to the new situation and began work on updating its popular *Insight Guide: Yemen* with all the latest information. The book's Project Editor, **Joachim Chwaszcza**, was one of the first foreigners to visit the newly created Republic of Yemen after the Gulf War. A freelance writer and photo-journalist living in Munich, he has written reports in various journals, has published a picture book about Mahayana Buddhism, and was responsible for Apa's Insight Guides to Sardinia and the South Tyrol, and its Cityguide to Prague. After numerous trips to Yemen, he knows and appreciates the country and its culture.

Chwaszcza assembled for this book a remarkable collection of authors and photographers. **Dr Werner Daum**, for example, the ambassador of the German Federal Republic in Albania, spent many years at the German embassy in Sana'a and Aden. He is one of the most respected experts on Yemen. Daum has published numerous books and essays, including a book about the Queen of Sheba, and arranged the famous Yemen exhibition in Munich.

Dr Yusuf Muhammed Abdallah has written the article about pre-Islamic history. The author is known as one of the most prolific scientists and archaeologists in Yemen. In addition to his lecture activities in Sana'a, he also holds visiting professorships in Minnesota and Marburg. As dean at the University of Sana'a, he is involved in research and science teaching.

Rudolf E. Bollinger is a freelance journalist who works as a consultant for various institutes in a number of countries. He is a member of the International Institute for Strategic Studies in London and of the European Institute for Security in Luxembourg. He wrote about the independence struggle in the South and the civil war in North Yemen for German journals such as *Die Zeit*.

Fritz Piepenburg has been living since 1975 in Yemen, where he works as a translator and language teacher. He is the Yemen correspondent for the weekly *Middle East Times* and the author of numerous articles in various English and German journals.

Joke Buringa is a Dutch anthropologist interested in medicine and the role of women. She lived in the Yemen Arabic Republic for

Chwaszcza

Daum

Bollinger

Piepenburg

three years and participated in field studies and development projects.

American **Jeff Meissner** lived in Sana'a for several years and was head of the American Institute for Yemeni Studies there. Meissner wrote his doctorate on the tribes of Yemen and is regarded as one of the experts in this field.

Jalel Buagga was born in Tunisia and lives in Paris. He is an ethnologist and sociologist who has travelled in Arab countries, particularly Yemen and Ethiopia, for many years. For this book, he has written the sections describing the southern regions and the Harraz mountains.

Frenchman **Pascal Privet** lived in Ta'izz in the early 1970s and took some of the first tourist groups through North Yemen. At that time, one could enter Yemen only via Ethiopia and Ta'izz. Privet produces documentary films on ethnological themes.

The third Frenchman in our team of authors is **Marc de Gouvernain**. Like his compatriots, his connections with Yemen go as far back as 20 years. Marc de Gouvernain has explored many of the country's walking treks and acts as a guide for tour groups going trekking in Yemen.

Werner Lingenau is a specialist in the development of Arab towns and worked for a number of years in the Office for the Restoration of Old Towns in Sana'a.

Peter H. Hellmuth is a teacher who has pursued his interest in the Arab world through many travels in the region – to both Yemeni states since 1975 – and has developed a deep commitment to the area. He has been vice-chairman of the German-Yemen Society responsible for Tourism since 1982.

Ahmed O'Shaish, who was born in the town of Rada'a and trained as a technical flight engineer in the United States, wrote the section on practical travel hints in Sana'a, where he now lives.

True Impressions

Most of the pictures in this book are by Joachim Chwaszcza, who tried not to produce romanticised clichés about Yemen but to give the reader a vivid impression of the true conditions there – without, however, impinging on the strict rules laid down in Yemen about taking photographs.

The majority of the remaining pictures were taken by **Lyle Lawson**, who in particular contributed the pictures of women.

Special thanks are due to Mr **Abdul Wahab Sadaka** of the Frankfurt office of the Yemeni airline Yemenia, who generously and unflinchingly lent his support to the task of updating this book to take account of the latest political changes. In Heidelberg, **Burkhard Schild** of Minitrek was always ready with help and advice for the editor, and in Munich **Tony Halliday** supervised the translation of the new material into English. In Yemen itself, Mr **Abdulkarim Abu Taleb** contributed to the success of this often far from easy project.

—APA Publications

Buringa

Buagga

Privet

Lawson

Hellmuth

History and Culture

Places

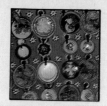

Maps

TRAVEL TIPS

**For detailed information
see page 313**

Whether or not she actually came from from Ma'rib in modern-day Yemen, the Queen of Sheba is surrounded by a sense of mystery and an air of unimaginable wealth and luxury. She was able to attain this wealth because the trade route for frankincense led through this country on the shores of the Red Sea. It came to be known as *Arabia felix*; the "fortunate Arabia" of the ancient world, fortunate not only because of the wealth generated by its trade, but also by the climate, considered favourable by the standards of the Arabian peninsula– the "green Yemen".

Hundreds of years later, coffee was the source of wealth, and even now a type of coffee bears the name of a port in Yemen–Mocha. And Aden, the "white man's grave", became the bridgehead to India.

Again and again over the centuries, explorers and adventurers have tried to enter the forbidden kingdom: Lodovico di Varthema, Carsten Niebuhr, Joseph Arnaud, Hermann Burchardt, Freya Stark and Hans Helfritz. Their reports and the artifacts they brought with them hint at fantastic splendours. In 1952 the Imam of the time, Ahmed, gave the American, Wendell Phillips, permission to carry out excavations in Ma'rib, but only for a short time–then the team had to leave the country in a hurry.

Even today, there is an air of adventure and romance about Yemen. Sana'a, with its breathtaking beauty, the dark suq and the veiled women, seem to transport the traveller back to the Arab Middle Ages. The proud *gabilis*, tribal warriors armed to the teeth, make many a visitor feel distinctly nervous. Simple *funduks* or inns, windows with coloured glass, and especially the plump cheeks of the men, full of *qat* (mildly narcotic leaves), are all aspects of Yemen's image. The feeling of being in some tale out of the Arabian Nights is easily sensed when you take an evening walk through a Yemeni town.

Many people are also attracted and fascinated by the unique beauty of the landscape. Deep canyons and evergreen wadis in the mountains contrast with the sand dunes of the Rhub al Khali. The "green Yemen" and the Wadi Hadramaut were well-known even in antiquity. However, the Tihama coastal strip, with its African-like villages of huts, or the mountain Tihama, with its beautiful euphorbia plants, also have their own charm.

Yemen is an Islamic country, without being subjected to stern fundamentalism. Here the Islamic tradition of hospitality still lives on, and in Yemen you will meet a dignified and proud people.

Preceding pages: an antique *djambia* can be worth a fortune; ornate façade of a house in Sana'a; Shibam, the Manhattan of the desert; in the mosque. **Left**, guard at the Wadi Dhar Palace.

Little is known about the prehistoric era in Yemen. Material that has been the subject of recent research by archaeologists has provided useful information about the Bronze and Stone Ages. It is assumed that Yemen had some part in the development of the ancient cultures of Mesopotamia, Egypt, the Indus Valley and the Levant. Geographical proximity to these early centres of civilisation and its own natural factors which favoured human life make it probable that Yemen had an early and highly developed culture–perhaps a response to the neighbouring civilisations. However, since the early days of archaeological discovery the country has not been at the centre of any scientific research. For this reason, united efforts are necessary to gain an overall archaeological view, and exact scientific excavations, in order to help this country, rich in traditions, to discover its cultural heritage and to write the missing chapters of its early history.

Early beginnings of Yemen: The ancient history of Yemen can be divided into two main periods. The first begins in the first millennium B.C. and ends with the decline of the eastern cultural centres towards the end of the pre-Christian era. In other words, it begins with the rise of the frankincense trade and ends when the land route was losing its importance and was finally replaced by a sea trade route in the western part of the Red Sea. The second era begins with the founding of the Himyar kingdoms and the rise of centres of civilisation in the high plateau with its basins and unconquerable mountains. It ends with the decay of these cultures, i.e. it lasts from the first to the sixth century A.D.

It is not possible to state exactly the time when the civilisation of Yemen first flourished. The earliest reliable information proves the existence of a highly developed

Preceding pages: the southern sluice of the ancient dam of Ma'rib. **Left**, the Queen of Sheba and Solomon. **Above**, Himyar inscription on a stele in Ma'rib.

culture which goes back to the tenth century B.C. The evidence refers to Saba, which unites the whole historical symbolism of ancient Yemen and was both its centre and its heart during this period. The historical and cultural development of the kingdom of Saba had a great influence in the early history of Yemen.

According to the genealogists, Saba was the father of Himyar and Kuhlan, ancestors of all Yemenis. The famous epic describing

the emigration and dispersion of Yemenis throughout many neighbouring countries refers to Saba and is reflected in the proverb: "They were scattered like the Sabaeans." The "good earth" mentioned in the Koran is in fact the land of the Sabaeans; it was the Sabaeans who built Ma'rib, the crowning achievement of ancient Yemen. Yemen owes its mention in the Koran to the great respect in which the Sabaeans and their capital Ma'rib were held.

For these reasons, the history of Saba forms the most important phase of the early history of Yemen, and the kingdom of Saba represents the greatest and most important political unit of this early era. The other kingdoms, such as Ma'in, Qhataban and Hadramaut were mere "satellite states." Himyar was amalgamated with Saba, and its kings called themselves "kings of Saba and Dhu Raydan"–the latter being Himyar.

The Ma'rib region along the Wadi Adhana was the original territory of Saba. It expanded more and more–as far as the Al Jawf valley in the north, to Kuhlan, Arhab and Al Bayn in the highland and plateau regions, and as far as Sana'a in the west. During its periods of dominance it extended its influence from time to time to cover the the Mediterranean. Frankincense was one of the most desirable and the most expensive of incense materials in the Middle East and the Mediterranean lands. This substance enriched the air with its heavy perfume in temples, on ritual occasions and public festivals. The best frankincense came from the southern coast of the Arabian peninsula, because the most favourable conditions for the cultivation of the plants prevailed here. Increased demand for frankincense and other valuable raw materials provided the stimulus for the development of intensive trading activity along the frankincense route.

However, such long journeys could never

whole of Yemen.

A Majestic past: Ma'rib was the most famous of the ancient cities of Yemen. On the left bank of the Wadi Adhana, the scattered ruins surrounding the modern city still provide evidence of the glory, splendour and majesty of times past. Archaeological finds have led to the assumption that Salhin, the site of the royal palace of Saba, once lay where old Ma'rib, now a deserted village, is now. From its strategically important position on the edge of the great desert, the city controlled the frankincense route, which ran from the Indian Ocean through Arabia to have been made without an efficient means of transport. It is assumed, therefore, that it was the domestication of the camel and its use as a beast of burden that made the development of the trade route across the Arabian peninsula possible. All indications point to the camel being domesticated as early as the Bronze Age, i.e. in the final centuries of the second millennium B.C. This assumption is supported by several passages in the Bible which refer to the visit of the Queen of Sheba (Saba) to King Solomon in the tenth century B.C. The trade route must have been in existence at the time of this visit. These reports also lead to the conclusion that trade links between Yemen and the Levant must already have existed in those times. There is mention of the large quantities of perfumes and incense which the Queen brought with her on her visit. The story of this visit in the Old Testament is the earliest source of information in existence about Saba and its development. It became famous and spread throughout the world. For centuries it has caught people's attention, it is mentioned in the Koran, and it survived in different versions as part of the cultural heritage of various nations, but more notable in Yemen. For Yemenis today, the

come to thee from Saba:
23. I found a woman reigning over them, gifted with everything, and she hath a splendid throne;
24. And I found her and her people worshipping the sun instead of God; and Satan hath made their works fair seeming to them, and he hath turned them from the Way: wherefore they are not guided..."

The economic wealth piled up in ancient Yemen by the Sabaeans more than any other people was based not only on income from trade but also on agriculture. The irrigation system of the Ma'rib dam, which still exists,

Queen of Sheba represents the former highly developed civilisation of their country.

The Queen of Sheba and her visit to Solomon is also mentioned in the Koran, for instance in the sura "The Ant", in which a bird, the hoopoe, reports to the King:

22. Nor tarried it long ere it came and said, "I have gained the knowledge that thou knowest not, and with sure tidings have I

Above, mighty and imposing, the old Minean city Baraqish with its 50 fortified towers above the outskirts of the city of Wadi Al Jawf.

leads to the conclusion that the system of cultivation must have been highly developed. Archaeological research at the site of the dam points to a date at least as early as the first century B.C. for the foundation walls. This fact confirms the evidence mentioned above for the existence of a highly developed civilisation at this time.

South Arabian inscriptions mention a long line of Mukarribs, religious rulers and kings, who reigned after the Queen of Sheba. A famous German scholar has tried to put together a chronological list for the first millennium B.C. Fifty Mukarribs and kings can be identified between the eighth and the first centuries B.C. Among them was Yatha Amar Bayyin, who is mentioned in the Assyrian annals (dating from around the year 715 B.C.) in connection with the Assyrian king Sargon II. In South Arabian inscriptions he is connected with the building of several works such as the dam and the city walls of Ma'rib.

Also mentioned in the list of rulers is Karibil Watar, who sent a gift to King Sennacharib, as inscribed above the Akitu building in Assur (685 B.C.). This is probably the same king as the one mentioned in the great inscription of Sirwah. The latter

which have some connection with his name, such as the Awwam temple or the so-called Mahram Bilqis in Ma'rib, the temple of the moon god in Sirwah and the temple of Al Masajid to the south of it–both difficult places to get to.

Up until the fifth century B.C. Saba remained the most important state. After this date, a series of political groups proclaimed their independence and established their own states. They began to compete with Saba for power and economic influence. These were the states of Ma'in, Qataban and Hadramaut.

Ma'in arose in the Al Jawf valley. Its rise

records several campaigns undertaken by him almost all over Yemen, with the aim of reinforcing the central power of the state of Saba and punishing rebels. From the inscription it can be assumed that he succeeded in establishing a powerful centralised state, as well as in unifying the Sabaean tribes and establishing a single religion, that of the major deity Almaqah, the god of the moon.

His building activities probably made the Mukarrib Yada il-Dharih the most famous of the kings. Yet another inscription tells of his buildings, especially the temples, many of

was made possible after the cities of Al Jawf, led by their religious centre Yathul (Baraqish) had succeeded, with the help of Qataban and Hadramaut, in gaining control of the frankincense trade route. The Minaeans expanded their area of influence to the north and built their own settlements as trading stations along the route. This was the origin of, for example, Dedan in the Al-Qura valley to the north of Yathrib and along the route from Najran to Ghaza. Merchants from Ma'in travelled from their capital Qarnawu (Ma'in) on strong camels (which came mainly from the Amir region to the north of

Al Jawf) to the international markets in Syria, Palestine, Egypt and even further afield. The tomb of a Minaean merchant has been found in Egypt. His name, Zaid bin Zaid, was inscribed on the sarcophagus; he was trading in myrrh and cinnamon during the rule of Ptolemy II (264 B.C.). The classical writers of antiquity also mentioned the Minaeans in connection with the incense trade. These same ancient sources also mention the inhabitants of Qataban and Hadramaut in the same connection.

Qataban first appears in the inscription of Karibil Watar, King of Saba, mentioned above. At that time it was still dependent on

Jubah, a day's march away from Ma'rib, and southwards as far as the sea. The people of Qataban developed a magnificent system of agriculture: they built efficient irrigation systems in the valleys as well as dams, and made considerable profit out of their situation on the trade route. They also passed laws intended to regulate economic activity. There is still a stele in the old market place in Hajar Kuhlan on which are inscribed the rules for the town market. The tolls and taxes which the traders who bought and sold in the market had to pay are also mentioned, as are other instructions on similar matters.

Hadramaut, which bordered on Qataban,

Saba and was supporting it against Axum in modern Ethiopia. However, in the fifth century Qataban succeeded, just as Ma'in did, in establishing its independence and in extending its influence, with the help of Hadramaut, at the expense of the kingdom of Saba. Its capital Timna lay in the Wadi Baihan. Qataban reached the peak of its power in the third and second centuries B.C. and extended its rule as far as the oasis of Al-

Left, inside the walls of Baraqish. **Above**, the walls of ancient Timna in modern South Yemen.

was once under Sabaean rule. In the fifth century B.C. it became independent and set up its own state in the course of the decrease of Saba's power. Thanks to the fact that the area of Dhofar, where frankincense was grown, was in Hadramaut's territory, the importance of that state gradually increased. Its capital was Shabwa on the outer western edge of the Hadramaut valley, which lies at the edge of the desert. Pliny describes its power in a famous passage: "The frankincense is taken after harvesting to Sabota (Shabwa) on the backs of camels, and one of the city gates is opened for them. The king has declared it a grave crime for any of the camels laden with such goods to leave the main road. In Sabota a tenth part, measured by eye and not by weight, is taken aside by the priests for their god Sabin (properly Syan), and the frankincense may not be sold until this has been done."

Towards the end of the first millennium and particularly in the final two centuries B.C. the population of Yemen paid less and less attention to agriculture and relied on the wealth which flowed so lavishly into their coffers from the trading caravans. The country was divided into political units which existed side by side: Saba, Qataban,

time, gradually acquired the necessary knowledge for sea travel in the Red Sea and discovered the secrets of the monsoon winds in the Indian Ocean. They could now navigate and trade along the entire coastline, without needing any help from the Yemenis, who up until then had controlled the frankincense route which ran through the towns of South Arabia. Trade, therefore, gradually moved over to the cheaper sea route. As a consequence, the land trade declined. The results of this process were also felt by the towns along the trade route; they began to lose their fabulous wealth, after getting used to the profits. It came as no

Ma'in, Hadramaut, and finally the rising power of the kingdom of Himyar.

The capitals of these states (apart from Himyar) were caravan cities, ruled in the first instance by influences beyond their control. Their fate, their rise and their fall depended on the ups and downs of the international markets and the related power politics of the great powers of the time. They suffered the same fate that befell the famous flourishing caravan cities of North Arabia several centuries later–Petra, Hatra or Palmyra.

The Ptolemies, who ruled Egypt at this

surprise, therefore, that the Bedouin along the route became restless and began to attack the caravan cities, as they had lost the support of the towns. Many of them lost their work, and most of them existed with only the minimum necessary to sustain life.

They began to use horses, which were already well-known among the Bedouin. These proved very successful in raids on the caravan cities, and thus contributed to the spread of Bedouin culture in these regions.

A Roman governor of Egypt named Aelius Gallus dared to take an army along the frankincense route to Ma'rib, with the help of a Nabataean guide, in 24/25 B.C. The campaign was a failure, but it revealed that "Arabia felix" was no longer unconquerable. The campaign spread alarm throughout the country, and for many of the inhabitants of the eastern valleys the situation became critical. An exodus to the highlands began, with "Bedouinisation" the only alternative for those who stayed.

Himyar, the rising power of the highlands, profited considerably from the unrest in the east. It became the main power in the entire region and began to compete with foreign trading nations along the new sea route. The new capital of Zafar was built in the central highlands, together with ports such as Muza on the Red Sea. The Himyar capital was linked to Sava, the most important caravan city of the highlands, by an overland route. Muza and Sava are both mentioned in the classical navigation guide Periplus of the Eritraean Sea: "Three days of overland travel from this port (Muza) will bring you to a city named Sava (now Sana'a) in the midst of a region named Mapharitis (Al Ma'cafir), and here there reigns a vassal ruler named Cholaebus (Arabic: Kulayb), who lives in the city. After nine more days you will reach Saphar (Zafar), the metropolis where Charibael lives, the rightful king of two tribes, the Homerites (Himyarites) and their neighbours, known as the Sabaites (Sabaeans); because of his constant embassies and gifts, he is a friend of the Emperor."

Agricultural highlands: Gradually new cities and states arose in the highlands at the expense of their sister cities in the eastern valleys. The decline of the land route and the lack of protection forced the population of the eastern regions, in particular the Sabaeans, to move west and to build up a flourishing agricultural system once more, this time in the highlands. Here there were fertile basins which received more rain than the valleys of the east. The cities in the centres of these basins were mostly ruled by Qayls (leaders) and began to compete with one another for power. So it was not only the established dynasties in the east and the

Himyarites who were competing for power, but also the smaller tribal dynasties in the highlands. The traditional title of the kings of Saba became, for a while, the dream of all the existing states. The country suffered from internal strife, and towards the end of the first century A.D. two of the traditional states, Ma'in and Qataban, had ceased to exist. Saba and Hadramaut continued to exist, but had become a target for Himyar and other ambitious states of the surrounding highlands.

In the final quarter of the third century A.D. Himyar, as the sea power and wealthiest state, emerged as victor in the

struggles, took Ma'rib, the capital of Saba, and subjugated Hadramaut. The kings of Himyar became sole rulers of Yemen, but kept the traditional titles "King of Saba", adding "and Dhu Raydan" (Himyar). Ma'rib was no longer the capital, and Zafar became the metropolis of the whole of South Arabia.

Himyar was the last of the ancient kingdoms of Yemen. It arose towards the end of the second century B.C. The year 115 B.C. is counted as the beginning of the Himyar era, which collapsed with the establishment of the kingdom. However, Himyar did not become a powerful state until the first century A.D., when it had totally conquered Saba, and it rose to be the major power in southern Arabia towards the end of the third century. The true founders of this kingdom were three rulers, whose fame and deeds became the subject of several epic poems, which still survive today in the memory of the Yemenis.

The first was King Sha'ir Awtar, who claimed the title "King of Saba and Dhu Raydan". He fought bravely against the Abyssinians, inflicted a severe defeat on the people of Hadramaut and towards the end of the second century A.D. he had become the most powerful ruler in Yemen.

The second was King Il Sharah Yahdub, who ruled as co-king with his brother Yazil Bayyin. He was one of the kings who made Sana'a one of his capitals and who attempted to found the huge kingdom of "Saba and Dhu Raydan." This attempt failed in the middle of the third century.

The third king was Shammar Yuharish. During his time, around the turn of the third century, the whole of Yemen was united under a central government. Shammar claimed an even longer title. He was "King of Saba and Dhu Raydan and Hadramaut and Yamanat". Yamanat represented the coastal region in the south of Yemen.

In the early fifth century Abi Karib Asad came to power, and gave himself an even longer title. His kingdom was larger and included the northern parts of Arabia as well. The Bedouin were also included in the kingdom of Saba and Dhu Raydan. Kindah, an allied state in central Arabia, also came under the influence of Abi Karib. He undertook campaigns which reached as far as central Arabia and is even supposed to have gone as far as Yathrib, named Al Medina two centuries later by the prophet Mohammed. From Yathrib he brought the Jewish faith to Yemen.

The second epoch in the early history of Yemen is considered to have ended with the death of King Yusuf Asar Yathar (Dhu Nuwas) and the occupation of Yemen in 525 by the Abyssinians. However, historians usually add the events of the sixth century up to the appearance of the prophet Mohammed. But by that time the Himyar kingdom no longer existed. There was only the Abyssinian occupation. It was followed by the final collapse of the dam of Ma'rib and the arrival of the Persians, who shortly before its conversion to Islam included Yemen as a province in their Sassanid empire. These events were a mere epilogue. The decline of the ancient civilisation had begun many years before the sixth century.

It is not always easy to visit the historic sites of Yemen. Many of them lie off the beaten track and are very difficult to get to. They are often to be found in tribal areas whose leaders have no particular interest in research or excavation and may even attempt to hinder such activities, if they should occur. In Ma'rib in particular it is becoming obvious how necessary specific measures to preserve the ruins and protect the entire site have become.

However, over the next few years important excavations will be taking place in Yemen, with the co-operation of universities and research foundations all over the world. This could mean that some of the sites will not be open to visitors.

Above, Sabaean alabaster head. **Right**, ruined temple in Ma'in.

سورة البقرة مائتان وثمانون

بسم الله الرحمن الرحيم

الم ذلك الكتاب لا ريب فيه هدى للمتقين الذين يؤمنون بالغيب ويقيمون الصلاة ومما رزقناهم ينفقون والذين يؤمنون بما أنزل إليك وما أنزل من قبلك وبالآخرة هم يوقنون

وست آيات أنزلت بالمدينة

سورة فاتحة الكتاب سبع

بسم الله الرحمن الرحيم
الحمد لله رب العالمين الرحمن الرحيم
مالك يوم الدين إياك نعبد وإياك نستعين
اهدنا الصراط المستقيم صراط الذين أنعمت عليهم
غير المغضوب عليهم ولا الضالين

آيات أنزلت بمكة

The history of Yemen is obscured by considerable confusion. Major events in this period of almost one and a half thousand years were the result of outside influences.

The interest of foreign powers in southwestern Arabia during all the phases of its history was not so much a matter of ruling the country itself than of controlling the trade routes which led through and around Yemen. Yemen was the key to the Red Sea. This was the strategic position that the rulers

ning of modern history: the fall of Constantinople in 1453, the discovery of America and–in the same year, 1492–the driving out of Boabdil from Granada and the completion of the Reconquistada, the discovery of printing, the Renaissance, and the Reformation. While the Spaniards and the English were concentrating their attention on the Americas, Vasco da Gama succeeded in sailing around the Cape of Good Hope in 1497. This was the beginning of Portuguese

of Suez, Cairo, Alexandria and Constantinople, have all wanted to possess if they possibly could, in recent times as well as during the Islamic period.

The history of Yemen, therefore, is often more than a piece of regional history of the Middle East; it is part of the world-wide struggle for power, influence and trade. One of these periods, the era around 1500, is the first period which we are going to look at more closely.

The Portuguese and the Osman Turks: In Europe, changes within and outside marked the end of the Middle Ages and the begin-

rule in the Indian Ocean. Da Gama landed as a conqueror in Mozambique, allied himself with Malindi, and landed in Calicut in 1497. Within a few years the Portuguese–among them Vasco da Gama on his second voyage in 1502–had occupied Mombasa and Lamu on the coast of Africa, and Goa, Diu and Cochin in India. In 1507, Afonso de Albuquerque landed on the island of Socotra, in order to take control of the trade between Egypt and India, via the Red Sea, from this point and thus to gain control of the entire European spice trade.

In Cairo tax revenues dropped so

drastically that the Mamelukes prepared a fleet against the Portuguese. After two battles outside Bombay and Diu, however, the ships had to flee back to the Red Sea. For his part, Afonso de Albuquerque now realised that he could only exercise lasting control over the Red Sea from Aden, but his attempt to take the city in 1513 failed. The Egyptian Mamelukes now decided to conquer Yemen using land forces. In 1515 their troops landed first in Kamaran, and

While Egyptian Mameluke troops, without supplies or reinforcements, had to surrender to native forces (in particular those of the Imam), the Turkish admiral in the Red Sea, Salman Ra'is, made a report to the Osman governor of Egypt in 1525. The admiral described the Turkish fleet with its ships and its cannons lying at anchor in Jedda. How easy it would be to use this mighty fleet against the "infidel Portuguese" and their Indian bases, he wrote, and added: "The

then just outside Zabid, where they inflicted a devastating defeat on the penultimate Tahirid Sultan, Al Zafir 'Amir II. Finally they conquered Ta'izz and Sana'a. In 1517 the Sultan was captured in the vicinity of Sana'a and was beheaded. In the same year the Osman Sultan Selim I besieged the Mamelukes in Egypt and also took control over their political power and position.

Preceding pages: magnificent copy of the Koran in the Great Mosque of Sana'a. Left, the courtyard of the Great Mosque. Above, the Al Janad mosque near Ta'izz.

province of Yemen is more fertile than the province of Egypt. The tax revenues of Zabid amount to 180,000 pieces of gold a year. One and a half days away lies a beautiful city named Ta'izz; it has well-farmed fields, vineyards and gardens. Yemen is worthy of becoming a fine province of ours. Here also lies the city of Aden. It is rumoured that even India has no such harbours. The revenue of the port amounts to some 200,000 gold pieces a year."

The Osman Turks could not resist the temptation to defeat the infidel and at the same time regain control of trade and acquire high tax revenues. In 1538 the Turkish fleet under Suleiman al-Arnauti took Aden by subterfuge, but had to retire without success from Diu to Aden and the Red Sea.

The first Turkish occupation, 1538-1636: Within a few years the Turks had succeeded in occupying many places in southern Yemen and the Tihama. By this time, their only remaining opponent was the Imam.

During these years the Turks were faced with an unusually vigorous period in the history of the Imams. Al Mutawakkil Yahya Sharaf al-Din and his son Al Mutahhar ruled (including the usual internecine struggles) from 1508-1573. From time to time the

Porte replied by sending a well-equipped troop under the command of Sinan Pasha.

Sana'a was occupied again, but despite the use of artillery Kawkaban and Thula could not be conquered. Soon both sides came to a sort of unofficial arrangement whereby the Imam retained the actual control of an area between Kawkaban, Thula and Hajjah as far as the Tihama, and the Turks controlled the lower part of Yemen and the lowlands in the Tihama. Among the structures built during this period are the great castle in the pass of Sumarah, and the road and fortifications on Mount Shamsan above Aden. In Sana'a one of the most beautiful buildings in the city is

Imams managed to regain Ta'izz, Aden and even Zabid. However, the better discipline and artillery of the Turks finally secured them the conquest of Sana'a (1547). Yahya Sharif al-Din withdrew to his family seat of Kawkaban, Mutahhar to Thula. The appearance of both these fortresses has hardly changed at all since the defensive works undertaken at that time by the Imams. The two rulers continued to resist the Turks from these fortresses, where they were also buried. In the meantime, the fortunes of war appeared to change. Yet when Al Mutahhar reconquered Sana'a in 1566, the Sublime

a reminder of the Turkish occupation. This is the Bakiriya Mosque, which the governor Hasan Pasha had built in 1597 in the same style as the great mosques of Istanbul, probably even following plans sent from the capital. The minaret, typically Yemeni, with its ornamental brick construction was originated in Afghanistan and Iran.

After the death of Al Mutahhar, a new dynasty of Imams came to rule Zaidi Yemen. One of them, Imam al-Qasim ibn Muhammad (1597-1620), the legendary hero and freedom fighter of the country, is still one of the great national heroes with whom Yemenis identify even nowadays.

The Zaidi Imams did not follow a direct line of succession throughout their history of over a thousand years. The only essential prerequisite was that they should be of the family of 'Ali and therefore of the line of Prophet Mohammed. Al Qasim came from a branch of family which had last supplied an Imam 600 years before.

Al Qasim (he later received the title "the Great" and ruled in the name Al Mansur billah–"Victorious through God") proclaimed himself Imam in the year 1006 of the Hijra (1597)–or possibly at the end of 1005 H–and was soon confirmed on his leading

fought against the local Yemeni rulers imposed by the Turks. The battles–they rarely involved more than a few hundred warriors confronting each other on either side– mainly took place in the traditional Zaidi regions: Kawkaban, At Tawilah, Hajjah, Huth, Sa'dah and Shaharah, the Eagle's Nest in the north. Here Al Mansur billah died, and immediately after, his son Al Mu'ayyad billah Muhammad was recognised as Imam. With the same degree of courage and a great deal of luck, he completed the work of liberation undertaken by his father. In 1629 the Turks withdrew from Sana'a (because of the war against Persia the Porte had been

role by a consensus of respected men. Al Qasim had, at this time, a reputation as an outstanding Koran teacher, and his military and political skills soon became apparent. He found his first followers among the Sanhan tribe (just to the south of Sana'a) and from then on led a life composed of nomadic wanderings and guerilla warfare, fighting almost as often against Sinan Pasha as he

Left, fragment of the Koran from the House of Manuscripts next to the Great Mosque in Sana'a. **Above**, teacher and pupil in the mosque and tomb of Queen Arwa in Jiblah.

unable to send more than a few reinforcements to Yemen). In 1636 they left Zabid, Mokha and Kamaran.

The coffee trade and its consequences: The course of the 17th and 18th centuries was determined not so much by political events as by the new economic importance of the world markets which Yemen gained through the coffee trade. For about two centuries coffee was the most important product on world markets and Yemen had the trading monopoly of coffee.

The Turkish occupation had exterminated all political rivals of the Imams, and by this time, after the Turks had been driven out, the next Imam, Al Mutawakkil 'ala Allah Isma'il bin Al-Qasim (brother of Mohammed and son of Al Qasim) was the sole ruler of northern, central and southern Yemen. His long rule (1644-1676) is considered a period of order, justice and prosperity—but most importantly it offered him the opportunity to include Hadramaut in the state of Yemen once more for the first time in many years. After extensive fighting Shibam (Hadramaut) was occupied, and governors were placed in Al Shihr and even in Zafar (Dhofar in modern Oman).

The subsequent Imams could barely keep

The rise of Mokha had led to the decline of Aden, but it was not able to affect the potential strategic importance of the latter which was determined by its natural harbour. When the British occupied Aden in 1839, once again with a view to securing the Red Sea, the population of this ancient and medieval city had fallen to 1,289.

Great Britain also used the occupation of Aden as a warning to Egypt, whose ruler Mohammed Ali had first of all led his troops against the Wahhabites and then (1833-1840) conquered the Tihama. As similar attacks had done three hundred years before, the British attack on Aden provoked a

control of the centrifugal forces in the country, in which every tribe wanted to rule itself and every tribal warrior wanted to be his own prince. With hindsight, the revolt of the 'Abdali prince in Lahej (Lahij, 30 km north of Aden) during the period between 1728-1731 can be seen as the most significant historical event. The prince murdered the Imam's governor and—with the help of the Yafa'i tribes—managed to defeat a punitive expedition. The modern division of Yemen into two states can be traced back to this event, which also made the British occupation of Aden in 1839 much easier.

counterreaction from the Porte. In 1849 the Turks occupied Hudaydah and Sana'a, but were driven out of the capital again after only a few days. The opening of the Suez Canal in 1869 strengthened the importance of the Yemen, but it also allowed the Turks to transport troops directly from Istanbul to Al Hudaydah. In 1872 the Turks re-occupied Sana'a, and only withdrew again in 1919 because of First World War.

Ayyubids and Rasulids: The year 1174 was one of the crucial points in the medieval Islamic history of Yemen. For the first time a sizeable foreign army forced its way into the country (it was not even an Arab army, but a Turkish and Kurdish force), and for the first time the previously rather diffuse variety of rival principalities, dynasties and tribal domains were brought together in a system of government that was highly advanced for its time, for the first time a centralised modern administration was formed, and the previously geographic term "Yemen" ("the South") came to mean a political entity which comprised the whole of southwestern Arabia, including Hadramaut and Najran. Also for the first time, Islamic schools (madressas) were founded, and this means that the Ayyubids gave Sunni

some members of the house later supplied themselves with a fictional Arab genealogy. The man who gave his name to the dynasty, Ayyub (= Job) ibn Shadhi ibn Marwan, left his homeland in Armenia/Kurdistan in the early 12th century with his father and his brother Shirkuh. In Baghdad the talented and active family was able to make important contacts in a short time and make use of opportunities for advancement. Ayyub's father was made commander of Takrit, and after his death, Ayyub took up the post.

In 1132 the Seljuk ruler, based in Mossul, attempted to conquer Baghdad–the seat of the Caliph–in vain. When he fled, Ayyub and

Yemen handsome buildings and reinforced religious traditions. In short, a new era began in the year 1174; the short period of Ayyubid rule acted as a foundation on which the later Rasulid dynasty could build and develop into the longest and most magnificent epoch of medieval Yemeni history.

Saladin and the Ayyubids: The Ayyubid family was of Kurdish origin, even though

Left, detail of the dome of the Great Mosque in the medieval town of Jiblah. **Above**, entrance to the ritual cleansing basins in the deserted fortress of Djebel Umm Layla.

his brother Shirkuh helped him cross the Tigris; this was the beginning of a friendship which was soon to prove profitable. In 1138 Baghdad relieved the brothers of their posts in Takrit. They fled to Mossul, where they were welcomed with open arms. In the same year Ayyub's son Yusuf was born. His full name was Salah ad Din Yusuf ibn Ayyub, the most important figure of the dynasty. The first part of his name became, in Westernised form, Saladin. By a mixture of good planning and good luck, military talent and political calculation, the Seljuk ruler of Mossul managed, through the efforts of his two generals–the above mentioned brothers–to include Damascus together with the north of Syria in his domain. In 1154 Ayyub became governor of Damascus; Shirkuh was his army commander.

In Cairo, during this time, one of the great Arab dynasties was in decline. These were the Fatimids, whose allies and co-religionists in the Yemen were the Sulayhids. The Fatimids came originally from Syria and had created a kingdom for themselves in Tunisia. From there they had moved east, conquering Fustat (now Old Cairo) in 969 and founding a new capital, Cairo, in the same year.

One of their viziers now fled to Damascus, looking for support for his own cause in the internal power struggles of Cairo. Shirkuh, accompanied by his nephew Saladin, marched to Cairo and reinstated the vizier who had fled. The latter, however, simply dropped his allies and called on the crusader knights of Jerusalem to aid him against Shirkuh and Saladin. The battles, which had less to do with religion than with power politics, were indecisive in outcome.

Not until 1138, in a third campaign did Shirkuh and Saladin firmly establish themselves in Cairo. In 1169, after the death of Shirkuh, Saladin became Vizier of Cairo, and a little later his brother Turanshah ibn Ayyub arrived with reinforcements from Syria. In 1172 the last Fatimid caliph died in Cairo, and now Saladin was officially the ruler of Egypt.

After a series of battles with the crusaders Saladin moved his forces south. In 1174 his brother Turanshah took a strong army via Mecca to the north of Yemen (Harad in the Tihama), where at the same time, the Ayyubid fleet disembarked with horses and reinforcements.

The Fatimids had long since replaced Baghdad as the economic centre of the Islamic world. The political rise of Cairo and clever trade policies had moved the main artery of the trade of that time from the Gulf to the Red Sea. Trade between India, Malaya, Sumatra and China on the one hand and Constantinople, Italy and Europe on the other all went through Aden and Cairo. In addition, the Egyptian Fatimids had, in their trade with India, relied upon their co-religionists in Yemen, the Sulayhids. No wonder their political successors, the Ayyubids, made their first move towards Yemen, and followed a short time later by establishing their own governments in Damascus, Aleppo and Diarbekir.

Back to the Yemen campaign. Turanshah marched southwards from Harad, occupied Zabid (on the 9 Shauwal 569 H = 13 May 1174) and eventually moved north once more towards Jiblah and Dhamar. Sana'a and also Shibam and Tarim in Hadramaut were not finally conquered until the rule of the next Yemeni Ayyubid (Tughtakin,

another brother of Saladin), in 1189. Further north, however, the previous rulers of Sana'a and particularly the Imam were able to assert themselves again and again.

This Imam, 'Abd Allah ibn Hamza–he ruled from 1187 to 1218–was one of those great figures brought forth from time to time by Zaidi history. The Imam relied as much upon his religious function as upon the building of a ring of mighty fortresses at

Above, a glorified portrayal of a battle between British colonial troops and Arabic tribal warriors, dating from the last century.

Shibam/Kawkaban, Thula, At Tawilah and Kuhlan, which in part still bear witness to his rule even nowadays; his architecturally most impressive "capital", however, was formed by the castle and mosque of Zafar-Dhi Bin (near Raydah), where his tomb lies (he died in 1217 in Kawkaban).

In order to understand the course of history it must be emphasised once again that the Zaidi Imams did not inherit their office, but had to gain it by "recognition". Their "calling", the *da'wa*, could be successful or it could not. 'Abd Allah ibn Hamza's first *da'wa* in 1187 had almost no or very little success. His second term, ten years later, perhaps succeeded because Yemen's need was at its greatest. Tughtakin now had the whole of Yemen except for Sa'dah under his control. Shortly after Tughtakin's death (1197) 'Abd Allah was finally recognised as Imam under the name Al Mansur, because of his scholarship (more than 40 books are attributed to him), his piety and his military capabilities.

Imam 'Abd Allah ibn Hamza (and also his son and successor) were the main military opponents of the Ayyubids and the early Rasulids. It could be said that their resistance led to renewed territorial consolidation of the Imamate and to the partition, still in evidence today, of Yemen into Zaidi north and Shafi'a south.

The Ayyubids, too, have left some beautiful buildings in Yemen. Their general Wirdashar had one of the minarets of the Great Mosque in Sana'a built in 1206/7; Tughtakin had the mosque of Al Janad renovated around the year 1184; and the minaret of the Great Mosque of Zabid also dates from this time.

The Rasulids (1228-1454): The sixth and last of the Ayyubid kings of the Yemen, Al Mas'ud Yusuf, conquered Mecca in 1220 and gave it as a fief to his general, Nur al-Din 'Umar. As so often happened in the Middle East, 'Umar made himself independent after Yusuf had left Yemen, two years later in 1230. Four years later, in 1234, 'Umar was recognised as the new Sultan by the caliph in Baghdad.

The Rasulids were of Turkish origin. 'Umar's grandfather had been an ambas-sador (*rasul*) in the service of the caliph, hence the family name.

It was possible for the Rasulids to build on the state organisation of the Ayyubids. A well-organised army allowed the first Rasulids to exercise their power over the whole of Yemen as far as Mecca and Zafar on the Indian Ocean, even though they remained mainly in the south of the country. In their capital, Ta'izz, some buildings still bear witness to their vigorous building programmes and their love of the arts. Many scholarly manuscripts, written by the rulers themselves and covering topics such as agriculture, equestrian skills, medicine, poetry and genealogy, have survived. Sultan al-Ashraf 'Umar is probably the only king in history to have designed an important scientific instrument, the astrolabe, and written the appropriate explanatory tract to accompany it (1291).

Among the many buildings of the Rasulids (among them the madressa in Mecca built by Al Malik al-Muzaffar Yusuf I and another, built by Al Mujahid 'Ali) we will only mention here the mosque of Al Mahjam in the northern Tihama and the Muzaffariya in Ta'izz. Both were built during the rule of Sultan Al Malik al-Muzaffar Shams al-Din Yusuf I (1250-1295), the most important by far of the Rasulid rulers. Later the Rasulids had further magnificent buildings erected in Ta'izz, which are still the grace and pride of the city: the Ashrafiya (built during the rule of Al Ashraf I and Al Ashraf II) and the Mu'tabiya mosque (built around 1400).

In a sense, the short-lived Tahirid dynasty, which took power in Yemen in 1454 and thereby finished off the Rasulids as a political factor, could be seen as their cultural heirs–at any rate, if you compare the beautiful mosque of Rada'a, completed around 1512, with those Rasulid buildings that still survive in Ta'izz.

The Tahirid dynasty marks the end of the period from 1174 to about 1500. The following Egyptian and Turkish conquest marked the coming not only of a new set of rulers, but also of a new epoch.

Islam comes to Yemen: Two events remain for us to examine, and both of them still affect Yemen today. The first is the conversion of the Yemenis to Islam, the central moment of the country's three thousand year history and perhaps not coincidentally the symbolic and historical mid-point of this same long history. Islam has done more to form Yemen than any other influence. This is evident not only in the visible signs, such as the minarets which tower above towns and villages, the call to prayer, the mosques, schools, pious foundations, fountains, customs and traditions, but also the Yemeni feeling of belonging to the faith, the belief that the faith is as important a part of home and identity as the country or the tribe.

The other event is the foundation of the

respected only for its past, but had otherwise declined to a quite unimportant settlement, while in the west the new Sabaean centre of Sana'a and to the south (near Yarim) the Himyar capital Zafar had developed into the dominant cities of the country. The centre of world politics had moved much further north, to the struggles between Byzantium and the Sassanid empire. Both sides tried to reinforce their power, even in the less important arenas. The last Himyarite king, Dhu Nuwas, believed that he could escape this rivalry by converting to Judaism. During the conquest of the newly-converted Christian, Najran had many Christians put to

Zaidi Imamate in 897 (= 284 H) by the Imam Yahya (his full name was Yahya bin al-Husain bin al-Qasim), who ruled under the name of Al Hadi ila 'l-Haqq ("he who leads along the right way to the truth").

The history of the conversion of Yemen to Islam was not recorded by the chroniclers until later, so that some of the facts cannot be dated precisely. In order to understand the circumstances better, it is necessary to look back at the events of the 6th century.

South Arabia had long lost its importance as one of the great cultural and economic centres of the ancient world. Ma'rib was

a martyr's death by burning (523), and the news of this terrible event spread so rapidly that Byzantium could not remain inactive.

Supported by the Byzantine fleet (Egypt was part of the Byzantine empire), the Ethiopian ruler crossed over to Yemen. The Abyssinian governor Abraha, once installed in Yemen, soon declared himself independent. However, an attack on the now flourishing trade centre of Mecca in 570, the year in which Mohammed was born, failed.

A nationalist reaction in Sana'a once more brought a native dynasty to power. In order to drive out the Abyssinians, they successfully approached another foreign power, Persia. The Persian armies came, stayed and put in their own satraps.

In the meantime Mohammed had begun to preach Islam in his own home town of Mecca. He did not view it as a new religion, but as the return to a faith in God such as had been revealed to humanity by earlier prophets–from Abraham to Jesus.

Mohammed soon discovered that a prophet is without honour in his own country. For this reason, he met in strictest secrecy (in 620 and then again in 621) with men from Medina, which at that time was still called Yathrib. These declared their sup-

inaccurate. "Hijra" is a term taken from the traditional law of South Arabia and refers to the founding of a protective relationship between a tribe and a member of a respected pious family who has come from outside. "Hijra" status obliges the protecting tribe to defend the new arrival as if he were one of their own. The immunity of the person also applies to his dwelling, where peace brings prosperity and trade also allows a town (old south Arabian "Hajar", linguistically related to "hijra") to develop. Mohammed and the men of Medina had indeed founded a "hijra" according to old Yemeni tribal law.

The following years saw a bitter struggle

port for him, converted to Islam and swore to protect him as if he were one of their family. A little later Mohammed left Mecca, which was by now very hostile to him, for Medina, the city which for this reason can be considered the cradle of Islam. This happened in the year 622, which in the Islamic calendar is counted as the year 1 of the so-called "hijra".

Few would seriously dispute today that the earlier translation of "hijra" as "flight" was

Left, watering hole in the Rub al-Khali. **Above**, camel caravan. Both paintings reflect an earlier, idealised view of Arabia.

between Mohammed and the men of Medina on the one hand and the citizens of Mecca on the other, which the prophet finally resolved to his benefit. In 630 he returned to Mecca– he met with almost no resistance–and, by clever policies of reconciliation, he won the city and the people over to his cause. His increasing success brought more and more Arab tribes from all over the peninsula, including Yemen, to join him. The early chroniclers reported that on the first Friday of the month of Radshab of the year 6 (= 628) Badhan, the last Persian satrap, was converted to Islam, and with him the tribes of the

Hamdan federation. If such a rapid conversion could be seen as a little doubtful, it is a matter of historical record that Badhan, appointed by Mohammed as the first Islamic governor in Sana'a, did indeed accept Islam.

From the earliest years Yemenis had sought out the Prophet and had joined his cause–for example (also in the year 628) Abu Musa al-Ash'ari from the region in which later Zabid was to be founded. His powerful tribe, the Asha'ir, followed, and Zabid was Islamic by 631.

Together with the deputations from Yemen, Mohammed sent some of his companions to the south. The most famous was

the mosque of Al Janad in the first week of Radshab will bring the same blessings as a pilgrimage to Mecca.

In order to understand the importance of the date, it is necessary to take a short trip back to Mecca. Mohammed took over the traditions of pilgrimage of the city of his birth, including the cult of the Ka'aba, the *'umra*, known in pagan times as Radshab-'umra, because it was celebrated in Radshab. It was nothing more than the form which was current in Mecca of the ancient Arabian Radshab festival. No wonder the new victorious religion also chose the date of the highest pre-Islamic festival for their

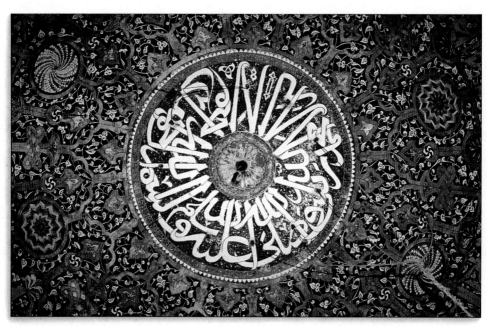

Mu'adh bin Jabal, who was sent to the Ta'izz region and there founded, somewhat to the north of the present city of Ta'izz which did not exist in those days, the mosque of Al Janad, the main town of the southern province, which formed part of the new administrative system together with Sana'a and Hadramaut. The mosque, impressive and majestic in its plainness, is supposed to have been founded by Mu'adh bin Jabal on the first Friday of the month of Radshab. That strange date keeps cropping up again and again! Much later it is reported that according to local tradition a pilgrimage to

triumphs in Sana'a and Al Janad.

While nothing remains in Mecca to point to the meaning and origin of the pre-Islamic 'umra, Yemeni sources allow us to assume that the pagan Radshab festival celebrated irrigation, spring and fertility. Just as with the "hijra" mentioned above, the Yemeni tradition allows new light to be thrown on this important religious aspect of Islam.

It is an interesting question: which of the two venerable mosques of Yemen–the Great Mosque of Sana'a or the mosque of Al Janad–is the elder. On the side of Al Janad, the date of 630 is very likely to be correct. It is more difficult to date the Great Mosque of Sana'a. According to the scholars and qadis, whom you can see at their prayers and studies, it was built in the year 6 of the Hijra, i.e. in the year of the conversion of Badhan, by Wabr ibn Yuhannus, following express instruction by the Prophet. Wabr later became the third Islamic governor of Sana'a. The early chronicles also give other dates for the building of the Great Mosque. There are also various dates for the conversion of Badhan.

Badhan, the unpopular representative of a foreign power in Sana'a, may have joined the rapidly increasing popularity of a new religion first and foremost to secure his own position. However, this could hardly have happened before Mohammed's final entry into Mecca. There is much to be said in favour of the view that Badhan's confirmation as first Islamic governor caused him immediately to display his new religious fervour by laying the foundation stone of the mosque in the garden of the Ghumdan palace–that would make it the year 630.

So we can assume, together with Al Razi (11th century), that the two oldest and most venerated mosques in Yemen were founded within a few months of one another, without being able to decide even nowadays which is the elder. The Yemenis followed the call of Islam in large numbers. The battles which established the new empire would certainly have had different outcomes without Yemeni warriors and Yemeni cavalry in particular. However, it is certain that the new faith, whose rites still contained elements of the old South Arabian religion, also answered a deep spiritual need of the Yemenis, who a few centuries ago had already developed a somewhat diffuse monotheism and whose word for the Supreme Being, Rahman-an "the Merciful", also foreshadowed the epithet for God in the Koran, ar-Rahman ar-Rahim or the Merciful, the All-Compassionate.

The first Zaidi Imam in Yemen: In the year

859 a child was born in Medina and it is unlikely that anyone at his cradle imagined that he would one day be a founder of a government of Yemen. This Yahya was a direct descendant of the Prophet and also of his cousin 'Ali ibn Abi Talib, who later married Mohammed's sole surviving child, his daughter Fatima. The children of the marriage, Hassan and Hussain, head the ever-diversifying branches of the family tree of the Prophet's descendants and of 'Ali's (the 'Alids). Hussain's grandson Zaid died, as did most of the early 'Alids, in battle against the central Islamic power which ruled in Damascus, and later his son Yahya,

who had fled to Khorassan and Afghanistan, was killed.

The blood descendants of the Prophet and 'Ali were the representatives of the party of 'Ali ("party" is shi'a in Arabic, hence the term Shi'ites), which was convinced that the religious and political leadership of the Islamic community should have been given to 'Ali immediately after the Prophet's death and then to his and the Prophet's descendants. How all this came about had only one explanation, which is the central principle of all the Shi'ites; they found new adherents again and again despite persecution by the established caliphs and their power structure has not been satisfactorarily explained to this day. The fact that the Shi'ites had most success in establishing themselves in the east of the Islamic world may possibly have some connection with the national sense of value and the assertiveness of the Persians, but for the Zaidi state in Yemen another tradition, the old Arabian one of "hijra", may have played a part.

The aforementioned Zaid's name was given, without any actual logical reason, to the Zaidi version of Islam. Certainly, Zaid did receive some recognition from theologians even in his lifetime, but his name was not given to this particular doctrine, previously known as "Hadawiya", until many centuries after his death–and it was given in Yemen. One reason was that the name Zaid was linked with concepts of impeccable justice, of monotheism and the rejection of evil, another was the effect of his martyr's death.

The older name "Hadawiya" came from the Yahya mentioned above, who later–in Yemen–ruled under the name Al Hadi ila'l-Haqq ("he who leads along the right way to truth"), normally shortened in general use to Al Hadi.

This Yahya–or Al Hadi–was a direct descendant of 'Ali's other son, Hassan. Yahya's grandfather, whose full name was Al Qasim ar-Rassi Tarjuman ad-Din, lived a few generations after 'Ali.

Al Qasim was a productive scholar, author of several religious works, perhaps less an original than a systematic thinker. At any rate it was he who compiled the essence of the Zaidi doctrine and by this means became the spiritual and intellectual father of this sect. Al Qasim was born around 785 and died in 860. His additional name of Ar Rassi came from the estate of the family, Ar Rass, a day's march or so from Medina. This is the third important name for the history of the Zaidis in Yemen. Writers as early as Ibn Khaldun referred to the dynasty of the Imams as the Rassids, after Al Qasim ar-Rassi, and this term for the dynasty has become current in Western historical writings.

To complicate matters a little further,

another 'Ali named Al Hassan bin Zaid founded another form of Zaidi theology at about the same time as Al Qasim and was able to apply it politically in a small state in Tabaristan, on the southern edge of the Caspian Sea, from about 864 onwards. This northern Zaidi state survived until the 12th century; links between the two Zaidi states at the northern and southern edges of the Islamic world were often surprisingly close. Once Al Hadi even received a small number of military reinforcements in Yemen from the Caspain Sea. There were also tensions. When the talented young Yahya, who obviously represented great hopes of the

future for his family, made his way some time after 883 to Tabaristan with a noticeable desire for some political position, he found the local branch of the family to be so reserved that he came back again and, a few years later in 893, was pleased to follow up a request of Yemeni tribes to come as a judge to Sa'dah.

Yahya failed in this first attempt to establish the Zaidi doctrine in Yemen and soon returned to Medina. Somewhat later the

Above, magnificent portrayal of the Queen of Sheba.

feuding tribes of Sa'dah approached him again; to the surprise of many he came back to Sa'dah, this time accompanied by about 50 faithful followers, and pitched his tents outside the city walls in 897 (on the 6 Safar of the year 284 H).

This date marks the beginning of the Zaidi Imamate in Yemen, which was to flourish as the longest lasting of all state systems in south Arabia–right up to the 1962 revolution. Over this period of more than a thousand years the Imamate was always able to keep control of the region around Sa'dah, often of the mountainous north of the country, frequently of the central highlands. Sana'a and Dhamar, sometimes also of the south as far as Aden and the hot Tihama in the west, occasionally even Hadramaut and Dhofar in the east.

Al Hadi, during the course of a few eventful years, was successful as a judge in matters of tribal disputes and as a religious leader of respected men, and was recognised by the people as an administrator of justice, particularly in matters of taxation. He was soon able to prevail in a military sense in Najran in many wars–small skirmishes and major battles, and then in broad areas of Hashid and Bakil, in Huth, in Raydah and finally, although only for a short time, he was able to march into Sana'a–on the 22 Muharram of the year 288 of the Hijra.

In the same year of 288 he had his first coins made in Sana'a, which display in very fine calligraphy the Koran verses 81 and 82 of the 17th Sura:

"Truth is come and falsehood vanished: verily falsehood is a thing that vanisheth, for by the Koran we revealed that which brings salvation and mercy to the faithful."

This was the first time that these verses appeared on a coin–and were clearly intended to express new and revolutionary claims, for "truth" is "al haqq", so that the inscription could be read as "Al Haqq has come." In an even more provocative manner, the inscription "al-Hadi ila 'Haqq Amir al-Mu'uminin bin rasul Allah" emphasises that Al Hadi was terming himself "Amir al Mu'uminin", "Commander of the Faithful"

(and "descendant of the Prophet of God"), placing himself in the position of the caliph, who alone had the right to this title.

Al Hadi died in Sa'dah, aged 53, on the 19 Dhu al-Hijja of the year 298 H (= 18 August 911). Even in dying he is supposed to have shown the strength of will that marked all his life: he died sitting up, giving his son advice and regretting that he had not succeeded in destroying all those who were unjust and lived impious lives. Al Hadi still lies today in the mosque in Sa'dah which bears his name and which he himself founded in 901. The outer walls probably date back to the original building, the great minaret dates from the 10th century.

Like all the great Imams, Al Hadi was a man of faith and of politics, of the pen and the sword. Of his works, two extensive commentaries on the Koran, a few shorter Koran treatises, and writings on the rights of 'Ali have survived, together with another work in which he attacked the legality on the Imamate positions of the caliphs Abu Bakr and 'Umar. There are also many writings on the function, purpose and history of the Imamate, other writings with a specifically theological content, and yet more writings taking one side or another in the theological disputes of his time.

Al Hadi came to Yemen within the frame-work of the ancient institution of "hijra". He was invited by parties in Sa'dah to judge their disputes, and in return the tribes offered him security and protection. For this reason he could, in his "hijra", establish his interpretation of the law, of Koran law, and also of the Zaidiya school of law. However, there was probably a third factor also at work, which also dates back to early South Arabian tribal society: it is not just anyone who can found a "hijra".

Among the prerequisites are the membership of a "holy" (in pre-Islamic times) or "pious" (after the coming of Islam) family. It was only because Mohammed belonged to the holy family of Mecca (the grandfather of 'Ali was the keeper of the key of the Ka'aba) that his founding of a "hijra" in Mecca had a hope of being recognised, and Al Hadi, too had some part in the particular blessing with which his family had always been associated, especially in Yemen.

We should not forget, though, that the Zaidi Imams had to establish themselves as foreigners, as Northern Arabians, in South Arabia, and were forever meeting bitter enmity on nationalist and on religious grounds (the latter was based on a "Protestant" reading of the Koran, in which sola scriptura was the only thing that counted). Added to this was the claim by Shi'ite and Zaidi Imams that only a descendant of the Prophet could fill the highest spiritual and secular position—which denied the Imamate even to highly talented local (South Arabian) pretenders. On this subject, we will quote just a few lines by the Yemeni scholar and poet Nashwan al-Himyari (1117-1178):

"When I speak with my opponents about the Koran,
Some of them quote me the words of Yahya.
And I reply: God's word is revelation!
And for you, it is the words of Yahya?"

The second Queen of Sheba: One of the shortest-lived dynasties of the Yemeni Middle Ages should be mentioned here: that of the Sulayhids and their Queen Arwa, which ruled for about half a century (from 1074 or 1086 to 1138) from Dhu Jiblah in the southern part of Yemen. The dynasty originated with a convert: 'Ali bin Muhammad al-Sulaihi. The family were Shafi'ites from the Harraz region. A friend of the family was a missionary sent by the Fatimid dynasty in Cairo to the Yemen. 'Ali was converted, and began to found a new kingdom based on Harraz in the year 1047.

After a series of battles he occupied Sana'a, but for about another 20 years he had to struggle with the black rulers of Zabid and the Zaidis in the north, until he could count Sana'a and the whole of Yemen south of the capital as part of his domain. 'Ali and his family went on a pilgrimage to Mecca, following the Tihama route, presumably in 1066/67. In Al Mahjam, the second largest city in the Tihama next to Zabid—later one of the three Rasulid capitals, along with Ta'izz and Zabid—a member of the Egyptian

Mameluke dynasty, ousted from power by 'Ali, laid an ambush for him. 'Ali was killed, and his wife 'Asma was taken prisoner. His son, Al Mukarram Ahmad, soon found his forces pushed back to Sana'a, which he was able to hold with difficulty. But he soon succeeded in reconquering the former Sulayhid possessions. He freed his mother in 1068, and one year later he married Arwa bint Ahmad (who is usually known in the chronicles as Al Saiyida al-Hurra al-Malika).

Presumably in 1086 he transferred all state authority to her and devoted himself—as a later chronicler reports—to the pleasures of wine and music. It appears that Arwa did not get on too well with her husband any more, but we do not know what the reasons were that persuaded him to give up his rule in favour of his wife. A little later (probably in 1087) Arwa moved her residence to Dhu Jiblah, that beautiful city in the warmer and more fertile southern highlands, which Al Mukarram's brother had founded some 20 years before as a governor's seat and which was praised by Arwa's court poet in the following lines:

"Neither Cairo nor Baghdad
Can be compared to the city
Which lies there, bounded by two rivers,
With its mighty fortress, the high Ta'kar,
Yemen belongs to that city!"

The following 50 years—Arwa died in 1138, and the dynasty ended with her—were full of the clash of weapons, but also of the sound of music and poetry in the palace of Jiblah. Arwa was an active and decisive ruler. She provided a lasting monument to her piety by turning her palace into a mosque, which still exists today, and where she is also buried. Arwa's long period of rule has remained in the memory of the people as a time of kindly and happy government. Her tomb in the mosque of her former residence of Jiblah is still visited by many people even nowadays.

Right, Solomon in his palace garden—covers of a rare and artistically remarkable Persian miniature.

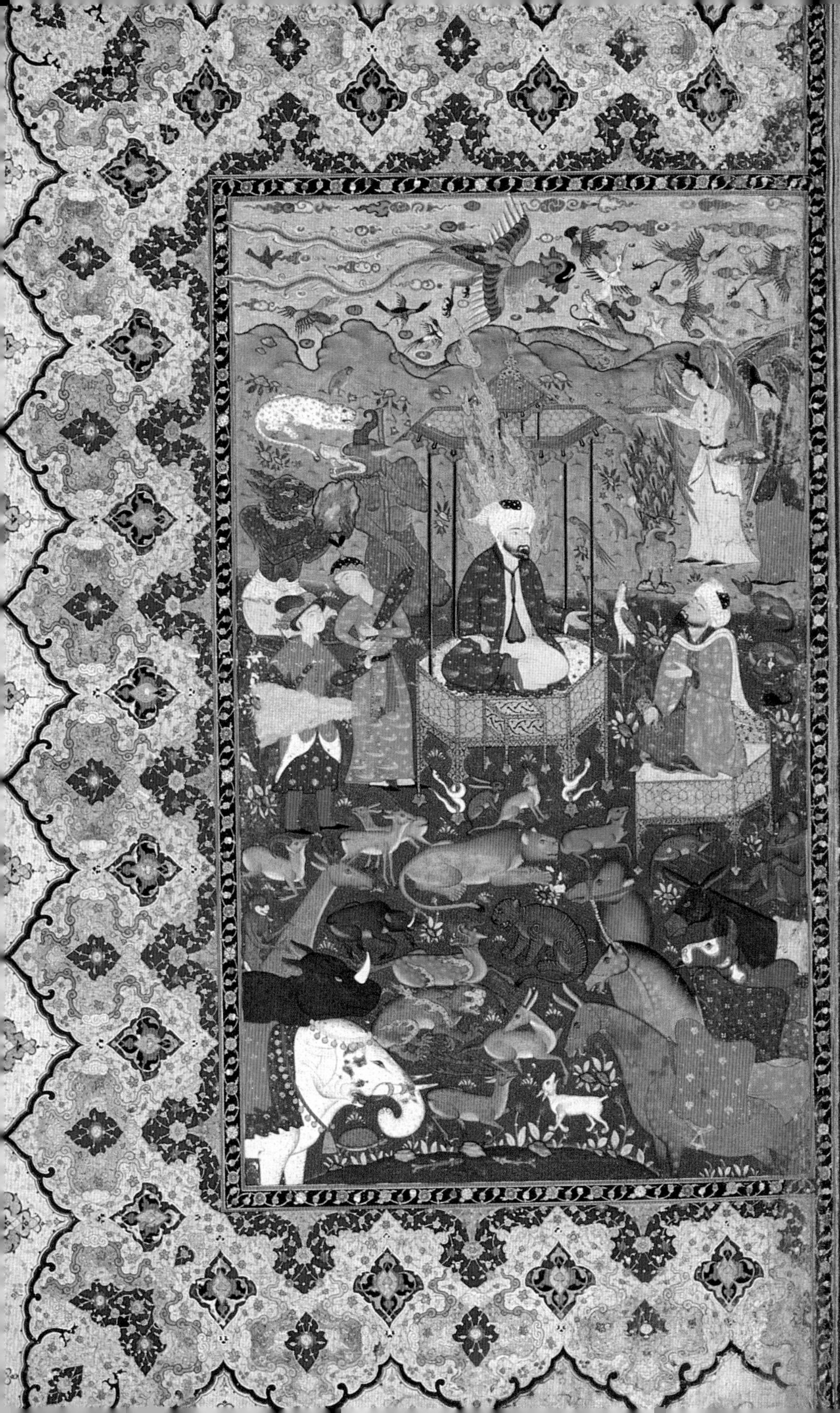

Which revolution in Yemen has been the more successful? The question has been asked again and again. There is no possibility of coming to a definite political conclusion, as both Yemeni revolutions were too different in the course of events, and even more in their results. In the north the quarrel was with the unequal social structure, which nearly all the theocratic Imams reinforced by their absolute rule, instead of finding some compromise.

In the south, however, the opposition was to colonial exploitation and to British imperialism, which added class differences to racial ones: white Britons, white Europeans, Indians and – last but not least – Arabs of higher or lower status, all cemented together by the British and southern Yemeni *raj*, a colonial administration along Indian lines.

Horseback fighters: Not until the end of the second Turkish invasion did all the tribes unite under Imam Yahya (1904–48). During World War I, which also spread to Arabia, Britain was worried about its base in Aden and tried to enlist the skilful horseback fighters of the Yemeni tribes against the Turkish garrisons. Although Yemen never joined the Entente, Imam Yahya, with the British at his back, saw the perfect opportunity to drive the ancient Turkish enemy out of the country once and for all.

Once the British colonel Lawrence of Arabia had succeeded in disrupting the Hejaz railway, essential for Turkish supplies and reinforcements, the greater part of the Turkish expeditionary force was defeated by Imam Yahya's federation of tribes and almost exterminated. The Turkish bases at Ta'izz, Al Mokha, Zabid, Hudaydah and the capital Sana'a were stormed despite dreadful losses, and the garrisons slaughtered.

Although the Yemenis were often openly in dispute with their Imam Yahya – he allied himself with or against the Turks according to the profits to be made from taxation – they were solidly behind their leader from 1916 to 1919, after his decision finally to drive the occupying power out of the country. When

the Turks were forced to withdraw in 1919, Britain honoured Yahya's valuable support in protecting the rear of Aden. The Treaty of Sèvres in 1920 gained Yahya international recognition as King of Yemen. However, nothing changed in the conditions of the Yemeni people, who had hoped for contact with the outside world. Treaties of friendship signed in later years – with Italy in 1926, the Soviet Union in 1927, Holland in 1933, Ethiopia in 1935, France and Belgium in 1936 and the United States in 1946 – remained almost meaningless.

Forces from the opposition soon arose in Yemen, with the aim of ending despotic rule. Young intellectuals, tradesmen and a few important local figures (owners of large estates and tribal leaders) were striving for political reform for a variety of quite different reasons. Most of these "rebels", though, were arrested and finally imprisoned. The original underground groups, Hai'at an-Nidal (Sana'a, a fighting organisation, 1933–44), the Free Yemeni Party (Aden, from 1944 on) and the Gamiyat al-Islah (reforming organisation, ibid from 1944 on) did not combine into the newly founded umbrella organisation Free Yemeni Movement until 1944.

The active phase of the first open rebellion against the Imamate in the modern history of Yemen began on 4 June 1944, when four prominent Yemenis fled from persecution to Aden: Sheikh Mohammed Ahmed Noman, Seijid Zaid al-Mukki, Al Qhadi Mohammed Mahmud az-Zubairi and Mohammed ash-Shami. The refugees were welcomed in Aden as "the best men of Yemen." Imam Yahya protested to the British authorities against their constructive criticism, published in the Aden newspaper *Fatat al-Jazirah* (*The Youth of the Peninsula*), and the authorities warned the paper to stop their attacks exposing conditions in Yemen. The

Preceding pages: Ali Abdullah Saleh and Ali Salem Al-Beedh celebrate unification. Right, a somewhat younger President Saleh.

fact that the British colonial power was making common cause against the "Free Yemenis" caused some waverers to return to Yemen out of fear and despair.

Those who remained openly addressed the following demands: first of all, he should permit a constitutional council of lawyers, bearers of high office and prominent figures; secondly, establish a special ministry of capable experts; and thirdly remove all his sons from positions of tribal rank. They were also not to be permitted to interfere politically in administrative matters. They were to receive pensions as a pay-off.

To fulfil these conditions would have

nation was set for 17 January 1948, and Imam Yahya was to be killed in his palace in Sana'a. The would-be assassins were successful in gaining entry to the palace, but were discovered by the chief of the bodyguard, Emir Amber, and forced to flee.

Without making certain of the event, the rebels notified the outside world by telegraph that the Imam had died on 17 January 1948 – and the false news did indeed go all round the world. However, the disappointed rebels did not give up easily. Patiently they waited for another chance. This came when the ruler had set out on a trip to inspect his estates near Hazayiz; they waited in ambush

shaken the theocratic Imamate to its foundations. Imam Yahya replied that it was his dearest wish to smash the provocative opposition. However, the "Free Yemenis" received some unexpected attention on 21 November 1946. Imam Yahya's eighth son, Prince Ibrahim, joined the rebels in Aden. They gave him the name *saif al-Haqq* (sword of truth) instead of his original title *saif al-Islam* (sword of Islam), and made him one of the leading figures of the resistance. Constantly in touch with their secret cells in the north, the "Free Yemenis" decided to assassinate the despot. The date for the assassi-

for his Cadillac, protected by bullet-proof glass. Pierced by more than 50 machine gun bullets, the "Unifier of the People" of 1916 met a dishonourable death in 1948.

The 1948 revolution: Without delay, the Crown Prince Ahmed made his way to the unconquerable Mountain Fastness of Hajjah with 180 soldiers, a truck full of US$100,000 and a sack of gold pieces. Immediately the "Free Yemenis" began their revolutionary march on Sana'a. Abdullah bin Ahmed al-Wazir, the candidate for the "secular Imamate", was proclaimed "leader of the country and head of state".

However, the leader of the Shafi'ite wing, Mohammed Ahmed Noman, and of the Zaidi camp, Mohammed Mahmud az-Zubairi, argued so much about whether the princely defector should await the successful outcome of events in the security of the southern town of Ta'izz or accompany the march to Sana'a that the unity of the front was broken. The consuming fear that favouritism would affect the expected distribution of posts also played its part. The ninth son of Imam Yahya, Al Abbas, gathered a tribal army of more than 20,000 warriors and on 11 March 1948 he stormed the "rebel city" of Sana'a. On 8 April 1948 the "People's

this had been seen in all the history of Yemen. This bloody sack of the city formed the basis for the successful revolution of 26 September 1962.

For 14 tortured years Imam Ahmed, an unreliable man given to violent rages, ruled from his capital of Ta'izz. He escaped several attempts on his life with difficulty, and was often severely wounded. Towards the end of his life his health was noticeably deteriorating due to his daily use of the hard drug morphine. He died a despised man in Sana'a in 1962 from the after-effects of an assassination attempt.

The revolution of 26 September 1962: In the

Imam", Al Wazir, was publicly executed and his head displayed as a warning to others on the Bab al-Yemen. The court cabal came up with new state slogans: "Down with the Constitution!" "Long live Imam Ahmed!" Thus Yemen's first revolution ended in a political, religious and human tragedy.

The new Imam Ahmed ad-Din allowed his tribal warriors to plunder and burn without hindrance in the city of Sana'a, a peaceful enclave among the tribal lands, protected since the days of the Prophet. Nothing like

Left, Aden, c. 1900. Above, Sana'a, c. 1960.

meantime, a potential avalanche of resistance to the house of Ad Din had built up. The conservative tribal faction expected the designated successor Crown Prince Al Badr to be a progressive thinker who would take care of their interests and be a just Imam. But the progressive underground movement, prepared for revolution, was already working towards a free republic and a final end to the secular and spiritual rule of the Imamate.

However, events took their own course, unexpected for both parties. The new Imam had held power in his hands for no more than a week before a coup by his confidant and chief bodyguard, Colonel Abdullah Sallal, swept him off the throne. Whether Al Badr had first been arrested by Sallal and Lieutenant Ali Abdalmoghny had then fired the shot, either with his pistol or with a tank gun, to signal the revolution in Tahrir Square in Sana'a–the course of events was obscured by the general hulaballoo. However, the all too premature celebrations were to have very serious consequences. In the midday heat, while the guards, euphoric with victory, were having a doze, Imam al-Badr, already proclaimed dead by popular opinion, rode unharmed out of the jail on a donkey.

He fought his way through to the Royalist

fighting constantly at the front, inflicted heavy defeats on the poorly equipped republican troops.

In order to avoid a total military defeat, Sallal appealed to the federal agreement with Egypt, ratified, oddly enough, by the crown prince at the time, Al Badr, on 8 May 1958. He asked Gamal Abdul Nasser for weapons and help. In 1964 the Egyptian expeditionary force, confident of victory, landed in the Yemeni Red Sea port of Hudaydah. However, Nasser's heavily armed troops could not prevail in the wild, rugged mountain terrain against the Malakis. The fact that Sallal had called in these former foreign

tribes in the north and, with their help and that of Saudi Arabia, fought a civil war which was to last for almost eight years and divide the country, the tribes, clans and families. Sallal, who appointed himself Marshal, soon lost the popularity of those first hours. He was neither a strategist nor could he win respect for the young republic in the eyes of the world. Again and again the Malakis, the Royalists led by Prince Mohammed al-Hussein, the commander in chief and political leader, Prince Abdullah al-Hussein, the co-ordinator and planner, and Prince Ahmed al-Hussein, the only royal representative

satraps from the Nile, hated since the days of the Turkish occupation, and the fact that they were soon plundering the Republican part of the country, finally split the freedom faction.

Many prominent Republicans opposed the new "occupation force" and their agent Sallal; among them were the former Minister of Defence and leader of the Council of the Republican Tribal Federation, Al Qhadi Abdarrahman al-Iryani and Hasan al-Amri, Lieutenant General and Commander in Chief of the Republican troops. In 1965 both opponents had become too uncomfortable for Sallal's liking. He sent them to Cairo on a pretext, where they were all placed under house arrest on Nasser's orders. Not until 1967 – Nasser had just suffered a catastrophic defeat in Sinai, and King Faisal was threatening to stop topping up Cairo's state treasury if Egyptian troops were not withdrawn from Yemen – did Nasser allow the detainees to return to Sana'a, knowing that Sallal was no longer capable of ruling.

It was only a short time later that Al Iryani forced the isolated Sallal to retire and he himself took over the newly created post of First Chairman of the Republican Council. Al Amri became Prime Minister and *fariq*, "Chief of the Generals of the Armed

Forces". From a historical perspective Al Iryani's correction of the 1962 revolution, undertaken on 5 November 1967, is an important date. From now on, in this almost exhausted republic, a handful of politicians was in power who were soon able to win the trust of all Yemenis. Without Al Iryani's "quiet revolution", the shaky republic would soon have fallen to the attacks of the Malakis.

As early as the winter of 1967–68 the

government was forced to show that it could stand up for itself. Sana'a was completely encircled by the Royalists for 70 days – from 1 December 1967 to 8 February 1968. Only the military genius of the commander in Chief Hasan al-Amri and the almost fatalistic, death-defying courage of the city militia, fighting for their lives, and the people of Sana'a, who feared another sack of their city like that of 1948, were able to break through the ring of besieging forces and liberate the city.

The battle of Sana'a, won by the Soviet Union despite delays in delivering the promised weapons, signalled a political change of course. Away from over-powerful allies and towards a peace with honour, that was the new state slogan. Every large tribe which left the banner of the Imam Al Badr, fast sinking into the dust of history, brought new life to the Republican forces. Secret meetings were held with federation leaders. Al Iryani, Abu Luhum, the powerful governor of Hudaydah, and Moishin al-Aini, a brilliant politician of the younger generation in his days with the "Free Yemenis", began the round of hard bargaining with the notables of the royalist tribes about subsidies, value and position in the young republic – decisive talks about the future of the country.

However, one man took the main courageous step to contribute to the survival of a liberal form of government. Qasem Munassar, tribal general of the Royalists and one of their best men, moved to the Republican side in the late summer of 1968 with his tribe of Beni Husheich and a total of 60,000 allied warriors. This took away the numbers that made the Yemen war militarily viable. Munassar had had enough of the suffering of his people. The crowd of princes, arguing among themselves in the Royalist headquarters, no longer provided a model of a reformed Imamate for the tribes. Munassar's selfless gesture, which ended with his murder by envious tribal leaders on 29 June 1969, prevented the total destruction of the Yemeni people.

On 16 March 1969, Al Iryani called together the first constitutional meeting of the elected parliament of Yemen and declared for a liberal political course: "Freedom and independence for every citizen of our republic. Sovereignty and no dependence on the great powers of this world!" The luckless Imam Al Badr had left Yemen on 8 March 1969 and had gone into exile in Saudi Arabia. However, King Faisal still supported some anti-Republican troops which fought on, trying to gain a strong bargaining position against Sana'a. Al Iryani signalled his readiness for peace in a reply during a radio interview on 22 March 1970: "We are calling for peace, because we believe that blood should no longer be spilled in useless war amongst ourselves." King Faisal got the message. He opened the palace gates of

elite followers, who now became ministers with and without portfolios.

The return of these politicians marks a date which was important for healing the rifts between the Yemeni people of the young republic after the long civil war. The kingdom of Saudi Arabia recognised the Arab Republic of Yemen as early as 23 July 1970, without conditions. This marked the official end of nearly eight years of conflict between the neighbouring states with their widely differing social systems. And from this point on the republic of Yemen could put its undiminished effort into rebuilding the country destroyed by war.

Jeddah to the waiting Yemeni peace delegation led by Premier Al Aini. The discussions ended successfully. After positive agreement had been reached, the sheikhs, ready to go home, and the prominent politicians of the Royalist side arrived on 24 May 1970 at the airport of Sana'a. After many years of absence the former foreign minister of the Royalists, Ahmed Mohammed ash-Shami, and his former deputy, Abdalquddus al-Wazir, stepped onto the now Republican soil. Ash-Shami was sworn in as a newly appointed member of the Republican Council, as were some of his

The war of independence in the south: For a long time Britain's grip on the South Arabian coast was a thorn in the side of the Turks in the north of Yemen, particularly after the opening of the Suez Canal in 1869. Imam Yahya, too, saw his claims to the southern part of Yemen fading away. The divisions among the Imams, the fighting between the Turks and the Yemenis and the growing resistance of the people to both systems practically put all the aces in the colonial power's hand. In 1839 a fleet of ships appeared off the lava coast of Aden, led by Captain Haines. The British, supported by cannon fire, attacked the only minimally fortified walls of the Arabian port. The sultans and sheikhs, who had been quarrelling with each other for many years, had nothing but camel cavalry to counter this attack. From this day onwards, the British crown ruled the coast of South Arabia with a firm hand, later adding the entire hinterland.

From the beginning they worked to the well-tried slogan "Divide and Rule!" It became the guiding light of all the British governors and high commissioners in Aden and in the protectorates. Not until the "Free Yemenis" marched on to Sana'a in 1948 did a common nationalist impulse go through all

onwards, they were to play a leading role in the development of the independence organisations *National Liberation Front* (NLF) and the *Nasserite Front for the Liberation of South Yemen* (FLOSY). While FLOSY wanted to win the war by peaceful means, the cell and cadre party of the NLF, supported from the beginning by the Eastern bloc, was never in doubt that only armed struggle, which began in 1963, would ever bring them success in their aims.

From 1963 on, their charismatic leader, Qahtan Mohammed ash-Shaabi, unified the movement and had all the strings in his own hands. For four long years the street battles

of Yemen once more. However, once the revolution had failed, the disappointed southern Yemenis fell back into their well-tried fatalism. Not until the early 1960s did underground groups in South Yemen began to resist the colonial power of Britain, which was becoming more and more oppressive. However, the trade unions in Aden had united in the Aden Trade Union Congress (ATUC) as early as 1956, and from 1961

Left, the return of tribal leaders to Sana'a. **Above**, the representative of the Yemen Arab Republic, Moshin al-Aini, addressing the UN.

were fought in Aden's Crater City and then throughout the whole hinterland. In December 1963 London sent Sir Richard Turnbull, an experienced diplomat, out to Aden. Armed with his bloody experience of the East African Mau-Mau revolt, he was to reign in the rising South Yemeni nationalism. However, his mission failed due to the unrelenting opposition of the NLF and FLOSY and he was replaced in May 1967 by Lord Humphrey Trevelyan. He, too, was unable to quench the nationalist fires, and in a secret agreement the British and the NLF decided to exterminate the Nasserite FLOSY. In Britain, giving up power to the NLF seemed the lesser evil when compared with the expansion of the Panarabic influence of Nasser in the South Arabian area. In three murderous days FLOSY was decimated to the point of insignificance.

After four years of fighting which had led to a dreadful loss of life the British decided to withdraw before the agreed date. Qahtan ash-Shaabi, designated the first "Bedouin and peasant president" of South Yemen, demanded £100 million as reparations for 128 years of colonial rule. However, the British would only allow a small sum. This put an end to all plans of rebuilding the

cil made up of three members led by the new President Salim Rubaia Ali. The main ideologue, Abdul-Fattah Ismail, became General Secretary and in May 1971 he was made chairman of the highest People's Council in South Yemen. However, the economic crisis of the 1970s allowed the left wing of the NFL to topple Rubaia Ali, who was interested in reunification.

On 26 June 1978 Rubaia Ali tried to force through his policy of reunification with the North, against the opposition of the party hierarchy, by means of a military coup. He failed and was later executed by firing squad. His successor, Abdul-Fattah Ismail, sought

country, and South Yemen thus became totally dependent on the Eastern bloc. The last British Highland regiment left Aden on 29 November 1967. South Yemen was free at last, but threatened to sink into party political squabbling.

Coups and presidential murders: The coup (or correction of political course) in South Yemen occurred as early as June 1969. On 22 June Qahtan ash-Shaabi was toppled by the radical left wing of the NLF, without the masses having dared to spill one drop of blood for their idol. The business of government was taken over by a Presidential Coun-

even closer ties to orthodox Marxism, and he united all the various factions of the NFL in the Yemeni Socialist Party (YSP), based on the principles of "scientific Socialism".

Ismail was put under pressure by the army and by various tribes and finally resigned in April 1980 "for reasons of health." He was exiled to Moscow, but returned to Aden in 1985 and was once more appointed to the highest party offices by the ruling President Ali Nasser Mohammed. The party and power struggles, which had been going on for nearly 20 years, reached a climax on 13 January 1986, when the President, pressurised by ultra-radical groups, tried to exclude the Politburo from decision-making. Abdul-Fattah Ismail and other high-ranking members of the YSP were shot during the process. However, the balance swung in favour of the party militia, which inflicted heavy losses on the forces of Ali Nasser Mohammed.

The South Yemeni civil war, which lasted from 13 to 24 January and in which various parts of the army hastened to help each of the factions, is said to have claimed the lives of 10,000 Yemenis. Large parts of Aden were destroyed. Ali Nasser Mohammed was forced to give up and flee to exile in North

formed a governing council of seven members, which took control of the country. A number of parliamentary and democratic elements built up by Al Iryani were dissolved. Colonel Al Hamdi tried to strengthen the power of the army at the expense of the tribal federation, probably because defeats were barely avoided in the border wars with South Yemen in 1971 and 1972.

Yet another factor was Al Hamdi's desire for reunification with the South, which did not fit in with the plans of Saudi Arabia or the tribal fundamentalists. This led to his being shot by a fundamentalist group of assassins on his country estate on 11 October 1977.

Yemen with 20,000 followers. Haier Abubaker al-Attas became President, and he is the present head of state. The fates of those responsible for the government were no less turbulent in North Yemen. The peace-making president Al Iryani was forced by pressure from Saudi Arabia, the conservative tribes and the army to submit his resignation on 12 June 1974. The following day Colonel Ibrahim Mohammed al-Hamdi

Left, Partisans fighting British colonial troops in the mountains of South Yemen. **Above**, victory dance after a successful battle in South Yemen.

His successor, Colonel Ahmed Hussein al-Ghashmi, recalled the National Parliament, which unanimously elected him president on 28 April 1978.

Once again it was to become obvious that only a strong army and a powerful central administration could keep control of Yemen, holding off coups and the tribal federation. However, this suited neither Riyadh nor Aden, both of whom agreed to all plans for unification on the surface but in fact attempted to undermine them. Just as Al Hamdi had been killed one day before his planned journey to Aden, his successor, Al

Ghashmi, suffered the same fate one day before his planned arrival in Aden. He was blown apart by a bomb hidden in a briefcase left in his study by a South Yemeni emissary. The explosion in the President's room had barely subsided before the former military governor of Ta'izz, Lieutenant Colonel Ali Abdullah Saleh, had acted, presenting himself as the new head of state. Just two days later, the members of the National Parliament confirmed him as Commander-in-Chief of the army and President of Yemen.

Saleh's darkest hour came seven months after he took office. The border war of 1979 with the People's Democracy of South Yemen had brought the armies of the Republic to the brink of defeat. It was only thanks to the tribal confederation that the South Yemeni plans for conquest failed. In May 1983 the National Parliament confirmed the President in office for another five years. Free elections held in June 1988 legitimised Ali Abdullah Saleh for another period of office. Even though his actions are sometimes controversial, Saleh remains a strong president who has succeeded in keeping control of his government and in pressing ahead with the rebuilding of the republic.

Oil paves the way: After their revolutions, the two states of Yemen were both in an extremely precarious situation. North Yemen was deeply in debt due to shipments of arms, mainly from the Soviet Union; South Yemen remained isolated in the Arab world for a long time because of its socialist orientation. Gradual reconstruction began in the Yemen Arab Republic with the re-establishment of outside contacts, including those with the West.

The infrastructure in particular was improved and expanded by road building, the building of new airports, water supplies and other projects involving technical and financial aid. The constant deficit of the state budget was reduced by capital aid from Saudi Arabia and the supply of Yemeni labour to work in Saudi oilfields. Naturally, when the recession in Saudi Arabia and the Gulf states came, this had disastrous consequences. In 1987, the budget showed a chronic deficit of US$390 million (1987).

The commencement of oil exports from the oilfields of Ma'rib and Al Jawf, discovered in 1986, and from those near the former South Yemen border near Shabwa gave some grounds for cautious optimism concerning the future economic development. The stabilisation of internal politics in North Yemen, the activities of a series of investors in trade and in the medium levels of industry, as well as the rising production of oil, were all signs of a positive development. The interest of foreign states in investing in North Yemen was increasingly noticeable.

With the closing of the Suez Canal after the Six Day War in Sinai, South Yemen, meanwhile, had lost its only opening to the outside world – the much frequented free port of Aden. It also faced bankruptcy after the struggle for independence and the refusal of the British to grant compensation. Foreign debts were high, officially standing at US$1.4 billion. For this reason, the totally impoverished though militarily well-equipped country could make only slow progress towards economic reconstruction.

Even today, despite great efforts, the infrastructure in the south does not match up to requirements. With its annual per capita income of US$550, South Yemen was one of the poorest countries in the world. There was no industrial production in the region; fish, salt, cotton, tobacco, honey and animal hides being the main exports. The socialist planned economy allowed no private enterprise. Some 200,000 South Yemenis earned their living as migrant workers in Saudi Arabia.

A brighter future: After the unification of the country in 1990 (see panel), remittances sent from Saudi Arabia ceased altogether when the Saudis expelled citizens of Yemen during the Gulf War. However, it seems likely that in the future the united Republic of Yemen will no longer have to be so dependent on neighbouring states. The continued exploitation of the country's vast oil reserves should help to put the economy back on its feet. And having regained its free port status, Aden will also have a key role to play in the country's fortunes.

Right, **President Ali Abdullah Saleh casts his vote for the new constitution.**

YEMEN UNITED

After 1970, it became ever more apparent that North and South Yemen were developing in opposite directions. While the north became an Arab Republic based on the Egyptian model, in the South the radical Marxist faction prevailed and founded the People's Democratic Republic.

Countless people who had lost all their possessions through the nationalisation policies desperately sought sanctuary at the other side of the border. This had already been set in the border treaty signed between the British colonial power in the south and the Osmanic power of occupation in the north.

The tensions between the two Yemens erupted in 1972 with the first border war. Through Arabic mediation the fighting could be halted after four weeks. Under the provisions of the subsequent treaty agreed in Cairo, Yemen was to become a united republic with a freely-elected parliament. Sana'a would be the future capital, and Islam the state religion. In certain sectors of the economy there were to be state-run monopolies, elsewhere developments would be left to the forces of private enterprise.

Despite a good deal of optimism on both sides, it soon became clear that unification was not going to be easy. In 1979 relations reached a new low-point when a second border war broke out. This time it was Kuwait that intervened and succeeded in bringing the two presidents to the negotiating table. Both sides promised a serious new beginning on the road to unification. The most important step in this process was the creation of a new constitution. A National Committee was formed to this end and presented its draft in 1981. But the question of when the constitution was to come into force remained unanswered.

The Yemen Council was founded, with the two presidents at its head. A joint commission at ministerial level worked on the standardisation of the education system. Commissions were also established to resolve the problems of land and water transport, as well as tourism.

The newly-discovered oil fields in the eastern border region demanded a speedy resolution of the differences between the two sides. The Kingdom of Saudi Arabia lay claims to this disputed area and stood poised to take advantage of the conflict between North and South Yemen.

Then in 1986, President Ali Nasser Mohammed was the victim of a coup in South Yemen. Ali Nasser, a personal friend of President Saleh, was welcomed in the north and permitted to station the sections of the army that had fled with him along the frontier. The new rulers in the south declared that they no longer felt bound to existing treaties; it seemed that the days of the cold war had returned.

But then came the astonishing events in Eastern Europe and these had a profound influence on developments in Yemen. President Saleh now wanted to force the reunification of the country. The south was beginning to feel the effects of the new policies of the Soviet government. But for a small sum outstanding, all financial aid from the USSR was cut. The leadership simply had to change course.

President Saleh conceded to practically all the demands of his bothers in the South and a transitional government was established in advance of parliamentary elections. The borders were opened and citizens of the Yemen could now travel to the other side without having to worry about being observed by the secret services of the respective territories. A presidential council with Ali Abdullah Saleh as chairman and Ali Salem Al-Beedh as his deputy was proposed.

Events then began to accelerate rapidly. The joint constitution which had been accepted by both governments was presented on 21 May 1990. There was only opposition in Sana'a from the ranks of the Muslim fundamentalists who refused to be part of any treaty with the "infidel Communists". But the vast majority of the population supported the process of unification, a fact to which the later referendum on the constitution impressively testified.

May 22 1990 was the day on which the newly united Republic of Yemen was born. In Aden, President Ali Abdullah Saleh hoisted the new Yemen flag – this, too, a concession to the South.

Islam has developed almost as many religious trends as Christianity. The main division lies between Sunnis and Shi'ites; the latter comprise some 10 percent of all Muslims. The origin of the split lies in the question of the Caliphate. Caliph (Arabic: *khalifa*) means "successor". The matter in question was the succession of the spiritual and secular leader of Islamic society to follow Mohammed. Some were of the opinion that any member of the Quraish tribe was suitable for consideration as a successor to the Prophet. In accordance with the actual distribution of power at the time, they therefore recognised the choice of Abu Bakr, 'Umar and 'Uthman as the first three successors to the Prophet. The opposing body of opinion, later termed "Shi'ites", held that right from the beginning 'Ali, Mohammed's son-in-law, should have taken over the leadership of all Muslims and the post should have gone to his successors. The term "Shi'ites" comes from the expression "the party of 'Ali" (Arabic: *shi'a(t) 'Ali*).

The Imam holds a central position in the Shi'a. The primary meaning of Imam is "leader of prayers", but the word is also used for an outstanding religious leader. The word has a third and very specialised meaning for Shi'ites. For them, the Imam is more: the recognised leader of their community, in some branches of the Shi'a no less than the mediator of divine will, free of sin, infallible, more than a pope, or, in the words of Grünebaum, a superhuman man.

The Shi'ites: In addition, the main branches of the Shi'a harboured another singular belief: that of the "disappearance" of the Imam. These faiths are of the opinion that one of their Imams, the last of the line, in each case, did not die, but "disappeared" and lives on, in concealment, and that he will return one day as Mahdi. This belief has given the two main branches of the Shi'a their names–the

Sevener and the Twelver Shi'a, who believe their seventh and their twelfth Imams to have "disappeared", thus ending the "actual" line of Imams. The Zaidis, realistic theologians and thinkers in other areas as well and also quite closely linked to the Sunni branch of the faith, did not have this particular institution. Their line of Imams, therefore, continues historically; the Imams had none of the almost supernatural aura of the seven or twelve "canonical" Shi'ite Imams, but were

considered to be normal secular and religious leaders, so that the revolution and the republic did not present a theological problem in Yemen, simply a factual end to the rule of the Imams.

The origin of the Shi'a: The actual split between Sunni and Shi'a goes back to the rule of 'Ali, the fourth caliph. 'Ali had left Medina for southern Iraq and had made Kufah his capital. In Damascus, in the meantime, the provincial governor Mu'awiya from the Umayyad family (part of the Quraish tribe) had made himself the de facto master of Syria and was not willing to submit to the Caliph 'Ali. The first battle between him and 'Ali (657) was indecisive. In Siffin, beside the Euphrates, the fortunes of war were beginning to turn in the Iraqis' favour when the Syrians stuck pages from the Koran onto their lances and demanded that the Holy Book and not war should decide the quarrel. 'Ali had to bow to the majority of his followers who did not want to spill blood within the Islamic community. After 'Ali's murder in 661, Mu'awiya was able to consolidate his power in Iraq as well. 'Ali is buried in Najaf– one of the greatest places of pilgirmage for Shi'ite Muslims to this day.

'Ali's son, Hassan, renounced all his

rifice and dedication, all bound up with high hopes of the afterlife, up to and including a longing for death. The main branch of the Shi'a, after the death of 'Ali and his two sons, considered the son of Husain, 'Ali Zain al-'Abidin, and his son, Muhammad al-Baqir as the fourth and fifth Imam.

The Zaidis: At this point the Zaidis split off from the main branch of the Shi'ites. Zaid, another son of 'Ali Zain al-'Abidin, gave this name to the Zaidis.

The Zaidis are political realists within the Shi'a, so much so that they have been termed the "fifth school of law" of the Sunnis. Their pragmatic viewpoint, not at all ideological or

claims to the throne and moved back to Medina. Thus the Umayyads in Damascus were able to establish themselves as the actual rulers of the Islamic world, while at the same time Shi'ite propaganda, reinforced by the opposition of Syria to Iraq, found new adherents in the underground movement.

'Ali's second son, Husain, renewed the struggle. He was eventually killed in 680 at the battle of Karbala' (Kerbela in southern Iraq). His martyrdom gave the Shi'a its passion and denial of the world, its capacity for enthusiasm, its willing acceptance of sac-

extremist, is shown by the fact that their Imams can be of the line of Hassan or Husain, and that they do not recognise any supernatural qualities in their Imams. For the Zaidis, too, the Imamate was never hereditary. On the contrary, every new Imam had to distinguish himself by his own achievements from among the very numerous descendants of 'Ali and then had to have his merits recognised, in a kind of democratic process, by the leading men of the country. Among the preconditions were scholarship, knowledge of interpreting the law, natural common sense and the ability to succeed against opposition. The Zaidi Imams, therefore, never formed a dynasty. It was recognised that there could be times without an Imam or with rival claimants. In contrast to other branches of the Shi'a, then, the figure of the Imam in Yemen was considered to be completely human, and it was never denied that the Imam could commit sins or make mistakes.

The differences between Zaidis and Sunnis are few. The main differences are a somewhat expanded call to prayer and a strict disapproval of popular religious traditions. For this reason, you will see no "saints'" tombs or *wali* in Zaidi Yemen

a spiritual leader appointed by God, who would continue the work of Mohammed, with the sole exception that he could not improve any more on the Koran.

After Ja'far's death the Shi'a , which had already been left by the Zaidis, split into two main branches: the so-called Sevener Shi'a and the Twelver Shi'a. The "Seveners" recognised Isma'il as the son of the already deceased Ja'far, as the "disappeared" Imam, though some of them also recognised his son Muhammad. This gave them their name of Ismailis. After these two there were no more Imams (hence "Seveners"). We will not go further into the many subdivisions of this

although they form part of every settlement in southern Yemen and the Tihama.

Sevener and Twelver Shi'ites: The sixth Imam (in the Shi'ite system of counting), Ja'far al-Sadiq, can be seen as the actual founder of the "Imamites". The "Imamites" (mostly known as Twelver-Shi'a by outsiders) form the official Shi'ite trend in present-day Iran. Ja'far was of the opinion that humanity needed, from time to time, to have

Left, the Koran inside a mosque. **Above**, the mosque offers the faithful space to study religious scriptures.

group here, but confine ourselves to the examination of two branches which had a part to play in the history of Yemen.

The Qarmats in Yemen: Qarmat, one of the Ismaili missionaries, founded a sect often described as "communist" in principle, which established a state in Bahrain in 899 (it existed until 1076) and which included Mecca in 930. The Qarmats sent two of their followers (one was a Yemeni) to Yemen: Ibn Haushab Mansur al-Yaman and 'Ali bin al-Fadl, who brought large parts of Yemen under their control around and just after the year 900, in a series of rapid and bloody conquests. We know little about the content of their teaching, which must have contained a good deal of social dynamite. It remains uncertain whether 'Ali bin al-Fadl actually permitted wine and incest or whether this was propaganda by his opponents. One chronicler reports that 'Ali bin al-Fadl had announced in the chancel of the mosque at Al Janad that the prophet of the Hashimite family (= Mohammed) was dead, and now a new prophet had arisen! In 912 he conquered Sana'a, diverted the canals into the Great Mosque and flooded it. His path was reportedly marked by murder and death, by violence and extremes of behaviour. Ibn Fadl

was poisoned while Mansur al-Yaman had died a short time beforehand. With the deaths of both, the episode of the Qarmats in Yemen was ended, even if some of their ideas survived in one form or another.

The Taiyibiya Ismailis: The other main branch of the Ismailis were the Fatimids, who established their magnificent rule (910-1171) in Cairo in 969 and divided into the groups of "Assassins" and "Taiyibiya". The latter received their name from Al Taiyib, a Fatimid who presumably died as a young child, who was recognised by Queen Arwa as the rightful successor to the Fatimid line in

Yemen and as the "disappeared" Imam, whose incarnation she herself represented. In her lifetime, the leading scholars appointed an independent religious leader of the community who became the recognised head of the sect after Arwa's death (without making any claims to the title of Imam).

The Taiyibiya Ismailis are still to be found in Yemen today (in the Manakhah area), but soon found more and more followers in India who outnumbered their co-religionists in Yemen so that the spiritual head of the sect moved his seat to India (Gujerat) towards the end of the 16th century.

The Twelver Shi'ites: Back to the most important body of Shi'ites, the Twelver Shi'a. Their name comes from the fact that the eleventh Imam, Hassa al-'Askari, died in 874 without an heir. Most of his followers eventually came to believe that he had a son, who was however not visible (or recognisable) in this world, but would return one day in order to take over the world and realise the triumph of the Shi'a. This 12th Imam is the Mahdi ("the one guided by God"), an eschatological figure, who is similar in many respects to Christ and who will divide good from evil in the Last Judgement.

The hidden existence of the Mahdi led to a great increase in Iran of the importance accorded to religious scholars, who, until the Mahdi returns, are obliged to collect and interpret the teachings of the eleven Imams. The Twelver Shi'a today forms what is easily the largest group of Shi'ites and is therefore often equated to the Shi'a itself.

The Sunnis: The Sunnis teachings appear much clearer. This is probably explained by the fact that their sources of law–the Koran and the Sunna of the Prophet–were completed and can therefore only be explained and interpreted. Sunna refers to the practice of the Prophet: that which he said and that which he did, as it was reported by his companions. It is obvious that in this case criticism of the sources and an attempt to build up a reliable chain of reporting must play a central part.

There are four main schools of law in Sunni Islam today, the Hanafis (codified in the 8th century), the official school of the Turks; the Malakis (8th century), the

74

Hanbalis (9th century) and the school of Al-Shafi'i (767-820), mainly found nowadays in Lower Egypt, Bahrain, Indonesia, Malaya and Yemen. More than half of all Yemenis belong to the Shafi'i school of law, mostly in the southern part of the country, the Tihama and the Democratic Republic of Yemen.

The Shafi'ites: Muhammad Al-Shafi'i was born in 767 in Ghaza, grew up in Mecca and belonged to the tribe of Mohammed, the Quraish. He showed an early interest in poetry and practised his language skills on the ancient Arab poets. At the age of 30 he came to Yemen, but his concern with Islamic law dates from his later years in Baghdad and

religious school–did they become the dominant school of law in the southern part of the country.

If you look closely at the features of the two main religious groups in Yemen, it becomes obvious that–apart from the fact that both dislike religious extremes–the idea of scholarship is of paramount importance. For the Zaidi Imams, it was a formal precondition for the post, and the countless written works of the Imams still in existence bear eloquent witness to this. These works are the pride of the mosque libraries, especially the library of the Great Mosque in Sana'a. The same is true of Shafi'ite Yemen. It has its

Cairo. He laid the foundations of his fame as a scholar in Cairo, and that is where he died. His beautiful tomb, with the dome built by the Ayyubid King Al Malik al-Kamil in 1211/12 is still standing today.

From Baghdad and Cairo the Shafi'ites soon found followers in all Islamic countries, although the process was admittedly slow to start with in Yemen. Not until the institution of the madressa–the

Left, decoration on the Mutawakkil Mosque in Sana'a in Midan at-Tahrir. **Above**, the mosque of Dhi Bin.

scholarly centre in Zabid, where Abu Qurra Musa bin Tariq founded a higher, originally Hanafi college as early as 819, which, for more than a thousand years, was the university of Sunni Yemen. The University of Zabid is a good 150 years older than Al Azhar in Cairo which was founded in 972.

The faith of Islam: The subject is as wide as a continent; it is for this reason that delving further into it is not possible, instead few but important aspects are examined in detail.

The cornerstone of Islamic faith is God, Allah in Arabic. The word is identical with other Semitic words for God, Il or El, or the

Elohim of the Bible. It is linguistically connected to the word for "first".

The Koran–the word of God revealed to the Prophet Mohammed by the angel Gabriel–describes in words of great poetry the boundless power, but also the unbounded goodness and mercy, and in particular the uniqueness of God. *La ilaha ill Allah* can be translated as "there is no God but God".

For this reason, Islam is also opposed to the Christian doctrine of the Trinity, accusing it of falsifying the oneness and uniqueness of God. In any case, Islam does not see itself as a new religion, but as "the" faith, the true faith as it has existed from the beginning, as it has been revealed again and again by the prophets, and falsified again and again by the evil and indolence of human beings. Mohammed, therefore, refers to himself as the last of the prophets (the Seal), by no means higher in rank than Abraham or Solomon, Moses or Jesus, who is incidentally accorded a particularly honourable place among the prophets by the Koran. Jesus is the son of Mary, a prophet, but not of God himself.

The Koran is completion and the re-creation of the Holy Scriptures. It therefore allows the heathen no place within the Islamic state, but respects Jews and Christians, "people of the Book". They are permitted to follow their faith, but have to pay higher taxes.

The essence of the Koran can be seen most clearly in two of its Suras:

"In the name of God, the compassionate, the merciful. Praise be to God, the Lord of the worlds, the merciful, the compassionate, King on the day of reckoning! Thee only do we worship, to thee do we cry for help.
Guide thou us on the straight path
The path of those to whom thou hast been gracious,
With whom thou art not angry, and who do not go astray."
(Sura 1)

"In the name of God, the merciful, the compassionate!
Speak: He is God alone, God the eternal,

He begetteth not and he is not begotten,
And there is none like unto him."
(Sura 112)

The Koran was not written down until after Mohammed's death. The authentic edition of the text recognised to this day followed during the rule of the Caliph 'Uthman. The parchments discovered in 1972 in the Great Mosque of Sana'a, the most important find of Islamic manuscripts in this century, also contained a few palimpsests dating from the first century of the "hijra"–i.e. pages with text which had faded and which were re-used as writing material during the first century of the hijra. Those original lines which can still be recognised are the oldest known fragments of the Koran.

The creed of every Muslim of every branch of the faith is a single sentence, which is also heard from the minaret during the call to prayer:

"Ashhadu an la ilaha il allah: Muhammadun rasul Allah."
"I profess: there are no Gods but God. Mohammed is God's Prophet."

The words of this creed form the first and most important of the "five pillars" of Islam which are the distinguishing signs of a Muslim. The other four are prayer, the giving of charity, fasting and the pilgrimage to Mecca.

The Islamic calendar: The Islamic calender is a purely lunar calendar. A lunar year has around 354.5 days; a month has 28 or 30 days. For this reason, and also when compared to the Western calendar, the important religious festivals are moveable, such as the festival of sacrifice 'Id al-Adah, also known as the "Great Festival" 'Id al-kabir, as well as the festival that marks the end of the fasting month of Ramadan, the festival of fast-breaking, the "Little Festival" of 'Id al-saghir. During the month of Ramadan everyday life in Yemen is completely changed; day becomes night and the other way around.

Right, minaret with Yemeni-style decorative brickwork in Sana'a.

"Yea, thou art fair, my beloved,
Yea, thou art fair..."

Thus the Song of Solomon, which does indeed appear to be based on Solomon's meeting with the Queen of Sheba. In the Bible the queen remains nameless, but in the Koran, and in Islamic tradition she is Bilqis. She became a symbol of their country for the poets of Islamic Yemen at a very early stage, and is compared more and more frequently to their contemporary situation. The glory of the past, the power of the kingdom of the Queen of Sheba acted as a contrast to the deplorable current state of affairs. The 12th-century poet Nashwan al-Himyari wrote:

"Where is Bilqis, she of the mighty throne,
She of the castle, higher than all other castles?"

In this symbolic and political sense, Bilqis became a fixed image of Yemeni poetry, particularly in this century. "Bilqis" stood for the country of Yemen, its humiliation by the rule of the Imams and by colonialism were described as her suffering; at the same time, Yemenis believed her to be a mythical figure of the beloved, giving the politically minded contemporary poet the strength for revolution and the re-creation of a new kingdom of Sheba or Saba. We only have space to quote one of these poets, the most respected of Yemen's living writers, 'Abdallah al-Baraduni:

"From the country of Bilqis comes this melody
And this plucked string,
From its air these winds and this magic,
From its bosom these sighs, from its mouth
These songs, from its history these memories.
From Fortunate Arabia these songs
And from its dark shadow these evil shades .
And wicked images.
With their sorrowful song they surround my senses

Songs whose tune is played by the double flute,
Verses full of song and full of tears,
Full of magic and youth and blossoming grace.
The song arising from blossoming bushes
With every note it fills the air with scents
And yet it begins to lament the wound in its eye,
From which bloody tears drop to the ground."

The Queen of Sheba in the Bible: Solomon (he ruled from 965/64 to 926/25 B.C.), as the Bible reports in the First Book of Kings, had seven hundred wives of royal birth and three hundred concubines. The visit of the one thousand and first is described thus: "When the Queen of Sheba heard about the fame of Solomon...she came to test him with hard questions. Arriving at Jerusalem with a very great caravan–with camels carrying spices, large quantities of gold, and precious stones–...Never again were so many spices brought in as those the Queen of Sheba gave to Solomon."

This–even if the text was not written until later–is the earliest historical mention of the Queen of Sheba. Surprisingly, in all the many ancient inscriptions in Yemen, there is never any mention of the Queen of Sheba.

The capital of the kingdom of Saba or Sheba was Ma'rib, where the Wadi Adhana breaks out of the Yemeni highlands in a narrow gorge and flows out into the eastern desert. Irrigation was used in this favourable spot as early as the third millennium B.C. Soon the irrigation works had expanded to such an extent that a clever system of distribution had created a fertile oasis–the basis for the life of the city of Ma'rib.

Irrigation technology and civilisation have here reinforced and supported one another. The maintenance of the ever more complicated system of dams required a

Right, under the gaze of Solomon, Bilqis crosses the glass-covered water.

ران آب رحمید جیا ماه مردم که دوان میدان در آمدندی حیال لروندی که ابست جامه

لاکشیدندی واین کار لر برای آن کرد که چنداینجه دیوان ملعنت پس کفته تو بدند چنان هست

بن ملعنتین بکریاس سلیمان سپید

مینه دید اندیشه که آنست جانهای حوزرا بالاکشد خانکه سلیمان ساقهای او

centralised state administration, which developed into the historical era of the state of Saba, around the capital of Ma'rib, from about 1,000 B.C. on. As the Wadi Adhana had the most plentiful water supply of the seasonal rivers of eastern Yemen, Saba soon became the most important of the ancient South Arabian kingdoms and a fixed station on the so-called frankincense route, along which Sabaean caravan leaders soon dominated the long-distance trade between the Indian Ocean and the north.

There are several pieces of evidence for women rulers of the Arabs in those early years. In 733 B.C. the Assyrian king Tiglath-

figure of "the" Queen of Sheba–she is not, therefore, a purely mythical figure, but does indeed incorporate a bit of reality, even if there is no actual historical figure behind it.

The New Testament and the art of the Middle Ages: Jesus brought the Queen of Sheba out of the distant past and made her his ally. On the Day of Judgement, "The Queen of the South will rise at the judgement of this generation and condemn it; for she came from the ends of the earth to listen to Solomon's wisdom, and now one greater than Solomon is here." (Matthew 12:42 and Luke 11:31)

The word for south in the Semitic languages is "T-m-n" or "Y-m-n". Here, then,

Pileser II reports a victory over the North Arabian Queen Samsi:

"And Samsi, the Queen of the Arabians, at the mountain of Saquirri,
9,400 of her warriors I slew, 30,000 camels...,
5,000 sacks of spices of every kind I obtained as booty. And she,
To save her life, she turned her face to the desert."

In this way Sabaean trade and the surprise that women ruled there may have led to the

Jesus is speaking of no-one else but the Queen of Yemen.

This link between the Old and New Testaments kept the theologians busy as early as the first century of Christendom. The Queen of Sheba stands for the Church, which is on its way to Christ, the new Solomon. This parallel inspired sculptors from the 12th century onwards to create their majestic portrayals of the Queen of Sheba at the entrances of Corbeil and Chartres, Parma, Wells and Freiberg. Another theological parallel soon brought the Queen of Sheba inside our churches and cathedrals. Scenes from the Old Testament were linked to those from the New. Now the Queen of Sheba, offering Solomon her gifts of gold, frankincense and myrrh, was to be seen in the windows of Cologne, Canterbury or Strasbourg, next to the Three Kings, who were presenting the infant Jesus with their gifts of gold, frankincense and myrrh. These images survived until the time of Hieronymous Bosch, in whose "Adoration of the Magi" of c. 1510 the richly embroidered collar of Melchior is adorned with the Old Testament precursor of the same scene.

Ghiberti and Piero della Francesca drew political parallels with the meeting of

From 1452 to 1459, Piero della Francesca then created what is perhaps the most perfect representation of what was unfortunately to remain an imaginary combination of East and West, symbolised by the Queen of Sheba and Solomon. From Ghibertini and Piero it is not far to Raffael and Holbein, who re-interpreted the meeting of the two monarchs as a relationship between the Catholic and Protestant churches, Raffael for the Vatican and Holbein for its opponent, the English king Henry VIII.

On Raffael's fresco of 1519 a venerable King Solomon can be seen and it is not difficult to recognise him as representing the

Solomon and the Queen of Sheba, at the same time providing us with the most noble portrayal of the ruling couple. On a bronze relief on the Baptistry in Florence, a dignified ruler and a noble, serene female figure step towards one another, set amid idealised Renaissance architecture. Ghiberti's relief refers to the attempt to unify the Eastern and Western churches in the face of the Turkish threat, and to the Council of Ferrara (1438), at which both the Emperor Sigismund and the Patriarch of Constantinople took part.

Above, frieze of stone blocks in Ma'rib.

Catholic church, embracing in his arms the Protestant daughter who seemed to have strayed. The first to turn Raffael's image into its political opposite was Hans Holbein the Younger, around the year 1535. He chose Solomon and the Queen of Sheba as a test piece in the hope of obtaining the post as court painter to Henry VIII. Here King Solomon sits on the throne, obviously well pleased with himself, bearing the features of Henry VIII. Humbly and begging for forgiveness, the Sheban approaches. This was how Henry wanted to see the humble approach of Rome–and this was why he appointed Holbein as court painter!

The Queen of Sheba in Islam: In the Koran, the kingdom of Saba or Sheba plays a much greater role than in the Bible. The final bursting of the dam at Ma'rib, a few decades before the arrival of the Prophet, is explained as the punishment of God for the pride and sin of the ancients, and as a sign of the changing times. The visit of the Queen of Sheba to Solomon (Sulaiman in Arabic), too, is adorned with exciting and fairy-tale detail. At the end of the story, in sura 27, verse 44, it says: "It was said to her: Enter the palace, and when she saw it, she thought it a lake of water, and bared her legs. He said: It is a

the enticing reference in the Bible to the "hard questions" of the Queen of Sheba—which are, by the way, not mentioned at all in the Koran text.

It is said that the Queen of Sheba sent Solomon a small box which contained a large pearl with no hole through it and a jewel which had had a crooked channel bored through it. With the entourage came 500 boys disguised as girls and 500 girls disguised as boys riding on noble horses. "If you are a prophet, then separate the boys from the girls, bore through the pearl and thread the jewel."

Solomon had bowls of washing water

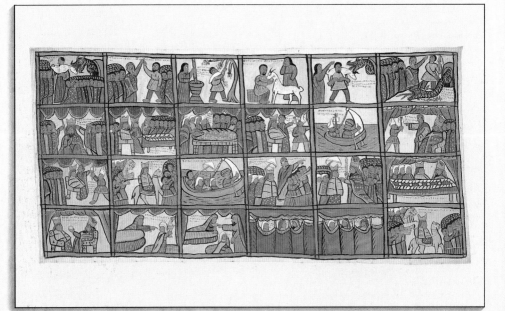

palace paved with glass. She said: O my Lord! I have sinned against my own soul, and I resign myself, with Sulaiman, to God the Lord of worlds."

Just as in the Bible, the heathen Queen converts to the faith of the true God—but the story of the "deep water" is so short and so incomprehensible to us that the background of the story must have been familiar to the contemporary readers and listeners to the Prophet Mohammed's words. Fortunately, the reports of Arab and Persian historians and commentators on the Koran are helpful.

First of all, they concern themselves with

brought to the young people, and it was seen that the girls delicately wet their hands, while the boys energetically plunged their arms into the water. In order to bore a hole through the pearl, Solomon called the termite, who appeared and ate her way through the pearl. In gratitude Solomon gave her the trees to live in. Then the King asked: "And who will put a thread through the jewel?" A little white worm appeared, took a thread in its mouth and pulled it through. In gratitude Solomon gave him and all his descendants the chance of a secure life inside fruits. Once Solomon had solved all the riddles, and the Queen of Sheba had finally decided to meet with him, Solomon ordered the spirits who served him to build him a palace into which he could bring Bilqis. The demons were frightened, because they feared that Solomon would fall in love with Bilqis and that she would bear him a son, then the demons would have to serve the son as well. So they thought of a trick. They floored the palace with a sheet of glass, under which the creatures of the sea were swimming. Bilqis, rumour had it, had hairy legs, and the spirits hoped that Solomon would be put off by this unattractive view. When the Queen of Sheba came, she did

them. "We do not know," was the answer. Then he called the Demons. "How can this be removed?" The same answer: "A razor." And Sulaiman replied again: "A razor would hurt the skin of a woman's thigh!" Then the demons let him wait for a long time, but eventually they brought him a paste of gypsum. And Ibn 'Abbas said of this event: "Verily, it was the first time any had heard of the paste of gypsum."

There you have it–the history of the invention of depilatories! However, it should become clear at the end of this chapter that there is more to this story– namely the recollection of ancient belief related to hair

indeed think that she had to wade through water, raised her skirts–and what was to be seen on both her thighs? Tightly curled hair!

When Solomon saw this, he turned away his eyes and called his subjects one after another. First, human beings. How ugly this was, he complained. "How can this be removed?" They answered: "With a razor, O Prophet of God!" Sulaiman replied: "A razor? That would hurt the skin of a woman's thigh!" Then he called the Djinn and asked

**Left, an Ethiopian illustration of the story.
Above, Bilqis in a comic strip.**

on the legs of supernatural beings.

The Queen of Sheba in Ethiopia: In Ethiopia the ancient legend was accorded more importance than anywhere else in the Middle East. Right up until Haile Selassie, who even had it written into the constitution, the rulers of Ethiopia believed themselves to be descended from Solomon and the Queen of Sheba. In a certain sense they were quite right, as the kingdom of Saba once belonged to the Ethiopians. As early as 500 B.C. and before South Arabian tribes (among them the Habash, who gave their name to Abyssinia) had settled on the opposite coast of

Africa. The Ethiopian church language, Ge'ez, is closely linked to ancient South Arabian, and the script is based on ancient South Arabian letters.

The earliest and, in a literary sense, most perfect portrayal of the Ethiopian legend of the Queen of Sheba is the "Kebra Nagast", "the Splendour of the Kings", dating from the 14th century. It tells of the journey to Jerusalem of the Queen of Sheba, an Ethiopian from Axum, the ancient Christian and pre-Christian religious capital of the country. The Queen–known as Makeda in the Ethiopian story–was impressed by Solomon's wisdom, and in her turn, she

attracted his interest. Solomon had a highly seasoned meal served, and when Makeda denied him the night of love which he suggested, he made a deal with her: if, during that night, she were to touch any of his property, she would have to submit to him... Thirst overcame the beautiful queen and she drank from a jug of water. Solomon was successful. Once again, water plays a part before the two are united.

A son, Menilek, resulted from their association. Once grown into a young man, he travelled to Jerusalem and, amid many miracles, brought the Ark of the Covenant to Axum. He then became the founder of the Ethiopian dynasty.

Another legend has survived in Tigre, a very interesting popular version of the story. A girl named Eteye Azéb ("Queen of the South") was to be sacrificed to a dragon. Seven saints appeared and slew the dragon. Some of its blood dripped onto the girl's foot, which turned into a donkey's hoof.

The people, delighted because of the death of the dragon, chose the girl to be queen. She travelled to see Solomon who healed her donkey's hoof. In this folk-tale version, the night of love with Solomon is, of course, described in a specially detailed fashion!

"I have come to thee from Sheba": In the Koran Solomon is portrayed as even more mighty than in the Old Testament. His authority, his wisdom and his faith are embellished even more magnificently. The visit of the legendary queen, the ruler of Yemen, is also, naturally enough, described in the sacred book of Arabia with particular interest and in lively imagery. Sulaiman is lord of all the creatures of the world: human beings, birds and spirits. One day, when all his subjects had gathered before him at his command, he noticed that the place of the hoopoe was empty. Obviously Sulaiman had not considered the fact that the hoopoe is a migratory bird. He became extremely angry and threatened the bird with dire penalties unless it could show a good reason for its non-appearance.

A little later the hoopoe arrived and had a good reason: it had flown as far as Yemen and there it had seen a wonderful green country, ruled by a mighty queen who worshipped the sun instead of God. "I have come to thee from Sheba with certain news," said the hoopoe. Solomon, determined to follow up the matter, sent the bird back to Ma'rib with a letter. The letter required the Queen of Sheba to renounce heathen ways and turn to God, the all-merciful, the all-compassionate.

Queen Bilqis sent an emissary with gifts and riddles; impressed by what she heard, she herself travelled northwards and turned to God. Al Tabari (c. 838-923), one of the early historians of Islam, further embroidered the meeting of the two rulers in the chapter on Sulaiman. He wrote that Sulaiman sent Bilqis back to Yemen where she married a prince of her kingdom. Then Sulaiman ordered the demons to build the gigantic castles of Yemen for the couple, first among them was the castle of Salhin in Ma'rib. By the time of Sulaiman's death, the demons had finished their work and, in an everlasting memorial to their work, had listed their deeds in Sabaean script on a wall:

> "Salhin we built
> In seventy-seven summers,
> One after the other.
> Siwah we built,

sidered the daughters of his princes as his own property.

Once upon a time, while hunting, the vizier heard voices singing–he had met the Djinn. He fell in love with the daughter of the King of the Djinn and married her. For the daughter from this marriage, Bilqis, he built a palace far away from Ma'rib so that the tyrant king should never get to see her. However, one day what the vizier feared finally happened. The king desired her, but Bilqis lured him to her chamber, made him drunk with wine and struck off his head. The people, however, were delighted and chose her to be Queen of Ma'rib.

> Marah and Bainun
> Our hands bathed in sweat.
> Hinda and Hunaida
> and the seven walled places of Qa'a,
> And in Raydah the castle of Tulfum!"

Other medieval chroniclers had plenty to say about Bilqis' descent. They claim that the father of Bilqis loved nothing as much as hunting. He was the vizier of the King of Sheba, a dreadful tyrant, who also con-

Left, Solomon and Bilqis. **Above**, Bilqis presents Solomon with gifts.

The parallels of this story with the Ethiopian folk tale (girl sacrificed annually to the dragon, which is finally killed by the brave Queen-to-be) are quite clear. The Yemeni fairy tales keep this same motif in many variations. The young woman appears as the sun (worshipped by the Queen of Sheba in the Koran, too), which is to be married or sacrificed to a demonic being. This demonic being is a water divinity, and the scene of passing through water in the Koran can only be understood with reference to the folk memory of the pre-Islamic Yemeni faiths.

EARLY TRAVELLERS

Many travellers, Arabs and non-Arabs, have described Sana'a. **Ibn Rusta**, who visited the city in the 10th century, wrote in his *Book of Useful Notes*: "It is the city in Yemen, which is without equal in the highlands, in the Tihama or in the Hejaz. It is unrivalled by any other in size, wealth, age and in tastefully prepared food..."

A century later, the Yemeni historian **Ahmed ar-Rasi** described the high buildings of the northern district of the city, Bab Sha'ub as: "They rise high up to heaven. Their upper floors are marvellous and built with great craft and skill. They serve as apartments for the governors who come from Iraq (the Abbasid governors)."

Even the famous **Ibn Batuta** visited Sana'a in 1331 and left an interesting description of the city: "The city streets are completely paved. When it rains, the rainwater washes the city clean."

The Englishman **John Jordain** visited the Turkish pasha in 1609 and remarked: "The city of Senan (Sana'a) is not a great city, but it is well positioned in a valley, surrounded by walls which are interrupted every 40 paces by a tower. The city has fertile soil, and the fruit and vegetables which are sold in the market are cheap. It is a pleasant city to live in with a mild climate—not too warm and not too cold."

CARSTEN NIEBUHR

Seven years later the Dutchman **Pieter van der Broeke** came to Sana'a. He was impressed by the legendary past of the city and wrote about a great mosque with more than 100 pre-Islamic pillars.

The German **Carsten Niebuhr** arrived in Sana'a in 1763 as the leader of a Danish expedition. He stayed in the city for only ten days, but in his book *Discoveries of the East* he left a very precise description and a map of the city. First he described an audience with the Imam: "A little later we were led directly before the Imam and instructed to kiss his right hand inside and outside and also his right knee. This we did, one after the other...

Each time we did so, a herald cried out loud: God save the Imam!" Niebuhr had walked through the city in order to take notes for his book. About the market of Sana'a, he wrote: "I saw in a market more than 20 different sorts of grapes. The local Jews make wine from the grapes, but cannot trade with it, as the Yemenis are great, indeed fanatical enemies of strong drink. If a Jew is caught bringing wine into the house of an Arab, the penalty is harsh..." As a farewell gift, the members of the expedition received "an Arab outer robe and undergarment and a letter addressed to the Dola at Mokha, which contained the instructions to pay us a farewell gift of 200 talers." Niebuhr reported: "I run ahead of myself to say that we received the money in instalments and that the Dola was most reluctant to pay up."

Left, Lintel with Sabaean inscriptions. **Above**, Carsten Niebuhr, an explorer of Yemen.

Turpin P.   Lambert J.sculp

Coffee is one of the most popular drinks on earth. A third of the human race drink it regularly, and, especially in Europe and America, they usually drink more than one cup a day. Members of the most widely differing races and cultures all have the same preference for a cold or hot brew of the roasted beans. Only a few consumers know that as late as 200 years ago all the coffee in Europe came from the little port of Mokha, a tiny town on the Red Sea in what is today North Yemen. The name mocha is the only reminder of the original home of coffee.

A story circulating in Yemen tells how Ali ibn Omar al-Shadhili, the "patron saint" of Mokha, offered passing Portuguese sailors some of his daily constitutional drink. He made the drink from the beans, which, after roasting, were grounded with mortar and pestle and boiled in water, he served this brew with the words "Qahwa, taman!" The sailors noticed with great surprise that the black brew renewed their strength and even healed them of some chronic ailments. They were so impressed that they took a few sacks of the green beans home with them. In this way the secret recipe of Ali ibn Omar al-Shadhili reached Portugal, and from there it conquered the whole of Europe and the rest of the world.

The saint lived towards the end of the 15th century. His tomb can still be seen in the great Al-Shadhili Mosque in Mokha. It is doubtful whether coffee actually did reach Europe via Portuguese merchants. The route via the Ottoman empire, which reached from the southern tip of the Arabian peninsula to just outside the gates of Vienna, seems more likely. Even nowadays a very strongly brewed coffee, with its grounds floating on top, is known as Turkish coffee. Coffee would, in this way, have made its triumphal progress through Europe in an easterly direction, so to speak. Whether it came via

Left, *coffea arabica*: illustration of a coffee plant. Above, coffee farmer in the Bani Matar region near Sana'a.

Lisbon or Istanbul, every single sack of coffee originated in the western mountains of Yemen and made its way on the backs of camels or donkeys along a 30 to 50 mile (50 to 80 km) route to the port of Mokha.

Sir Henry Middleton, director of the British East India Company, landed in Mokha in 1610 and, on his way back, took with him the first sacks of coffee to be seen in England. Six years later, Captain Pieter van der Broeke came to the harbour of

Mokha and enquired for his part about the possibilities of the coffee trade for the Dutch East India Company. In the meantime, the first coffee houses in Vienna and Amsterdam opened their doors. As early as the mid-17th century there were coffee houses and complete coffee shops to be found from Oxford and London to Boston and New York in the New World. An early poster, now on exhibition in the London Museum, praises the positive qualities of the new drink: "It enlivens the spirit and lightens the heart...it also helps to ease sore eyes...is excellently suited to prevent or heal giddiness, nausea or the loss of teeth...it is neither sedative nor stimulating." In many countries, coffee houses were soon discovered as comfortable meeting places and frequented by musicians, authors, artists and politicians. Johann Sebastian Bach even composed a special coffee suite in honour of the enlivening drink.

As soon as the colonial powers discovered the value of coffee they tried to bring the trade under their control. The English, the Dutch, the French and the Americans, one after another, established factors in Mokha in order to buy the treasured beans at the best possible price and then to store them in

out of Yemen and had them planted successfully in Ceylon and Java. The French had no less success with their overseas plantations.

The colonial powers had hereby achieved their long-desired aims and could now control not only the trade in coffee but also its production. No-one wanted to pay the price demanded by the Arabs any more. The various empires produced their own–more cheaply. Even so, up until the end of the 18th century 22,000 tonnes of coffee were exported annually via Mokha. The lion's share of this amount went to America. However, exports then declined rapidly, and

warehouses until the next ship arrived. It was not unusual for these factors to hold diplomatic rank and to be permitted, for instance, to fly the flag of their country from their enclave. For this reason, the claim is certainly justified that the first diplomatic relations between Yemen and Europe came about thanks to coffee.

Up to the end of the 17th century nearly all coffee for the world-wide trade came through the port of Mokha. However, the days of the town's flourishing trade were soon to be numbered. The Dutch had by now succeeded in smuggling young coffee plants

the coffee trade of Mokha almost ceased. During the first 80 years of the 19th century the population of Mokha shrank from 20,000 to the tiny number of 400 inhabitants. From then, coffee production became the privilege of the eastern colonies. From there, the production of coffee moved further east to South America and eventually to Africa.

Yemen, whose role as a coffee producer was almost forgotten by the rest of the world, has never given up growing coffee. The western mountain ranges fulfill exactly those climatic conditions in which the coffee bush flourishes. From Razih, near the town

90

of Sa'dah, to Wadi Warazan to the south of Ta'izz, the farmers nurture their coffee shrubs, planted in terraced fields, as their forefathers did before them. During the harvest period, from April to June, about 10,000 tonnes of hand picked red coffee beans are still spread out on the flat roofs of the houses to dry. After the drying process, the beans are packed into linen sacks and transported to the old market in the capital of Sana'a. Just as in earlier years, every single sack is weighed and then placed in the Samsarah, the former caravanserai. Later the dried husk is removed from the beans and packed in separate bags. A Yemeni custom

has a specialised use in the chocolate industry as a flavouring. Brands such as Matari (from the Bani Matar area) or Haimi (from Al-Haima), both examples of *coffee arabica*, are valued by coffee experts. Yemeni coffee is widely known for its strong aroma. It is just the right coffee for blending with other kinds from Brazil or Africa. The North Yemeni government wants to encourage and expand coffee growing. In 1980 the Ministry of Agriculture began a development project to expand coffee production. Using modern scientific methods, researchers are trying to increase the yield per acre of plantation. Also,

to do with the husks is very much to the advantage of coffee growers. This is the taste for *qishr*, a hot infusion of coffee husks, flavoured with ginger, cinnamon and cardamom. The price per kilo for the coffee husks is even greater than the price for the green, unroasted beans.

Seventy percent of these are still exported, mainly to Saudi Arabia, Japan, Europe, the Soviet Union and the USA. Yemeni coffee

Left, coffee trader in the Suq al-Milh of Sana'a. **Above**, only ruins are left of the famous port of Mokha.

everywhere in the country nurseries for young coffee shrubs have been set up, with the plants being sold to the growers for a small price.

Expert opinions differ on the hopes for an increased Yemeni share of worldwide coffee production, currently worth about two billion US dollars a year. On the negative side, the flat plantations in Africa and Latin America are less labour intensive to run and can therefore produce cheaper coffee. Positive hopes for a revival of coffee production lie in the powerful aroma and unique taste of Yemeni coffee.

Every afternoon the same ritual is carried out. Whether you are in the city or in the country, the afternoon is *qat* time. In the morning people arrange where to meet to enjoy *qat* together. Friends, colleagues, neighbours and relatives meet after lunch in the host's home and go up to the *mafradsh*, the best and the highest room in the house.

A *qat* party: After greeting each other, the guests make themselves comfortable, with the host taking up the central place at the rear

end of the long room. Usually, everyone brings his own bundle of arm-length twigs wrapped in plastic film to keep them fresh. Only if it is a special occasion, a wedding for instance, will the host also provide the *qat*. If a stranger is a guest and arrives without *qat*, he is generously given twigs by everyone there. Only the young tender leaves are carefully plucked off the leaves and chewed. The pulp is pushed into the inside of the left cheek until the latter is as round as a ball. What at first sight looks like bad toothache is actually the full cheek of a practised *qat* chewer. Beginners tend to swallow the green leaves instead of just the juice.

While the body relaxes, the spirit spreads its wings, and everyone takes part in lively conversation. After about two hours the conversation dies. You communicate with your neighbour without words and occupy yourself with your own thoughts. Eventually only the peaceful gurgling of the narghiles or the noisy slurping of the men is heard, followed on each occasion by "Al-Hamdu Lilah"–praise and thanks be to Allah.

Not until the sun sinks towards the western horizon, tracing beautiful patterns on the wall of the room as it streams through the coloured windows, does a change of mood befall some guests. The chewed *qat* pulp is spat into a container intended for the purpose and the mouth is rinsed with cold water. Tea with milk is served at the end of the party. The guests collect their *djambias* and jackets and leave the gathering.

Herbal side-effects: As the use of *qat* plays such a central role in the life of many Yemenis, it is a matter of vigorous controversy and is often sharply criticised. The Yemeni institution, Centre for Yemeni Studies, published a book on the subject in 1982: *"Qat in Yemen and its role in Yemeni life."* The opinions of prominent authors range from absolute rejection to total justification.

This dispute is a very old one. The central question is whether *qat* belongs to the drugs forbidden by the Koran or not. One typical answer is that of the Islamic scholar Ibn Hadshar al-Haythami (A.D. 1504-1567) to a question posed by the inhabitants of Sana'a and Zabid. In his opinion, *qat* belonged to the so-called *shubahat*, those dubious cases on which even the Koran cannot give a clear decision. He recommended that Yemenis should distance themselves as much as possible from this drug, even if the use of *qat* was not among the forbidden activities.

Chemical research by the World Health Organisation (WHO) has established that there are two substances in the young *qat* leaves which are responsible for the stimulating effect: cathin and cathinon. The latter is an earlier stage in the biosynthesis of cathin. Both substances are very closely related chemically to the amphetamines, and have almost identical effects. Just like amphetamines, cathin and cathinon are both responsible for the release of adrenalin. As a result, body temperature and blood pressure rise, the pulse rate increases and the emotional state of the person becomes excited. The after-effects of taking *qat*, which could be described as a sort of "hangover", are loss

days and Fridays. However, all attempts to restrict the use of *qat* in North Yemen have failed miserably up to the present time. Those in favour of *qat* describe the chewing process as a harmless habit which unites all ages and levels of society in a communal rite. Its opponents argue that that this habit swallows up to 30 percent of monthly income. In some families the purchase of *qat* is carried out at the expense of buying food.

Despite all this, Yemen is by no means the

of appetite and sleep, nervousness and even depression. However, the intensity of the "hangover" depends on the type of *qat* used. The very expensive kinds are supposed to have no after-effects, while the cheaper and probably poorer sorts produce ill effects.

Supply and demand: *Qat* is completely prohibited in other Arab countries such as Saudi Arabia and the Gulf states. In South Yemen the use of the leaves is restricted to Thurs-

original home of the *qat* tree. It is assumed that the *qat* plant was introduced about 700 years ago from Ethiopia. Only a few actually used the drug: the Sufis, Muslim mystics, used it in their search for a deeper insight into the nature of the divine, and rich merchants used it simply out of boredom.

Not until this century, and especially during the last thirty years, did *qat* cultivation increase, to the extent of driving out coffee plantations in some places. One can hardly blame the farmers, because a hectare of *qat*, given the demand, brings a profit five times that of agricultural products.

<u>Preceding pages</u>: *Qat* gathering in the mafradsh. <u>Left</u>, enough leaves for the afternoon. <u>Above</u>, *qat* seller in the Tihama.

TRADITIONAL DRESS AND FASHION

Up until the revolution of 1962 clothing was traditional, but afterwards it changed considerably, both for men and for women. You can still see some examples of traditional women's dresses, with their colourful, complicated and varied patterns, in the recently opened National Museum in Sana'a. Historical sources mention both the export of Yemeni textiles and the import of the finest textiles from various countries of Europe and Asia–right back to the days of the Queen of Sheba.

The *hadith* mentions that the wives of the Prophet Mohammed asked him for cloth from Yemen. In the sixth century, the Ka'aba in Mecca was covered with Yemeni cloth.

South Arabia had far-reaching trade connections from the earliest historical times, as there was great demand everywhere for frankincense and myrrh. As sailing in the northern part of the Red Sea was very dangerous and no-one knew how to make use of the monsoon winds, goods were transported by camel along the routes which link present-day Oman with South Yemen and also crossed the Silk Road to China. Over the centuries the range of available products increased due to the growth of trading links.

The fine imported textiles were so expensive that they were reserved for the elite. Ordinary people had to make do with cloth produced within the country. This was true both of cotton and of dyes. For centuries there was an important indigo (*nil*) producing industry in Al Dahi and in Zabid in the Tihama, and up until the revolution, indigo-dyed cotton was the main material for clothes. However, this skill has died out in the last twenty years. Today, dyed cloth makes up a small portion of Yemen's manufacturing industry.

The Tihama was still producing 552 tonnes of cotton in 1953/54, but the present figure is far below that amount. This cotton is prepared partly in the factory built in Zabid in 1957 and partly in the works built by the

Chinese in Sana'a in 1967. However, not much is left today of the traditional textile industry which was mainly based in the Tihama. The weavers first mentioned by Carsten Niebuhr after his journey in 1762 still exist in Al Duraymhimi, in Al Manzar and also in Bayt al-Faqih. In these places, they still weave according to the old methods, but nowadays, of course, they use chemical dyes.

After the civil war Yemen began to break down its inner and outer isolation. The large-scale migrant working of the men and the rise in purchasing power that this brought about made it possible to buy a rapidly rising number of imported goods, among them textiles and clothing.

The most important article of "clothing" for the men of the highlands is the dagger or *djambia*. Basically, there are two kinds of dagger: the J-shaped *asib* and the less curved *thuma*, which is only carried by the religious upper classes. The prices of daggers vary according to material and workmanship. A handle made of ivory or rhinoceros horn makes an enormous difference to the value of the dagger.

In the more remote tribal areas men still wear their long hair untied. Particularly in the mountain regions there are still old men to be found who proudly wear their hair in the traditional way and skilfully drape a cloth about their shoulders. The men in the Tihama prefer to wear straw hats–the fez-shaped *kufiyah* deserves mention. Many young men like to wear the "Palestinian" chequered headress, imported from Japan or Korea. Among young men, too, Western influences via tourism or TV have changed fashions in clothing and hairstyles.

The traditional garment of the men of the Tihama is the wrapped embroidery skirt or *futah*, wrapped around the hips and fastened with a belt. In the highlands a calf-length shirt, *zanna*, is worn, with a jacket over it. The belt is, of course, adorned by the *djambia*.

Women's dress shows a greater variety, as

Left, woman wearing the *sitara*.

it is a sign of their place of birth–except of course the wearing of the *sharshaf* (a black skirt, cape, veil and head covering) or the *abaya*, a loose black coat. The *sharshaf* was introduced by Turkish women to Sana'a only 50 years ago. The wives of the Imam were the first to wear this kind of dress, but it was soon copied by other upper class women. Today the *sharshaf* is widely worn in Yemen.

The veil is an important part of women's clothing. It acts as a symbol of proper male and female behavior. It makes it possible for women to keep their distance, and men are visibly reminded of the limits of decent behaviour. Veil, *sharshaf* and *abaya* are worn to protect women. They are also status symbols, however, for they are signs that a woman is well provided for.

In some towns, especially in Sana'a and Rada', women nowadays wear the *sitara*, a large, brightly coloured and patterned cotton cloth which covers them from head to foot. However, this is often made of cheap cloth imported from India, even if it is made solely for Yemeni women. Here too, the colours of the material used show regional differences. In Sana'a dark *sitaras* predominate, while the women of Rada' prefer a pale or white background. The *sitaras* in Machwit are blue with red dots.

In the Tihama women wear a variety of different styles. In the north, in the Wadi Mawr region, women wear translucent muslin dresses, *gamis*, in glowing orange, scarlet or yellow, and huge straw hats on top of their head coverings. In contrast to the women of the mountains they do not wear the veil. In rural areas the women wear a skirt, a fitted upper garment and a cloth draped around the head. Other fashions predominate in towns such as Zabid or Bajil: black or white poncho-style dresses, made of artificial fibre, with yellow or black machine embroidery about the neckline. The V-neck is sewn shut until the clothes are sold–a sign that the dresses have not been worn. The broad, long stripes of skilful embroidery on the old black cotton dresses of some women are usually still done by hand. Many regions of the Tihama have their individual styles. In Zabid, dark cotton dresses are worn, wide cut

and with a light-coloured square of some other material set into the upper part. In Bayt al-Faqih, a few miles away, you will see mainly long, close-fitting dresses in black or white, skilfully embroidered.

The clothing of the women in the highlands is quite different. Here they usually wear the *sirwal*, a pair of baggy embroidered trousers. For everyday wear, the trousers and the embroidery are usually fairly simple. It is difficult to obtain hand embroidered *sirwals*, as sewing machines have now taken over this job. In the suq, you can also buy the embroidered leg sections and attach these to the trousers. Normal dress consists of the *sirwal*, an under-dress and a wider dress over the top. The latter has a dropped waistline with a pleated skirt and is usually made of polyester.

Unfortunately, the old traditional dress has become an increasingly rare sight in Yemen. However, items of traditional clothing can be bought as souvenirs in the suqs of Sana'a, Ta'izz or Sa'dah. Here your can buy cotton dresses from the Tihama with very wide and long sleeves, *zinnyhi* adorned with brass rings, or the close-fitting black velvet dresses with costly silver embroidery from the Djebel Harraz region.

Their preference for bright and glowing colours is not the only typical characteristic of Yemeni women–they are also true artists in the skill of draping veils and head coverings. It is hardly a sign of a lack of talent for fashion among Yemeni women that Western eyes are usually too unskilled to pick up such niceties.

For some time, textile shops have been flourishing in Yemen since more and more women are making dresses to suit their own tastes. The cheaper fabrics come from the Far East, but the finest silks and textiles from Europe or China can also be found. It might perhaps be possible, so that this tradition should not be completely lost, to re-awaken an individual style once more, before the market is swamped completely by off-the-peg clothes from Morocco, Egypt, Indonesia or Thailand.

Right, an unveiled woman from the Tihama.

Just a quick glance at the street life in Yemen will show that women appear in public much more rarely than in many other countries and that they cover themselves with a variety of articles of clothing to escape unwanted stares, to keep their distance and to avoid unwelcome attentions.

In front of strangers and outside the house Yemeni women make themselves invisible, but this does not mean that they are considered unimportant. The veil is often written about the life of Yemeni women, another factor which helps this stereotyped view to survive. How do women live in Yemen today? It is of course impossible to generalise this. Just as in any other country, there are no homogenous groups, as the situation of women primarily arises from tribal law, and apart from the large number of tribes, there are also various regional factors to be considered.

Among these factors are the geographical

seen as as a symbol of the oppression of women within Islam. Yemeni women living in the countryside often do not wear a veil, but the veil, has until recently, been seen quite often in the city. Mixed company is very rare in this strict muslim country, but it is by no means unknown.

Men and women lead strictly separate lives, and for a visitor from a different cultural background, this is yet another sign of the supposed oppression of women. However, many Yemeni women would not recognise themselves in this particular image. In literature, very little has been features of the country. The practice of building settlements on mountain peaks and other picturesque sites, such as is done in the highlands, certainly increases the workload of Yemeni women. Food, firewood, water–it all has to be dragged up from the hillside to the homes. The isolation of individual settlements was increased, until very recently, by the absence of roads and motorised transport, and this factor still influences behaviour, clothing and language to this day. There are also considerable differences in women's opportunities for work and education in urban and rural areas.

According to the 1986 census, 86 percent of the population still live in the country.

Yemeni society consists not only of the various tribes, but also of various social classes: the *sadaah* or aristocratic elite, the *qudhat* or judiciary, the *gabili* or tribespeople, and right at the bottom the *akhdam* who perform the dirtiest tasks. The social class into which a woman is born will have a decisive influence on her prospects for marriage and employment.

within the tribe, even if its representatives to the outside world have always been men. There is no documentary evidence of the position of women within the tribes, but it is known that the women of Djebel Sabir in the Ta'izz region and those of the Wadi Al Jawf are strong and energetic personalities. In some of the more remote northeastern districts women are even said to drive cars and carry weapons.

The process of modernisation, however,

The rapid changes which the country has undergone since the end of the civil war in the early 1970s have had widely differing influences on the lives of women. Family and tribe are of great importance to men and women. Tribal structure and territories, such as the Hashid and the Bakil in the northern and north-eastern parts of the country, have remained essentially unchanged for centuries. Women had a strong position

has lessened the influence of women. The opening up of areas by newly built roads has restricted their mobility because there are far more strangers about. Other factors in this lessening of influence have been the large number of migrant workers who have returned from Saudi Arabia and the Gulf states to insist upon "proper" behaviour from their wives, and also one-sided development projects which portray women as housewives and mothers.

Yet another factor influencing the lives of women is the economic development of the last twenty years. The large-scale exodus of

Left, in the country women often do not wear the veil. **Above**, at the weekly market in Wadi Dabab.

migrant workers seems to be in correlation with the kind of farming which is carried out in some areas. The absence of men forces women to take over at least part of the work. In some cases this has helped them to be more independent, but often they have been placed under the supervision of a male relative. After the peak in the numbers of migrant workers in the 1970s more and more men are coming back to their home country. However, those who return often do not want to go back to the hard life in the country. Instead, they move to the towns and usually leave the care of the family land and the farming to the women.

of the population still live, work is still very scarce and hard to come by. The hardest tasks–according to information from the women themselves–are the evermore difficult task of fetching water and firewood and the cutting of alfalfa, the feed for the family cow. Just looking after one cow can take up to six or eight hours a day. Water and wood are mostly carried on the head, and women often have to carry between 20 to 25 kilos (44 to 55 lbs) for long distances uphill.

Apart from housework and bringing up children, Yemeni women often earn a little extra money by selling dairy produce or dried cow or sheep dung, animal husbandry

On the other hand, the migrant workers have sent huge sums of money back into the country, most of which benefitted their families, while the government, unable to secure its share, imposed taxation on the population. The government, therefore, is still dependent on help from outside the country, mainly from other Arab states. But many Yemeni families are now able to purchase modern consumer and household goods, which has led to a considerable reduction in workload for women, especially in the towns.

In the country, however, where 86 percent

or craft work. It is estimated that women do around 70 to 75 percent of the work in agriculture and animal husbandry.

Before the 1962 revolution there were hardly any schools in the country. Over the last twenty years their number has risen drastically, as has the number of students. This has improved prospects for men and women of securing a job and attaining different division of roles. The indirect spread of information via television, the presence of foreigners and greater mobility have also helped speed this process. It is no longer assumed as a matter of course that a daughter will follow in her mother's footsteps. Yemeni women are now beginning to show interest in learning. However, because of the numerous different dialects spoken in country areas, many women have difficulty in following television or radio programmes.

About 53.8 percent of men and 93.2 percent of women are illiterate, and the percentage in rural areas is much higher than in the towns. Although regular school attendance is increasing, the increase is greater among boys than among girls. There are still too few schools and far too few teachers, which has led to the large-scale employment of Egyptian and Sudanese teachers–all men, of course. As expected, the lack of women teachers has a particularly negative effect on the number of girls attending school.

International organisations usually measure the position of women by their share in the world of employment, their education, their legal status and their health care. Around 68 percent of women over the age of ten can be said to be actively taking part in the economy. They work almost exclusively in agriculture. Only 1.5 percent are active in the official employment sector, usually as teachers but also in banks, ministries and offices. In theory, all careers are open to women, except those of lawyer or member of parliament. The last two positions are still considered unsuitable for Yemeni women.

In many countries women live longer than men, but not in Yemen. Life expectancy is 43.3 years for men, as against 40.8 for women. Although the infant mortality rate has gone down considerably, it is still high: 176.7 per 1,000 for boys, 170.1 per 1,000 for girls, with the actual figures probably being somewhat higher. The reasons for the higher mortality rate among women over the age of 15 is probably due to complications during pregnancy or childbirth. However, malnutrition is also widespread in Yemen, particularly in the Tihama.

Men and women have equal rights in state law, and women have had the right to vote since 1983. Family law is influenced by Islam, which means that divorce is made more easy for men. Polygamy is permitted but not common.

However, we should not lose sight of the women's own perspectives. The frequent afternoon gathering of women, the *tafrita*, offers them space for their own lives and serves a number of useful purposes. Marriages are arranged, goods are sold, information and new experiences in all sorts of areas are exchanged. Women's support for one another, in family matters too, is very strong and is often underestimated by outsiders.

Little attention is also given to the fact that women make their own mark on their surroundings. In many areas it is the women who are responsible for the outer appearance of the houses. There is a remarkable similarity between the patterns on house walls, the henna painting and make-up of the women and their basket work.

It is a pity that language barriers, the division of the sexes and the modesty of the women–combined with the prejudices of travellers–can all too easily conceal the variety, the joys and sorrows of the lives of Yemeni women.

Left, young mother from the Tihama. **Right**, woman from Sana'a wearing the typical *sitara*.

Many visitors to exhibitions over the last few years have seen for themselves that Yemeni silver is among the most beautiful of the so-called "ethnic jewellery" available.

Museums all over the world have begun to open up collections of Yemeni jewellery–an unmistakable sign that an end has come of the living meaning, the natural self-evident role played by jewellery in Yemen. However, in the little shops of the silver suqs, you can still find such an astonishing variety of objects that not only souvenir hunters, but connoisseurs as well can still obtain good and even important pieces. In refinement and balance of material, form, technique and pattern, it is on a level with Classical gold jewellery, European jewellery between the Renaissance and the 19th century, and Ottoman and Indian court jewellery.

Compared to work from these periods, two things are obvious. First of all, Yemeni jewellery is also the work of a highly developed, settled, urban culture. There is practically no "nomadic" jewellery, as the adornments of the nomads in the east and the Hadramaut were made by settled smiths in the small and very ancient centres of culture of those areas. Secondly, you will quickly discover that the prices for good pieces, although by now quite respectable, are still only a fraction of the sums you would have to pay for comparable quality from the periods mentioned above.

Of course you can buy good pieces everywhere in Yemen, but you can be sure of finding them in the silver suq (Suq al-fedda or Suq al-muchlass) in Sana'a. Bargains at ridiculously low prices are as unlikely in Yemen as they are in the Paris fleamarket.

Jewellery in the Islamic world: Very little jewellery has survived from ancient times, despite the legendary wealth of Saba and Himyar. Most of that which has survived is gold and, apart from a few regional differences, it belongs to the broad spectrum of

Hellenistic or late Roman jewellery. None of it, not even the silver bracelets in the museum of Sana'a, have had a continuous influence until the present day.

The origins of present-day styles lie further back. When the Islamic empire conquered all the ancient Mediterranean world, in which Iran was included, it took over the Byzantine and Sassanid forms and traditions to such an extent that it was more of a continuation than a break. Within a few centuries, Islamic tastes in art had unified these traditions, infused them with a new spirit and, from about the 10th century onwards, developed and refined its own catalogue of forms.

The Koran and jewellery: "For them, the gardens of Eden, under whose shades shall rivers flow. Decked shall they be therein with bracelets of gold, and green robes of silk and rich brocade shall they wear, reclining them therein on couches."

Such is the promise made by the 18th sura, verse 30. On account of these words, a tendency has developed to view the wearing of gold in this world with distrust. Gold was the preferred metal of ancient times, but jewellery from the Islamic world is generally–and in Yemen almost exclusively–made of silver.

Jewellery in Yemen: The oldest surviving Islamic pieces of jewellery in Yemen are partially made of gilded steel and some are 500 years old. Silver jewellery may, in favourable situations, date back to the 19th century, as it was generally melted down when it became unattractive and re-worked, though, because of the fixed traditions of the craft, it was usually in more or less the same form. The raw material probably came into the country mainly in the form of Spanish and later Austrian coins ("Maria Theresia Talers", known as *Riyal fransi*), used in exchange for Yemeni coffee. This would explain the vast quantities of silver jewellery–an average married woman would own several kilos–and also the fact that fine old pieces can still be found today.

Left, young Yemeni woman wearing silver jewellery.

In order to guarantee the purity of the silver (there are two types–*mukhlas* made from pure Maria Theresia silver and *nusfi* with a 50 percent addition of copper), the pieces made in Sana'a were usually stamped. The older stamps usually name the ruling Imam. On those from the present century, this is replaced by the name of the silversmith (usually Jewish). Pieces by the Muslim silversmiths from the Tihama and Hadramaut are frequently signed. This, too, was mainly intended to guarantee purity of the silver, but just as with the pieces from Sana'a it was also a guarantee of excellent artistic workmanship.

Male adornment: The most noticeable adornment of a Yemeni man is the *djambia*, the South Arabian curved dagger. This is not so much a weapon as a status symbol but an indication of his social position and legal rights. Young Yemenis wear them as a symbol of manhood, often from the age of 14. In a court of law, after a verdict has been passed the dagger has to be given up, signifying the of loss of legal rights.

The name comes from *janb* or side, as the *djambia* is worn, by the upper classes of the country, at the right side of the body. It can be seen in exactly this position on the famous

bronze statue of the Sabaean prince, Ma'adi Karib (8th century B.C.), in the National Museum of Sana'a.

Of the three components of the curved dagger (blade, hilt and scabbard), the hilt is usually the most valuable part. It is made of ivory, narwal tooth, horn, wood and nowadays, even of plastic. The most common material is cattle horn, but the most treasured is a certain portion of the horn of the rhinoceros, *saifani*. Such a hilt only achieves its full value after it has been used by several generations.

Valuable blades come from the old centres of the iron industry: Hadramaut, Nisab, Al Juba and Rada'a. The smiths who make weapons in these towns are all descended, according to their traditions, from the same tribal ancestor. Good blades, not as famous however as those listed above, are also made in Sana'a and Sa'dah. Nowadays, most blades are imported from Japan! The prices of a good new local hand-made blade and an imported one are roughly in a proportion of 10:1, probably with good reason.

There are two main shapes of *djambia*–the curved scabbard worn in the middle of the body, a sign of a free tribal warrior or *gabili*, which is known in central and northern Yemen as *'asib*, in the Tihama as *jafir* and in the south and southeast as *jihaz*. Usually the 'asib is made of plain leather, as the hilt and the blade determine the value of a dagger.

The second most common form is the *thuma* scabbard. It is slightly curved, and is worn at the right side of the body, always underneath the belt. Until 1962 it was reserved for the *saijids* and *qadis* and was generally magnificently worked in silver.

Such silver scabbards for the upper classes were made almost exclusively in Sana'a and in Az Zaydiyah (in the Tihama). Jewish workmanship can be recognised by the fine filigree; Muslim silversmiths preferred inscriptions, often in verse form:

"O you who are sorrowful, be not sorrowful/ For sorrow is bitter!" or "By God! This is a scabbard for the sword/ Prepared for the hosts of death./ He who rightfully holds it,/ He shall achieve his aim./ It was made of silver and of gold,/ To adorn a brave man!"

The Imams were fond of magnificent

thumas, as is shown by the collection of gilded silver scabbards in the National Museum of Sana'a.

Women's jewellery in Yemen: Until about 30 years ago every woman in Yemen would own a large number of pieces of silver jewellery. As part of the bride-price (paid by the bridegroom and the father-in-law) the bride's father would buy silver jewellery, which formed the basis of the woman's personal possessions.

In country areas women wore their jewellery while doing their daily work. In the upper class families of Sana'a or Haban they would usually wear a few bracelets, rings

dowry. It is therefore not surprising that the greatest masterpieces of Yemeni jewellery are to be found, apart from the *thumas*, among the *labbas*.

The *labba* used to be the main product of the Jewish silversmith craft in Sana'a. The families of Bausani and Badihi were particularly famous. The quality of the workmanship and the natural attraction of the capital made the old suq the shopping centre of the upper classes of Sana'a, for most of the areas of Zaidi Yemen and the western highlands.

Yemeni silver jewellery is one of the most important forms of artistic expression of the

and necklaces during the day. Belts, anklets, headdresses, hair ornaments and earrings, and especially all kinds of necklaces would only be taken out of the domestic treasure chest on special social events.

The two main forms of necklaces are *lazim* and *labba*. The *lazim* consists of chains hung horizontally and is worn by girls, while the *labba*, a broad, flat peice of jewellery mainly formed of hanging parts, is part of a bride's

Left, finely worked curved *thuma* belonging to the aristocracy. **Above**, silversmith's shop in Ta'izz.

country. Its very best creations represent the pinnacle of excellence of jewellery from the Islamic world. Jewish silversmiths played a considerable part, especially in the making of jewellery in Sana'a. Jews were known as silversmiths in Medina as early as the time of the Prophet. In 1948, however, Jewish silversmiths, along with most other Jews, left Yemen for Israel.

There are still a number of Jewish silversmiths in the north of the country. However, the decline of traditional craftsmanship has less to do with the emigration of Jewish silversmiths than with changes in taste.

The day starts very early for the people of Yemen. The first call to prayer by the muezzin sounds when the houses of the neighbourhood can only be seen as shadows and the air is still bitterly cold in the mountains during winter. According to Islamic tradition, *al fajr*, the dawn prayer, begins in the first early light of dawn, as soon as a black thread can be distinguished from a white one. That is often possible a long time before sunrise.

hand curve, is buckled on around the hips and a cloth skilfully bound around the head. The jackets of the men hang on a nail in the wall, as do long strips of cloth, which are first thrown over one shoulder and then wrapped around the neck. In the cold months of winter the thick *baltu* is worn, this is a warm coat of blue fabric, fully-lined on the inside with lambskin.

Women stay at home for the *fajr* prayer. They usually wear colourful dresses over

The morning prayer: In the larger towns, the muezzins make their calls at the same time from all directions at once and cover the town with a melodious network of "Allah akbar"–Allah is the greatest–and "Hayya ilal Sala"–come to prayer. Whoever wakes up first wakes all the other family members in the room. Women have the same obligation as the men of the house. Women and men usually sleep in different rooms, even close family members.

The *zanna*, the white robe that also serves as a nightshirt, is kept on. The *asib*, the scabbard of the *djambia* with its sharp right-

long trousers and tie the *lithma* around their heads, a thin veil which *leaves* only the eyes free. At home, the whole face is left free. However, if a stranger comes into the house, someone who is not a member of the immediate family, the face can quickly be veiled right up to the nose and above with one deft movement of the hand. When Yemeni women leave the house they put on more clothes than usual. The *maghmuq* further covers the entire face, and the colourful *sitara* is laid over the head and shoulders and held shut in front with one hand. Another form of costume which is often seen is the black *sharshaf*, which comprises a wide skirt, a cape and a head covering. Women wear black gloves with it, so that they are wrapped from the head to the hands and feet in black.

Children are usually allowed to get up later. Nowadays they no longer wear the *qarqush*, the pointed hat with the little tail for girls and umarried young women. Boys dress in much the same way as grown men. They often have a small *djambia*, sometimes

One of the men who is close to the missing person will be given the task of calling in on his way home to see how the man is. If he is ill, neighbours will see to it that he gets medical attention. If he is on his travels, they will take care of any essential tasks. The mosque also plays a central role in other situations. If two families are in dispute, the sacred ground of the mosque is the ideal place to meet after prayers, to discuss the situation calmly and to settle points of

fastened with a nail through the scabbard so that it cannot be drawn.

The men go to the mosque, the centre and the meeting place around which the life of the whole quarter revolves. After prayers, the absence of a neighbour might be noticed. Of course everyone knows everyone else, and if a neighbour who takes part regularly is missing, the others quickly become worried.

Left, the call to prayer by the muezzin—help by modern technology. **Above**, hard work for the women—fetching water from the cisterns.

controversy peacefully. And if there is no other way out, the imam or some other legal scholar can act as arbitrator or judge.

Breakfast is not eaten until much later, when the sun has long cleared the horizon. It is a simple meal, either of scrambled eggs with tomatoes or cooked beans, *ful*. With it fresh unleavened bread from the *tannur*, the stove with its opening at the top, is served. The morning is the only time of day when *bun*, real bean coffee, is served. Others prefer the milder *qishr*, made from the husks of coffee beans.

The men then leave the house, and its five

to seven floors become the domain of women, who see to the housework. All work is done communally, constantly accompanied by lively conversation and, in recent years, by noisy background music from the radio. Old and young help to clean and cook until the work is done. The baking of bread is a particularly important task. The dough is laid in flat slabs over the *machbaza*, a mushroom-shaped instrument which is then used to press it against the hot oven wall of the *tannur*. Glowing charcoal is used to cook the other hot dishes, as well as butane gas. The preparations for the midday meal are so complicated that one woman alone could

day meal would comprise radishes dipped in a sauce specially prepared for them, *shafut*, a cold dish with soured milk, which tastes spicy and refreshing and has the effect of an aperitif, followed by *bint as sahn*, hot flaky pastry with honey and hot fat poured over it. *Selter*, a sharply seasoned liquid mixture of meat broth, onions, tomatoes, mincemeat, eggs and *hulba*, a mixture of fenugreek and grated leeks, is the main dish. The whole is served in a stoneware pot, which holds the heat for a long time and allows the meal to carry on cooking on the "table". This dish could with justification be described as the national dish of Yemen. Rice is also served,

hardly cope with them.

The midday prayer: The morning ends with the midday prayer, *ad zuhr*. The muezzins call to prayer once again when the sun has reached its peak and throws the shortest shadows in the city. Afterwards the whole family meets to eat the midday meal, which is usually taken together, except when guests have been invited. Then the men and their guests eat first, followed by the women of the house.

A large plastic sheet is laid in the hall or in a special room of the house, and all the dishes are arranged on it carefully. A typical mid-

as are vegetables stuffed with mincemeat, fish, poultry or boiled beef and mutton. The *maraq* or meat broth is particularly prized by all. It is drunk with a squirt of lemon juice. The meal ends with fresh fruit or a caramel pudding. Following the meal, tea and *qishr* are served in the *mafradsh*, where people settle themselves comfortably among the cushions along the walls and prepare themselves for an afternoon of prayer, *qat* and pleasant conversation.

The afternoon prayer: The call to the afternoon prayer, *ad asr*, goes out when the sun stands at an angle of 45 degrees to the surface of the earth. The men go back to work, or (a more frequent occurrence in Yemen) meet for their usual afternoon *qat* gathering. Where they will meet in the afternoon has already been decided in the morning. This is the hour of discussion, of the narghile and the chewing of *qat*.

Women have their own gatherings, known as *tafrita*, and both sexes always meet in different houses. Before the women enter the room they remove the black *sharshaf*, and their colourful and sometimes elaborately embroidered dresses can be seen once more. On formal occasions, such as the birth of a child or a wedding, the women enjoy

foreign women are soon accepted into the circle and asked about their own family life, just as if they were old friends.

Evening prayer: The sunset prayer, *al maghrib*, usually marks the end of the *tafrita*, and the women go home to prepare a simple evening meal. This meal is similar to breakfast, consisting of *ful* or eggs with tomatoes. Large amounts are not generally eaten, as *qat* has a strong inhibiting effect on the appetite.

The sun sets relatively quickly, and as soon as twilight has given way to the dark night sky the muezzins raise the call for the fifth and final prayer of the day, *al isha*. Sometimes the men stay in the mosque for

wearing gold and silver jewellery, visible to all. Almonds, raisins, popcorn and sweets are handed round, accompanied by cups of hot tea or *qishr*. Some smoke the narghile and others chew the bundles of *qat* they have brought with them. Lively conversation is conducted in a very sisterly atmosphere which knows no taboos. Intimate details of family life are also discussed freely. Even

Left, Yemeni boy. **Above**, there is always time for a bit of a chat. **Following page**, tribal warrior from Ma'rib.

the brief hour between al maghrib and al isha and use the time to study the Koran or to listen to a lecture by a religious scholar. After the evening prayer they all make their way home. School students do a little more homework, tradesmen check over the day's accounts once more, many women sew belts for *djambias* or crochet little caps. Ever since the arrival of television these traditional pastimes have, of course, had powerful competition. However, people still prefer to go to bed early, without waiting up for the end of the TV programmes. Tomorrow is sure to be another early start.

THE TRIBES–THE BACKBONE OF THE NATION

Thousands of years ago–long before the coming of Islam–the tribes were a basic element of the social structure of Yemen, and they have remained so to this day. Most of the inhabitants of the country who live north of Yarim–these make up more than two-thirds of the population of the country–belong to a tribe. However, great regional differences still exist even within a tribal community.

In some parts of Yemen which visitors can drive through–for instance, along the road from Sa'dah in the north or Ma'rib in the east–most of the men from the tribes are heavily armed. Visitors can even see armoured cars which are more likely to belong to the individual tribes than to the central government. Even if strangers are only very rarely threatened, harassed or touched by these weapons, it is obvious that they are used in feuds, skirmishes and tribal wars which are totally outside the control of the central government in Sana'a.

At the start of the 1970s, the total tribal population was 1,467,000 and the urban population of the Aden area was approximately 300,000. There is no other large town in the western part of the country where tribesmen, who form the predominant element, are mainly employed in agriculture, living grouped in or around villages or settlements along wadi beds and deltas down to the coast.

Nevertheless most Yemenis, whatever tribe they may belong to, share a feeling of national identity and solidarity which is based on a belief in the common origin of the Yemeni people and their tribes. Among Arabs, the Yemenis are considered the descendants of the tribe of **Qahtan**, the ancestors of the South Arabian tribes, as against the North Arabians, whose ancestors are known as **Adnan**. The different origins of the southern or Qahtanid and the northern

or Adnanid Arabs were of great political importance in the first centuries of the Islamic age and have not been forgotten to the present day.

This genealogical system, which is common knowledge in Yemen and a basic part of current general knowledge, was worked out in the 10th century by the geographer and historian Al-Hamdani. He vigorously disputed the assertion of some northern Yemeni tribes that they were descended from northern (Adnani) ancestors. The belief in a common tribal past became increasingly important in the years after the 1962 revolution and during the time of the consolidation of the republic, as it reinforced the solidarity of the Yemeni tribes in opposition to the deposed rulers, the Zaidi Imams, who traced themselves back to the northern Adnani.

Yemenis trace the greater part of their customs and traditions back to the ancient tribal custom. The grown men, for example, carry the *djambia*, a curved dagger, and they all dance the bara', a *djambia* dance, which was originally danced at weddings or on national or religious holidays. Nowadays there are official government-supported dance groups who dance the bara' as part of a Yemeni cultural events abroad, and the bara' is much more widely distributed in Yemen itself than it was many years ago. The inhabitants of Sana'a claim that only a generation ago the bara' was only very rarely danced at weddings in Sana'a. Nowadays the dance is considered customary on such occasions.

Another major important aspect of Yemeni society is a strict social system expressed in a language of honour (*sharaf, izz, ird*). Relationships of the men with one another, their behaviour towards women and towards guests is laid down and regulated in the most exact detail. This narrow and almost inflexible social order both demands and supports the solidarity of the community. What is a tribe, and what is a tribal territory, and what does being a member of a

Left, the word of elders still has great weight in the tribal community.

The Tribes–Backbone of the Nation 115

tribe mean in Yemen?

At its simplest level, the tribe or *gabila* is a political unit based on a particular region. It has fixed borders, a known number of members at any one time and a certain amount of political autonomy with which it interacts with other tribes and with the central government. Almost all the tribes in Yemen now lead settled lives. Most subsist on agriculture, planting their fields either with grain such as sorghum, millet, wheat or maize for their own use or with cash crops for the market such as *qat*, coffee, bananas or grapes. Some members of tribes earn their living as craftsmen, for instance as carpet

tribesmen elect his oldest or best qualified son as his successor. If a sheikh dies in advanced old age, one of his sons is bound to have taken over most of his duties some time ago, and is often addressed by the title of sheikh even before the death of his father. As well as the sheikh, individual families have their own leaders, the *agil*, who acts as a mediator between the sheikh and the ordinary tribes people. In some parts of Yemen, for instance in the east, there are many sheikhs and it is not always possible to tell how they are related to one another.

The tribes are often named after their ancestors. In some cases the name of an

weavers or smiths, and an increasing number are tradesmen and shopkeepers. However, certain skills such as those of butchering or barbering are carried out by men who are not part of the tribe.

Tribal rules and regulations: People are born into their tribe and they do not choose their tribe. But it is possible to change tribal membership and it happens only occasionally, but most people prefer to remain faithful to the tribes of their fathers and grandfathers. The office of tribal leader or sheikh is normally inherited within the family members. When the old sheikh dies, the

ancestor is preceded by *Beni* (sons of...), for example in Beni Suraym (in the Khamir region), Beni Husheich (to the east of Sana'a), Beni Mahwab (near Kuchlan), and Beni Marwan (in the northern Tihama). Some tribes replace Beni with *Dhu*, such as Dhu Mohammed and Dhu Hussein–sometimes referred together as Dhu Ghaylan–in the Barat region.

Other tribes simply name themselves after their ancestor, such as 'Idhar (north of Shaharah), Al-Karif (in the Dhi Bin region), Mura (to the south and west of Ma'rib) and the major tribes: Hashid, Bakil, Madhhij.

Some tribal names represent the plural forms of their ancestors names: Al-Usaymat (in the Huth region) and Zaraniq (in the Tihama around Bayt al Faqih and Zabid). Finally, geographical regions can also give their names to tribes, such as the Bilad ar-Rus (land of mountain peaks) tribe to the southeast of Sana'a.

The cohesion of a tribe may be expressed in the figure of a common ancestor, but there is always tension around the ancient traditional borders of tribal territory. This can be seen in the words applied to a newcomer accepted by the tribe. He becomes one with the tribe in its borders,

One of the most important tasks of a sheikh is the arbitration of disputes. Talk of tribal law and tribal justice does not mean that there is always a single unified code of laws. When tribal matters are brought before the sheikh or other notables they try to avoid social rupture by making use of a vaguely defined law that allows free interpretation. In this way formulas for compromise are easily found in order to settle disputes. In a dispute which is to be settled by tribal law each party appoints a guarantor or *kafil* who has to see to it that his party abides by the decision of the sheikh. Each party is also required to lay down some valuable items as

hadd, and its ancestors, *add*. Members of a tribe can always tell if a member of their community is descended from the same tribal line and particularly from the dynasty after whom the tribe is named. Checking facts with a knowledgeable member of the tribe will often establish that the origins of whole lines of descent and families lie in quite different tribes.

Left, the governor of Ma'rib–an important sheikh–taking a helicopter trip with his bodyguards. **Above**, discussions are always held in a circle.

guarantees. In a minor dispute the *djambia* of the two men will suffice. In important cases, and also in those between two different tribes, the guarantees comprise a certain number of guns. In addition, each party has to agree to abide by the sheikh's decisions.

These are, however, not always successful, as serious conflicts between two tribes are comparable to the disputes of two nations in international law. There is no higher authority which could enforce the judgement. Each tribe is responsible for its members. A tribal warrior who has killed a member of another tribe is usually protected by his own tribe. His tribe will negotiate with the tribe of the dead man and agree on a sum of financial compensation or *diyah*. The concept of honour is important between tribes and among members of the same tribe as well. If a tribal warrior has broken some law, his tribal companions take it upon themselves to protect him. However, if he has offended against the code of honour, he has to carry the consequences alone. If he behaves in such a dishonourable way that he goes right against the tribal code–for instance, if he leaves a travelling companion in the lurch during a fight and if this leads to the companion's death–the tribe can expel

the tribes mentioned by contemporary chroniclers are those tribes which still exist today, and an important role is played by the Hamdan, Al-Karif, Yam, Khawlan, Nihm and Murad.

The Zaidi Imam Al-Hadi Yahya Ibn Al-Hussein, founder of the state which was to become the Yemen Arab Republic after the 1962 revolution, came to Yemen in 893 at the invitation of the tribes of the northeast, the area between Sa'dah and Najran. For a period of more than a thousand years the tribes of the north were the most powerful military supporters of the Imam and, in the end, the strongest opponents of the new

him and announce this expulsion to other tribes in the suq. He then no longer belongs to the tribe, and the tribe has no further responsibility to protect him.

Many tribes which still exist today can look back on a line of descent which stretches a long way behind them into the past. Often they still live within borders which were already mentioned in pre-Islamic manuscripts. Around 630, in the early Islamic years, Yemeni tribes visited the Prophet Mohammed in Medina, announced their conversion to Islam and assured him of their political loyalty. Among

republic. Al-Hadi Yahya sent punitive expeditions against the stubborn tribes who had at first supported and then rebelled against him. The bulk of the military forces of the Imam was always drawn from the tribes of the north. The Ottoman Turks who occupied Yemen in the 16th and 17th centuries were driven out of the country with the armies of the individual tribes under the leadership of the Zaidi Imams.

One reason why tribal structures have survived so long in Yemen is their flexibility. Over the last 1,400 years–since the rise of Islam–nations have arisen and

118

disappeared once more. Yemeni tribes were incorporated in these nations, but remained responsible for the administration of their tribal areas. In those periods when central authority crumbled and fell apart they ensured the survival of social order by their traditions and laws.

In the southern mountain country between Ibb and Ta'izz the old tribal structures have by now almost disappeared. One reason may be that here, close to the old trading city of Aden, agriculture and trade, due to the nearness of the central government in Sana'a, have played a more important part. One possible cause which may have led to

incorporated them into their state and placed them under the rule of governors. They also forced the tribes eventually to suppress those of their number–the Dhu Mohammed and the Dhu Hussein–who were most vigorous in opposition. Apart from the fact that Crown Prince Ahmed ad-Din was a master in the manipulation of tribal alliances and managed to get the tribes to control one another, one reason for the defeat of the tribes was their poor weaponry.

During the years of the civil war which followed the revolution of 1962, both sides had sufficient weapons, the Royalists being supplied by Saudi Arabia and the Re-

the dissolution of tribal structures in this area may lie in the 13th and 15th centuries, when the Rasulid dynasty in Ta'izz and Zabid ruled over the land of Yemen.

Once the country had been formally declared independent of the Turks and had been constituted as the Mutawakkilid Kingdom of Yemen, the Imams ruled from 1918 to 1962. They suppressed the tribes,

Left, leaving the meeting place together. **Above**, tribal decisions are announced in the market–fighting is forbidden.

publicans were backed by Egypt. In consequence, some sheikhs in the northern and eastern regions in particular can offer stronger opposition to the central government today than they could during the rule of the Imam. However, recent research shows that the power of the central government is steadily increasing, as the state–the Yemen Arab Republic–is replacing the tribe as the immediate object of political loyalty. Gradually, the descent from a common tribe, the Qanthan, may finally become for the people of Yemen a symbol of a complete and united nation.

A wedding is a joyful celebration and considered a welcome opportunity for a social gathering. Customs and traditions are different from one country to another, and many Yemeni customs may seem strange to a Western visitor. Among these is the fact that bride and bridegroom are selected by their respective parents.

In a strict society such as that of Yemen it is easy to see why parents are essential to the choice of a suitable marriage partner. With the exception of relationships within the family, daily life is based on a strict separation of the sexes. A young man has little or no chance of meeting women, particularly those of his own generation. Instead, he has to rely on the advice of his mother, of older sisters and aunts.

The bride search: When looking for a bride, the mother and father of the son have to work closely together, as each of them knows one half of the neighbouring families. When the son has reached marriageable age (usually around 17 to 19), the mother looks out for a suitable bride. She can come from the neighbourhood or from their own family. The marriage of cousins is permitted and practised within Islam.

The mother knows the women of the neighbourhood very well. After all, they meet almost daily for the *tafrita*, the comfortable social gathering of women where the latest news and gossips are swapped. Once the mother has formed her own opinion, she confers with her husband, who knows the male side of the other family very well. The dignity and status of the house from which the prospective daughter-in-law may come are carefully examined. Only when father and mother are of one mind do they consult their son. It could well be possible that he knows the young woman slightly, especially if she is one of his relatives. However, it is equally possible that

Left, the bridegroom in festive array—which includes his rifle—at the ceremony.

he knows nothing about her.

A day is set for the father and son to go to the house of the bride's family in order to discuss the matter. This gives the future bride, who usually already knows what the visit means, the chance to take a look at her suitor. She may even have the opportunity of serving tea or *qishr* to the visitors. Of course, she will remain heavily veiled. Usually, she will know much more about him than he will about her. Men are simply more visible in public than women.

Once the father of the son has made his suggestion or choice, the potential father-in-law will ask for some time to think it over and to discuss it with his family. He will also mention that he will first ask his daughter if she agrees to the choice of suitor. Once all parties are in agreement, a time is fixed for the betrothal.

The betrothal: The betrothal feast is set for a Thursday or a Friday. Father and son, accompanied by three or four male friends or relations, visit the house of the father of the bride bringing raisins, *qat* and other gifts. The engagement ring is handed over to the father, together with clothes for the mother and daughter. Dates for the wedding are considered, and the bride price is decided upon. The major part of the bride price, which is paid by the father of the bridegroom, is later spent on jewellery and clothes for the bride. Valuable things bought with the bride-price remain the private property of the woman, which the husband cannot touch even after many years of marriage. It functions as a sort of insurance policy and remains entirely the woman's property even after a possible divorce.

The betrothal ceremony is very informal and verbal. Often the bride price has not been collected yet, and the parties have agreed on a time by which the money shall have been saved up to the agreed amount. Even so, the betrothal is considered a firm promise between two families to marry their children. A withdrawal or a dissolution of the betrothal leads to a severe loss of face by the family in question.

A three-day wedding: The wedding will last for at least three days. It usually begins on Wednesday and ends on Friday, the free day of the week in Yemen. On Wednesday afternoon the marriage contract is signed and concluded in the bride's house. The bridegroom and the father sit opposite one another in the presence of the qadi, an Islamic scholar of the law. The bridegroom then asks his future father-in-law: "Will you give me your daughter in marriage?" The father of the bride answers for his daughter: "Yes, I will give you my daughter to wife." The qadi then has to ask the father if his daughter agrees to the arranged marriage. Bridegroom and father clasp right hands. The qadi lays a white cloth over their hands and recites the *fatiha*, the first sura of the Koran.

The ceremony reaches its height when the father of the bridegroom throws a handful of raisins onto the carpet. All those present try to pick up as many raisins as possible for they are signs of a happy future for the couple. According to another custom, all those present give larger or smaller amounts of money, which are called out one after the other by a crier. The money is intended to cover the cost of the lavish wedding celebrations.

Laylat az-Zaffa, the most important and most public part of the wedding celebrations, takes place on Friday. The butchers come very early in the morning to prepare the meat for the lavish wedding feast. Several sheep and possibly even a calf have been purchased for the meal. Sometimes a hundred or more guests are invited for lunch and an afternoon *qat* gathering among the men is a common procedure.

Women from the neighbourhood arrive more often than not bringing their kitchen utensils in order to help with the tedious preparations. Several rooms, sometimes even in separate houses, are prepared for the meal so that all the guests can eat at once. The men go to the mosque before the midday meal and say their midday prayers. On the way back, the bridegroom, wearing a traditional brand-new costume and carrying a golden sword in his hands, is accompanied by dancing and singing men. Drums provide the beat for the dance. The meal itself is eaten, as usual, in a customary squatting position on the floor.

In the afternoon, the guests sit in various rooms or even on various floors. All of them chew *qat* and smoke the narghile. Incense burners fuelled by glowing charcoal release the scent of the incense and are passed from hand to hand with a pious blessing. A qadi recites old poems, with the guests joining him from time to time. The recitation contains reminders of Islamic duties and wish the new couple Allah's blessing and a long happy married life. Whenever the qadi takes a break, a man plays the lute and sings wedding songs. Sometimes he is accompanied by the other guests using hand drums or cymbals.

In the meantime, the women meet at the bride's house. A special make-up artist is responsible for arranging the bride's hair and painting delicate patterns on her hands and feet. The bride either wears a traditional wedding dress or a modern white dress in the Western style. Plenty of gold and silver jewellery is of course essential. The palms of the hands and the soles of the feet are reddened with henna. While the bride takes her place in the front on a chair, where she can be seen by everybody, the guests sit on the pallets along the wall and often also squashed together on the floor. Tea, *qishr* and fruit juice are served, accompanied by sweets, cakes, almonds and raisins. A lute player or–unfortunately more and more frequently these days–a cassette recorder with the volume turned high provides entertainment. The younger women dance in the main room while the older ones retire to the quieter neighbouring rooms and chat while taking to *qat* and the narghiles.

After the sunset and evening prayers the men go into the street and prepare for the Zaffa. They form a lane, standing to one side of the house entrance but still under the numerous lightbulbs strung right across the street or lane. At one end, with his face towards his own house, is the bridegroom, accompanied by his father, his brothers and his friends. Children carry vases or flat aluminium plates on their heads with strongly scented herbs and burning candles. Sometimes hen's eggs are added, symbolising the hope of plentiful offspring.

The qadi stands on the opposite side, between the men who have lined up into two lines. The qadi recites the *nashit*, often making use of a microphone. He takes turns with the men beside him, who sing the refrain at the top of their voices. The texts once more consist of good wishes and blessings for the newly-married couple. Slowly, step by step, the whole procession approaches the entrance of the house. The singing goes on without a break. In the meantime, the women of the entire neighbourhood have climbed onto the roofs of the houses and set up the trilling, high-pitched

is accompanied by her father, her brothers and other male relatives. As soon as she enters the house of her bridegroom she becomes part of her husband's family. However, she retains the right to visit her own family at any time and to stay for several weeks if she wishes. The husband then has the duty of arranging transport to her previous home and back again to her own house. The next day, celebrations continue, mostly only within the family circle together with a few close relatives.

Over the last few years, a tradition has emerged that the bridegroom and the other men travel to the edge of the Wadi Dahr in

zaghrada. The air is practically vibrating with the singing of the men and the high-pitched trill of the women.

When the bridegroom is close enough to the door, he runs into the house and following old tradition jumps over his own threshhold. This marks the end of the official ceremony. The guests continue to dance in front of the house, but soon go home. If the bride has not come yet, she soon will. She

Above, bridal procession with drummers in Shaharah.

order to dance once more, accompanied by drums. Sometimes on a Friday morning you can see several wedding parties dancing at the same time. The guests arrive in trucks, jeeps and Toyota pick-ups, accompanied by shrill singing and the rhythmic drumming of the musicians of Sana'a. Afterwards, bride and bridegroom visit the bride's mother and present her with more gifts. This ends the celebrations for the men, but the women, who were earlier busy with the preparation of the wedding feast, continue a well-deserved celebration for a few days more into the following week.

The types of houses and living accommodation in Yemen are as varied as the scenery of the different regions of the country. However varied the styles of building might be, they all make use of locally available building materials. The houses are excellently adapted to the climate and well suited to the daily needs and social customs of Yemen. The marked regional styles of Yemen differ in the choice of material and in building technology, as well as in the decoration of the façades and interiors.

The most remarkable buildings are the multi-storey tower houses. These buildings have up to eight or sometimes even nine floors and arouse considerable respect for the achievements of the architects of the old days. They are based on ancient South Arabian models. According to region, the towers are made of natural dressed stone, of mud brick or a combination of these materials.

Mud, in the form of air-dried brick or built according to various wet mud techniques, is the usual building material in the northern and eastern parts of the country, with stone being used more in the rocky mountain regions. The houses typical of Sana'a use dressed natural stone in the lower storeys and fired brick in the upper floors. The breadth of the wooden-beam ceilings in the houses is determined by the length of the beams available. For this reason, rooms wider than 10 feet (3½ metres) are a rarity.

The inside arrangement of the tower houses follows a strictly vertical plan. The ground floor is occupied by a stable for domestic animals, the floor above is storage space. The houses of the upper classes sometimes contain a second storage floor and rooms for servants. The next storey contains the living room of the family, in which the master of the house will receive guests. The family's private accommodation begins above this floor, with the *diwan* or parlour which is only used for special festivities, such as weddings or to celebrate a birth. Next to it and above it lie the bedrooms of the members of the family. The kitchen is usually found on the floor above the *diwan*. The floor above that usually has a roof terrace on which most of the work of the household can be carried out in the open air. The topmost room of the tower is the elaborately decorated reception room or *mafradsh* used for *qat* gatherings.

In all the living and sleeping rooms the furnishings consist of relatively flat pallets along the walls with cushions at the back to form arm rests. There is a bathroom or a toilet on each floor of the living accommodation.

Particular attention is paid to a style of building appropriate to the climate. The thick walls balance out even the great differences in temperature between night and day. The narrow windows protect against heat in the summer and in winter, when the sun is low, they allow the warming rays of the sun to enter.

The tower-like houses were originally designed for one single extended Yemen family, to whom as a rule they belonged to. However, especially in the larger towns, more and more houses are being divided into individual apartments and rented. The new ideal home, too, is modelled more and more on low-rise buildings in the Western bungalow-style.

The traditional reasons for multi-floored buildings–defensibility and the saving of agriculturally valuable land–are losing their importance, and it is impossible to ignore a growing disregard of traditional building and lifestyles. The new buildings of migrant workers who have returned and government buildings have introduced new Yemeni styles of building and ways of life even in rural areas. Unfortunately there seems to be no future for the regional styles which have matured in harmony with nature, particularly that of the tower houses.

Left, houses in Kahil in the Harraz range.

Yemenis who see strangers passing by on foot away from the paths and roads will often come up to them without any inhibitions. Sometimes they will accompany them for part of the way. They almost always ask the same questions. "You have no car, then? Why did you come over the pass when there's a path around the bottom? Why are you leaving so soon? You've only been in our village for ten minutes!" These remarks are certainly not confined to Yemen, but they

their dreams. On foot you can quickly get away from the busier travel routes, and without great difficulty you can be "the first European to come to this village". However, a new country also means a population who don't know what a tourist is. In some areas, without being actually hostile, people are rather reserved towards strangers, whether they are Europeans or come from another part of the country. For this reason you would be well advised not to go just any-

have a particular significance. The first cars appeared in Yemen in 1950, the first tourists after 1970, and the roads, built by bulldozers and with great effort in order to link up the highland villages, have only been in existence for about ten years. It is a blessing to be able to get to market in a few hours instead of a few days. For this reason the people cannot understand why some tourists prefer days of walking to a few hours in a car.

A new country: For those who search the world for places where not everything has spoiled yet and tourism has made no impact on the landscape, Yemen is the country of

where. There is plenty to discover in the easily accessible areas. Many people say: "Go to Yemen as soon as you can: in five years' time it will all be spoiled." The opposite is true. The modernisation of the country, the improvements to the road system and to communications will, in a few years' time, allow you to visit areas which are beautiful but simply not accessible at the moment.

A mountainous country: Any traveller hearing the word "Arabia" should not think of Yemen as a flat country. In the course of a day you can easily drop from 9,840 feet (3,000 metres) above sea level to 5,900 feet

(1,800 metres), or the other way around. The altitude, the strong sun and the sweat it produces will inform you that these mountains are definitely in Arabia. But they still remain mountains; there is frost at night in December and at altitudes above 6,560 feet (2,000 metres) there is thick fog in the evenings to prove it. If you're hiking in Yemen, you need good reliable equipment: good shoes with soles that won't melt on the boiling hot rocks and a quilted bodywarmer

you in the evenings. The main problems are the supply of drinking water and the weight of the packs. However, there are enough routes where you can travel on foot in stages through varied and interesting scenery, but at the same time enjoy the comfort of supplies brought every evening by a jeep driven by a Yemeni chauffeur. It is preferable to use a chauffeur who comes from the area to which you are travelling, or to put it another way, who will allow you to accompany him

for the cool evenings. Camping by the Red Sea is like a dream. But you should avoid sleeping in the open air. It is advisable to carry a good tent, especially in April, but also in July and August when short but heavy monsoon thunderstorms break over Yemen. It is difficult to hike for several days in succession in Yemen if you do not have a car with supplies and material which can meet

Preceding pages: asking the way will not always get you a clear answer. **Left**, on a lot of treks it is possible to have vehicle accompaniment. **Above**, camp near Bokhur on Djebel Kawkaban.

on a visit to his homeland.

Land of countless villages: Hiking and backpacking have their fanatical adherents, undoubtedly because, apart from the sporting activity, they offer a unique chance to get to know the people of the country. Arriving in a village on foot after coming down the mountain is quite a different experience from arriving by car along the asphalt road across the plain. Another thing that is so pleasing about Yemen is that its marvellous mountains are inhabited by a farming population who, over the course of centuries, have formed the slopes of the mountains into terraces of alternating shades of green and ochre. These people amuse themselves– there can be no other explanation for it–by putting the most beautiful houses on all the peaks and rocks which are hard to get to. Luckily for the hiker, the villages and the system of agriculture have led to the mountain ranges being criss-crossed by narrow donkey paths, which are carefully maintained by the Yemenis. They are very willing to show you the paths when you have given up hope of getting from one point to another on your map. Often, such a chance meeting will end with the remark: "Why don't you take this path, it leads up that way. I'll come

invitation to drink tea, eat or spend the night with them. However, you should not forget that the hospitable mountain people are not blessed with worldly goods. If you give some tins of fruit, some cloths for the woman of the house, or even a little money, it will be most gratefully received. It is not payment, but an exchange of gifts, as is customary in this country. It is also unnecessary to hurt or irritate these people. It is just not proper to walk through a field where the barley is just sprouting. It is also a good idea to be very cautious with your dressing. Don't take photographs as soon as you enter a house. Wait, and talk a while, take your time, and

with you, the view up there is beautiful."

There are paths everywhere: from one hill to two or three villages; from one side of the ravine to the other. Existing maps do not reflect the topography and its difficulties very well. The mountains are inhabited, and Yemenis would have great difficulty in understanding visitors who walk through their villages without speaking to anyone. The easiest way of making contact is to ask where the path leads or how you get to this or that village which you have discovered on your map. The Yemenis will always reply to such contacts with a smile, and often with an

the photo will come later. Talking is of course not easy. Only a few school children in the mountains will speak the odd word or two of English, and some of the men may speak French because they have worked in Djibouti. A smile, the photos that you show around, and gestures–this language is understood all over the world.

Places to walk: Apart from the fact that certain regions are difficult to get to and not very safe, it is not possible to hike or backpack everywhere in Yemen. The main reasons are shortage of water and no settlements. In the mountains, hikes lasting several days are possible. But there are also other areas of Yemen which offer opportunities for little-known but very exotic tours.

The Tihama: The Tihama is, in contrast to general opinion, a beautiful region with interesting people and villages. However, it is less suitable for hiking because of the dust and the heat. The same is true of all the regions lower than 4,265 feet (1,300 metres). Arid rock, water shortage and extreme humidity are among the prevalent conditions.

Those who are hungry for desert experiences, however, will have their reward. The whole chain of hills, some 37 miles (60 km) from the coast, which separates the Tihama

Yafrus to **Djebel Habashi** and the southern flanks of **Djebel Sabir**.

The coast of Yemen: Unfortunately, the coast is not particularly attractive. The long stretches of beach are often swampy, grey, without any palms or other trees to mark the boundaries, and have very little interesting scenery to offer. However, you can walk along the coast from **Al Khawkah** through **Wadi Mulk** and halfway to **Al Mokha**. Here you will find beautiful beaches with groves of palms reaching to the sea, many birds and some pretty fishing villages. However, you should have a car accompanying you, which for most of the route can drive along the

from the higher mountains, is pure delight for the senses. It is a chaotic collection of rocks in a bewildering array of shapes and possesses an astonishing flora. Some starting points for hikes in this region are:

Al Mahabishah to **Djebel Ash Shara fayn**;
Suq at-Tur at the foot of **Djebel Hajjah**;
Suq al-Khamis to **Djebel Hufash**
As Suqnah (near Al Mansouryah)

Left, the highland plateau of Kawkaban is a favoured area for hiking. **Above**, magnificent blooms at the edge of the highland Tihama.

seashore. The distance involved is some 19 miles (30 km), i.e. just about two days, with an evening dip in the sea. The rest of the way to Al Mokha offers very little of interest.

Inland: The **Djebel Sabir** near Ta'izz is very easily accessible, as it rises right behind the town. You can cross the many valleys which cut into the flanks of the mountain to the south and west. The women of Djebel Sabir are beauties of a type which is seen only in the Yemen. It is often the women who invite you into the house or to take a cup of *qishr*, the brew made of coffee bean husks.

Jiblah is also suitable for shorter hikes. If

you come from Ta'izz, you can leave your car up on the hill which towers above the valley of Ibb and Jiblah and walk to Jiblah on foot. The Djebel which dominates Ibb is also interesting. You can even trek across the heights as far as the **Sumarah Pass**.

In **Damt** you will want to do more than climb the volcano and see the crater lake. From the heights you can make out a row of other crater lakes and a splendid row of jagged peaks, which stretch out to the south for several hours' journey on foot. A tour of these dry, rocky ridges—without villages, but still worth while—can easily be managed in a day from a base camp in the plain.

The desert regions in the east are not recommended for hiking, because of the lack of security and the great heat. You can make a very good day's journey along the the old but well-preserved south road from **Jihanah** to **Ma'rib**. Once you have left the rocky plateau and the isolated rocky outcrops, you will come to a landscape of rounded hills and sandy hollows which is similar to the Sahara.

The mountains: These regions are the best-known in all of Yemen. The variety and the beauty of the scenery, the many villages with their marvellous architecture and a favourable climate make hiking here an unforgettable experience. However, it is necessary to memorise your daily location and the local topography very thoroughly every morning. Bad visibility can obstruct the tours all the year round because of the fog, which sets in the afternoon. A stretch of 12-19 miles (20-30 km—not more than 9-12 miles or 15-20 km on the map) can easily be coped with in one day. Apart from warm clothing, you should carry plenty of water in your pack (three litres at least) and sufficient sun protection.

Djebel Shaharah: The plain at the foot of the mountains at *Al Gabei* has dry steppe zones to offer, similar to the edges of the Tihama. The way up to *Shaharah*, once the refuge of the Imam, is like climbing up to an eagle's eyrie. The recently built unpaved road is as dangerous as the vertigo it arouses. Several paths cross the ridges, peaks and slopes around Shaharah, which is a good base for hikes in this area.

The Manakhah region: This is not only the undisputed region with the most possibilities for hiking, but also the most accessible. In the north of Manakhah is **Djebel Ismael**, where you can spend two or three days. To the south lies the long chain of **Djebel Shibam**, which has a wealth of splendid villages such as Zahra, Beni Mora and Al Houdaib, the place of pilgrimage for Ismaelis. The peak of Djebel Shibam is overlooked by the town of Kahil, which lies above Manakhah.

The southern massif is more for the adventurous. Here you will come to **Djebel Bura'** and to the **Tihama** via the old route used by Carsten Niebuhr, the route which once led from Sana'a to Bayt al-Faqih. To the west of Manakhah is **Djebel Masar**, also very beautiful and covered with villages on its southern slopes. From the summit you can descend to Hudaydah along the asphalt road and leave your car there.

Shibam and Kawkaban: Both are suitable for a short excursion from Sana'a. Following a magnificent path, you can get from Shibam to Kawkaban and continue the hike to your own satisfaction on the high plateau. Following the jagged edges of the mountains and passing through a fascinating landscape of wild canyons you come to **Thula** via **Az Zakatin**. From here you can hike in the wild, jagged mountain landscape as far as **Amran**, or, following the northwestern valleys, trek as far as the high altitude town of **Kuhlan** and further on to **Al Hajjah**. If you walk from Kawkaban in a westerly direction you will come to **At Tawilah** in the course of a day. The main route divides from here on, and without following it directly—it is too dusty—you will come to **Al Mahwit**.

Going further on, you can descend to **Djebel Hufash** and then, following the course of the wadi to the south, reach **Suq al-Khamis** in two days from Al Mahwit. From Shibam you have the chance of undertaking a magnificent ten-day tour which goes as far as Manakhah. This tour can be accompanied by a car. For all hikes it is necessary to obtain the permit for the region in question and to keep it with you at all times. This *tassarir* is obtainable from travel agents or directly from the Tourist Office at the end of Taharir Square in Sana'a.

Right, rocky outcrop at Hosn Bokhur.

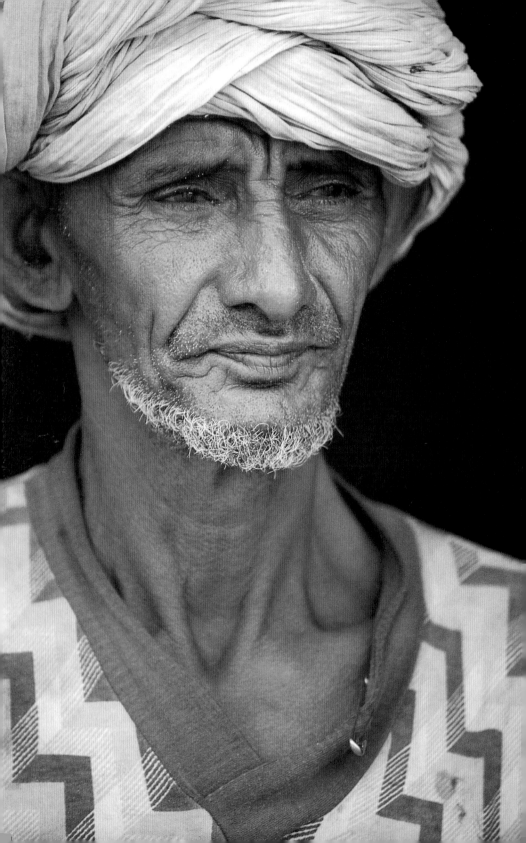

YEMEN: LAND OF ADVENTURE

The Republic of Yemen was proclaimed on 22 May 1990. In a step that came as a surprise to many observers, the erstwhile Yemen Arab Republic and the socialist People's Democratic Republic of Yemen had united. Then, hardly had people grown accustomed to the new situation than events became overshadowed by the Gulf War, and Yemen came under heavy fire for its neutral stance towards Iraq. But things soon began to settle down, and although the country continues to face immense economic problems, the government is confident that these can be overcome.

For travellers to Yemen, the political changes have undoubtedly made things much easier. Almost all parts of the country can now be visited without any burdensome restrictions. Routes and destinations, which up until a few years ago could only be dreamt of, can now be explored.

But this doesn't mean that the familiar destinations have lost any of their appeal. Sana'a, now the capital of the whole country, remains an Arabian dream. Aden, the economic metropolis of the future, is casting aside the depressing legacies of Socialism and is looking to regain its former prosperity. The mountainous interior, with its unique landscapes and imposing multi-storey clay houses remains as fascinating as ever, as do destinations such as Tihama, the "green Yemen" around Ibb and Ta'izz, and Sa'dah or the Djebel Umm Layla in the north of the country.

For those in search of new horizons, there is the old Incense Road with the ruins of the royal cities of Timna and Shabwa, cities whose wealth and splendour were already well known in antiquity. The visitor can now follow in the footsteps of such intrepid travellers as Philby, Freya Stark and Hans Hellfritz to explore the fascinating Wadi Hadramaut, which together with the Wadi Yashbum and the Wadi Doan is quite unique for its palm groves and the splendour of its clay architecture. The Ramlat as Sabᶜatayn – *The sands between the two Shebas* – at the southern edge of the vast Rhub al Khali desert, the Empty Quarter, has hitherto seldom been visited by foreigners.

Relations between Yemen and its eastern neighbour Oman have improved since unification, and so in the foreseeable future it should also be possible to follow the old Bedouin trails all the way to Salalah on Oman's Arabian Sea coast. No matter how much else may change in the years to come, Yemen is sure to remain a land of adventure.

Preceding pages: on the way to market; livestock market in Suq Al Dabab; the contrasts of the Wadi Hadramaut. **Left**, man of the highland Tihama.

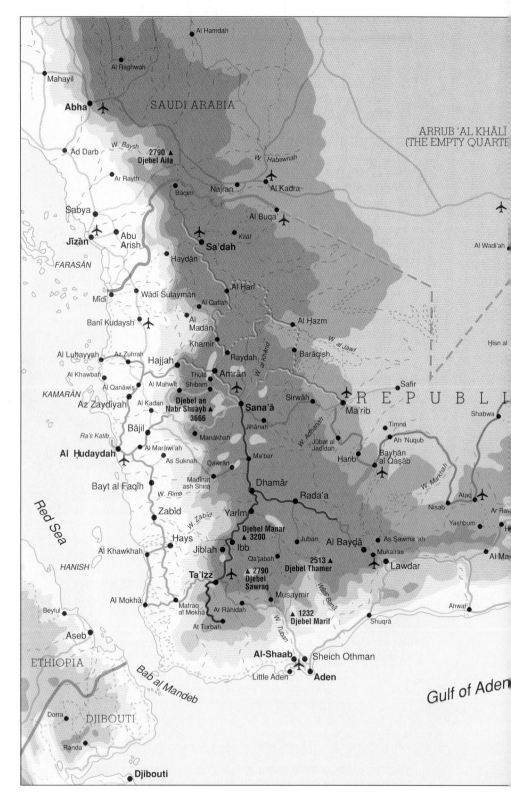

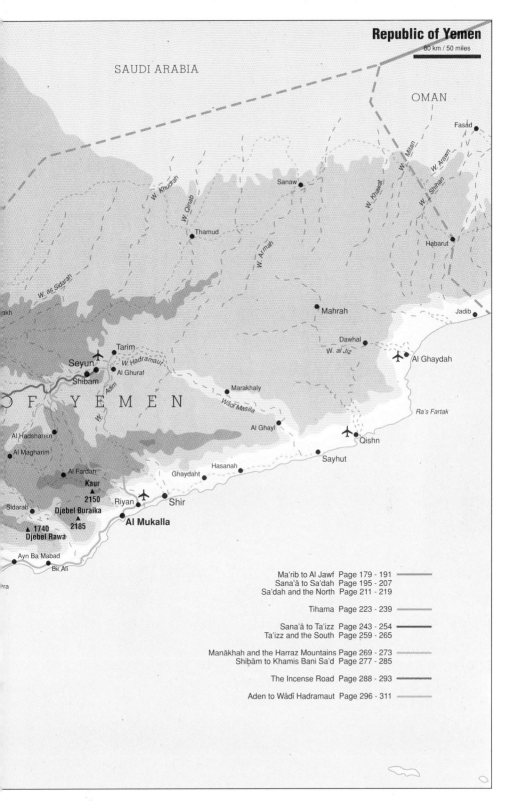

Republic of Yemen

80 km / 50 miles

SAUDI ARABIA

OMAN

Fasad

W. Khudrah

W. Qinab

W. Mitan

W. Khawat

W. Arawn

W. Shihan

Sanaw

Thamud

W. Armah

Habarut

W. as Sidarah

Mahrah

Jadib

akh

Dawhal

W. al Jiz

Tarim

Seyun

W. Hadramaut

Al Ghuraf

Al Ghaydah

Shibam

Adim

Ra's Fartak

O F   Y E M E N

W.

Marakhaly

Wadi Masila

Al Hadsharein

Al Ghayl

Qishn

Al Magharim

Sayhut

Al Fardah

Hasanah

Kaur

Ghaydaht

▲

2150   Riyan   Shir

Sidarah

Djebel Buraika

▲

▲ 1740   2185   Al Mukalla

Djebel Rawa

Ayn Ba Mabad

Bic Ali

ra

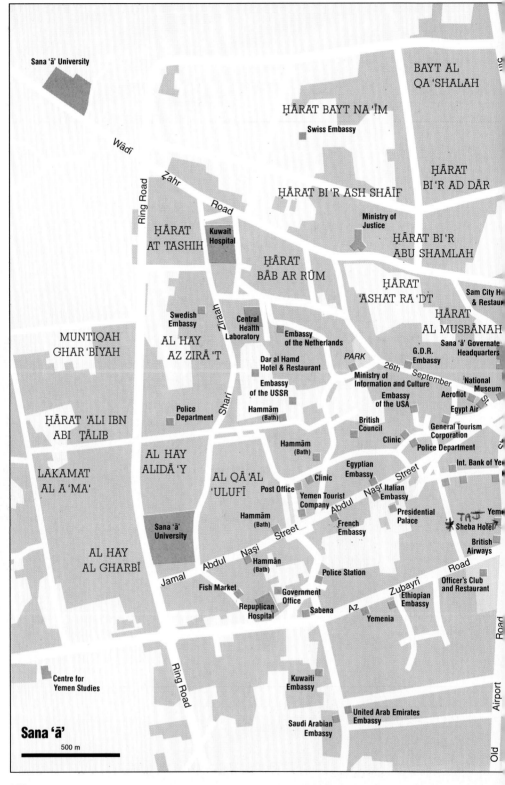

Sana 'ā' University

HĀRAT BAYT NA 'ÏM

BAYT AL
QA 'SHALAH

Swiss Embassy

Wādī

Zahr

Ring Road

Road

HĀRAT BI 'R ASH SHĀÏF

HĀRAT
BI 'R AD DĀR

Ministry of
Justice

HĀRAT BI 'R
ABU SHAMLAH

HĀRAT
AT TASHIH

Kuwait
Hospital

HĀRAT
BĀB AR RŪM

HĀRAT
'ASHAT RA 'DT

Sam City H
& Restau

Swedish
Embassy

Ziraah

Central
Health
Laboratory

Embassy
of the Netherlands

HĀRAT
AL MUSBĀNAH

Sana 'ā' Governate
Headquarters

MUNTIQAH
GHAR 'BÏYAH

AL HAY
AZ ZIRĀ 'T

Shari

PARK

G.D.R.
Embassy

Dar al Hamd
Hotel & Restaurant

Ministry of
Information and Culture

26th September St.

National
Museum

Embassy
of the USSR

Embassy
of the USA

Aeroflot

Egypt Air

HĀRAT 'ALI IBN
ABI ṬĀLIB

Police
Department

Hammām
(Bath)

British
Council

Clinic

General Tourism
Corporation

Police Department

LAKAMAT
AL A 'MA'

AL HAY
ALIDĀ 'Y

Hammām
(Bath)

Egyptian
Embassy

Clinic

Int. Bank of Ye

AL QĀ 'AL
'ULUFÏ

Post Office

Naṣr Street

Italian
Embassy

Yemen Tourist
Company

Abdul

Presidential
Palace

TAJ

Yeme

Sheba Hotel

Sana 'ā'
University

Hammām
(Bath)

Street

French
Embassy

British
Airways

AL HAY
AL GHARBÏ

Abdul

Naṣi

Jamal

Hammān
(Bath)

Police Station

Road

Zubayri

Officer's Club
and Restaurant

Fish Market

Government
Office

Az

Ethiopian
Embassy

Repuplican
Hospital

Sabena

Yemenia

Centre for
Yemen Studies

Ring Road

Kuwaiti
Embassy

Saudi Arabian
Embassy

United Arab Emirates
Embassy

Old Airport Road

Sana 'ā'

500 m

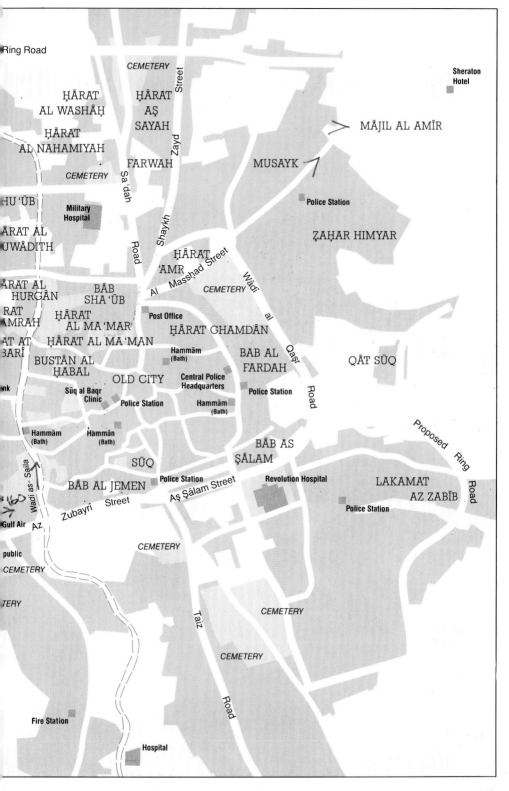

Ring Road

CEMETERY

HARAT
AL WASHAH

HARAT
AS
SAYAH

Sheraton
Hotel

Zayd Street

MAJIL AL AMIR

HARAT
AL NAHAMIYAH

FARWAH

MUSAYK

CEMETERY

Sa'dah

HU 'UB

Military
Hospital

Police Station

ARAT AL
UWADITH

Shaykh Road

ZAHAR HIMYAR

ARAT AL
HURGAN

HARAT
'AMR

Al Masshad Street

Wadi

RAT
MRAH

BAB
SHA 'UB

CEMETERY

al

AT AT
BARI

HARAT
AL MA 'MAR

Post Office

HARAT GHAMDAN

Qasr

QAT SUQ

HARAT AL MA 'MAN

BUSTAN AL
HABAL

Hammam
(Bath)

BAB AL
FARDAH

Road

nk

OLD CITY

Central Police
Headquarters

Suq al Baqr
Clinic

Police Station

Police Station

Hammam
(Bath)

Hammam
(Bath)

Hammam
(Bath)

Proposed Ring Road

Wadi as- Saila

SUQ

BAB AS
SALAM

AZ

BAB AL JEMEN

Police Station

Aş Salam Street

Revolution Hospital

LAKAMAT
AZ ZABIB

Gulf Air

Zubayri Street

Police Station

public

CEMETERY

Taiz

CEMETERY

TERY

CEMETERY

Fire Station

Road

CEMETERY

Hospital

147

SANA'A–CITY ON THE ROOFTOP OF ARABIA

If you have the good fortune to fly over the capital of Sana'a in the late afternoon you will witness an unforgettable sight. The tall houses of the old city are bathed in the warm yellow sun as it casts long shadows. The architecture of the old city is so varied and spontaneous that the eye is caught again and again by the rooftops and the upper storeys. Two notable sights are visible at once from the air. One is the dry river bed of the Saila which winds its way right through the centre of the city and is used mostly by cars as a roadway if it doesn't happen to be the rainy season. The other is the almost square construction of the magnificent Friday Mosque with its enormous courtyard. Again and again, the architecture will never cease to fascinate you.

"Sana'a must be seen": These are the opening words of an old proverb, attributed to such famous people as Imam Mohammed al-Shafi'a, the founder of the Islamic school of law of the same name, and Mohammed al-Hamdani, the famous Yemeni historian and geographer of the 10th century. The words remain relevant to this day, although no-one travels through the Sana'a Basin any more on the back of a camel "which hangs its head from exhaustion." It must have been an arduous journey, climbing up the "Rooftop of Arabia" from Saudi Arabia or the coastal plain.

With sufficient periodic rainfall to permit cultivation, Sana'a is very different from the other parts of Arabia. It is fertile in contrast to the dry character of the Arabian peninsula. This is due to its volcanic origin, high relief, and abundant rainfall. The country is characterised by its diverse physical geography which varies from the lowlands to the highlands. This diversity, fortunately, has a great economic siginifi-cance, since different types of soil are found in different areas of the country. The result is that various land cultivation has taken place.

Sana'a lies at an altitude of about 7,546 feet (2,300 metres) above sea level and is surrounded by even higher mountains. To the east lies Djebel Nuqum (9,488 feet/2,892 metres), with the walls of a fortress clearly to be seen on its peak. The even higher mountain to the west, Djebel Ayban (10,466 feet/ 3,194 metres), can only be seen from the eastern part of the city. On its peak you can see the structure of a relay station for Yemeni television.

The Sana'a Basin, some 50 miles (80 km) long and 10 miles (16 km) wide, descends from south to north. The floodwaters of the Wadi As Saila flow in the same direction during the minor rainy season which is between March and April and the major one which falls in July and August. The Saila then winds its way north past the garden city of Ar Rawdah and finally flows into the Wadi Al Jawf to the northwest of Sana'a. To the south of the city, on the slopes of the Haddah mountains, there is still a series of springs rising which in earlier years were channelled into subterranean passages and thus brought drinking water to the population.

The best preserved channel, the Ghazl al-Aswad, still served its purpose as late as 1973. Today many of these springs have partly or completely dried up, because of the uncontrolled use of water from the basin and the surrounding highland via deep wells equipped with diesel pumps.

2,000 years of history: Sana'a in the past was technically, economically and socially developed, but–because of political fragmentation and an isolationist policy–remained almost untouched by the outside modern world until well into the 20th century. It is still unknown and very much self-sufficient.

According to ancient legend, Sana'a was founded by Shem, who is the oldest son of Noah, at the foot of Djebel Nuqum. Mohammed al-Hamdani, the 10th-century Yemeni historian, describes vividly the founding of Sana'a in the 8th volume of his 12-volume work *Al Iklil*:

"He who built the place of Ghumdan and dug the wells was Shem, the son of Noah–peace be with him. He left his home in the north and wandered south. When he came to Yemen, the country pleased him...the valley of Sana'a pleased him best. When he began to build foundations on the western side of the valley, a bird came, took his plumbline in its beak and flew away with it. Shem followed the bird...until the bird dropped the plumbline at the feet of Djebel Nuqum. Then Shem knew that he was to build the palace of Ghumdan in the place where the bird had dropped the plumbline."

The oldest inscription known to date, which mentions Sana'a together with the more northerly settlement of Sha'ub, is dated by some historians to the first century A.D., which puts it into the reign of King Halak Amer bin Karibil Watar. Sha'ub is still the name of the northern gate, which unfortunately no longer exists.

Inscriptions dating from the early third century mention the two palaces Salhin in Ma'rib and Ghumdan in Sana'a together. According to Al Hamdani these two palaces were the main residences of the Sabaean kings. When the Himyar conquered Ma'rib half a century later and then spread their rule over the whole of Yemen, according to legend, it was probably Zafar (near Yarim) that served as their capital. At any rate, the sources are silent about Sana'a until the city became the centre of events once again in A.D. 525 after the Ethiopian conquest.

Most historians believe that the word Sana'a goes back to Sabaean root and

The rooftops of the Suq al-Milh in the old city.

means something like "the fortified one." It is assumed that the mountain on where the citadel Qasr as-Silha (the highest point of the city of Sana'a) stands now was once the site of this early Sabaean fort. Under the protection of the fort, people would have settled and, at first, carried on trade undisturbed in the form of a weekly market.

Mahram status has also been ascribed to the city from the earliest times. Mahram means "sacred place," which is well respected by all, and where no hostilities or disputes may be settled with weapons. The chequered history of the city proves that this "protected status" was not always respected by the northern tribes.

A homogeneous race: The people of Sana'a are a mixed race: the pre-Qahtania Mediterranean type and the Armenoid (Middle Eastern Alpine). In the highlands, the population shows a balance between the two types. Negro characteristics was introduced around the 5th and 6th century A.D., however,

a further mixture of early Indo-Aryan traits occurs in some parts of the highlands accounting for some eight to 10 percent of the population who are characterised by fair complexion, blue eyes and blond hair.

Ghumdan: The palace of Ghumdan did actually exist, and it has been described with pride by later poets, long after the coming of Islam. According to the poets, the palace was 20 floors high, with a roof of translucent alabaster. The four outer walls were built of four different coloured types of stone. On each corner there was a lion of bronze, with an open mouth which howled when the wind blew through it. Apparently Ghumdan was destroyed soon after the coming of Islam. According to a description by Al Hamdani, it was still possible to see the ruins of the palace in the 10th century. They lay on a hill to the east of the Great Mosque.

After the conquest of Yemen by the Ethiopians in 525, the ruler Abraha built a second palace, which was to become

A relic of Turkish times–the Bab al-Yemen.

famous far and wide outside the borders of the country. The Ethiopians were Christians, for them, the cruel persecution of Christians by the last Himyar king, Dhu Nuwa, was a welcome opportunity or revenge to bring Yemen under their rule. Abraha built a magnificent cathedral and was supported in his work by none other than the Emperor Justinian. Historical sources describe the cathedral as being 262 feet (80 metres) long and 82 feet (25 metres) wide. The ceiling was of teak and was held by gold and silver nails. The pulpit was made of ivory with adornments of gold and silver. The pillars and floor of the cathedral were made of polished marble. The most impressive part was the crypt, which was roofed by a dome 51 feet (15½ metres) wide. A gigantic alabaster window in the eastern section was said to have let in the light of the morning sun and of the moon "so brightly, that all inside who looked up to the window had to shade their eyes."

Abraha's ambition to make the build-ing into a place of pilgrimage for the whole Arabian peninsula led to his downfall. Soon the cathedral came to rival the (pre-Islamic) Ka'aba in Mecca, and disputes broke out. During a punitive expedition by Abraha to Mecca, after some people from Mecca had deliberately desecrated the cathedral, his army was almost completely destroyed by an unknown mysterious plague. It is still not clear what actually happened. The Koran reports that a huge flock of birds dropped little stones on the soldiers and forced them to retreat. It is a fact that Abraha died shortly after this defeat. Ethiopian rule in Sana'a came to a rapid end, as troops from Persia conquered the city with the support of the Himyar nobility, only a few years before the coming of Islam.

There is enough documentary evidence to prove that the Persian governor Badhan accepted Islam as the new religion in 628. Nowadays the first Friday of the Islamic month of Radshab is still celebrated by the people of the city in **Street traders beyond Bab al-Yemen.**

memory of this event.

Islamic history: During the early Islamic centuries Sana'a was ruled by governors, the so-called *walis*, who were appointed by the Ummayid caliphs in Damascus and later by the Abbasid caliphs in Baghdad. These governors were sent by the caliph or were Yemenis who were confirmed in their office by the caliphs. The latter was the case, for instance, with the Beni Yu'fir, who conquered Sana'a in the early 10th century and resided there for the next 150 years.

The Yu'firids were constantly in conflict with the rising power of the Zaidi Imams in the north, who were later to take over the rule of Sana'a and the whole of Yemen. The final period of Yu'firid rule was characterised by constant squabbling and frequent changes of governor. The Arab historian Al Tabari reports that during this time power changed hands in Sana'a more than twenty times in only twelve years.

Peace was not restored until Ali Bin Sulayhi, a follower of the Egyptian Fatimids, conquered Sana'a in 1047 and made it the capital of his kingdom. Forty years later his famous daughter-in-law Arwa bint Ahmed moved the capital to Jiblah.

In 1173 the whole of Yemen was conquered by Turanshah, the brother of Saladin, who also became quite famous in Europe. The Ayyubids built a new palace to the west of the Saila and added a new settlement to the fortified city. This area is still known as Bustan as-Sultan–the (Ayyubid) Sultan's Garden. When the Ayyubids eventually chose Ta'izz as their capital and fortified it, Sana'a suffered again and again from the territorial disputes of the Zaidi Imams in the north and the Ayyubids in the south. Not until the establishment of the Rasulid sultanate in 1228 with its capital in Ta'izz did Sana'a become peaceful again, after a peace treaty with the Zaidis. About a hundred years later Sana'a finally fell into the hands of the Zaidis, until the city was conquered in

Rain turns the streets into rivers.

1515 by fighting troops of the Mameluke dynasty from Egypt. The Mamelukes were very successful in their wars because they were the first army in the history of Yemen to use firearms in battle.

However, the success of the Mamelukes did not last long. Two years later their homeland of Egypt was conquered by the Osman Turks, who quickly spread throughout the entire Arabian peninsula. In 1538 Turkish armies first landed on Yemeni soil. Nine years later they succeeded in occupying Sana'a, after the northern water gate of the Saila was opened for them by a traitor. From this time on the Turks were constantly fighting the Zaidi Imams of the north.

The Osman Turks made great changes to the appearance of Sana'a. They extended the fortifications and built their typical domed mosques (such as the Al Bakiriya, in the east of the city, built in 1597). The system of government was restructured, state property was registered and a simple educational system was introduced.

In the meantime, the Zaidi Imams of the north collected their forces and increased their pressure on Sana'a. Qasim the Great and his son Mu'ayyid eventually found themselves in such a strong position in 1623 that they were able to force the Turks to leave the city and even the whole of Yemen. From that time until the second Turkish invasion in 1872 Sana'a was the capital of the Zaidi kingdom.

After nearly 250 years of Zaidi rule, the Turks returned to Sana'a under Ahmed Muchtar Pasha and placed the city under the rule of the Sublime Porte. On this occasion the Turks settled in the garden quarter of Bir al-Azab which they surrounded with its own wall. The old city and Bir al-Azab were linked by the royal palace and grounds of Al Mutawakkil (the Museum of Sana'a is part of the palace), built 150 years earlier by the Zaidi Imam Al Mutawakkil Al Qasim.

The prophet came from a merchant family background, too.

The Zaidis continued to resist the Turks, and Imam Yahya besieged the towns under Turkish rule in 1904, Sana'a was among them. After discussions, which seemed hopeful at first, open war broke out between the two sides, during the course of which the greater part of the population of the city either died or was forced to flee the country. The end of World War I marked the final withdrawal of Turkish forces, and Imam Yahya ruled the kingdom from his capital at Sana'a up until his assassination in 1948.

Sana'a in the 20th century: Imam Yahya Hamid ad-Din settled into the old palace district of Al Mutawakkil and had two further large buildings erected, Dar ash-Shukr and Dar as-Sa'ada. The latter now houses the recently opened National Museum. Imam Yahya was known for his policies of absolute control and his jealous exclusion of outside influences from his country. Yahya, like his son Ahmed after him, saw himself as a ruler by the grace of God and the rightful successor to the Prophet.

Resistance movements were already forming during the reign of Imam Yahya. When the latter fell victim to an assassination attempt in 1948, a new Imam was proclaimed in Sana'a, who announced parliamentary-style reforms. Crown Prince Ahmed who heard about the assassination of the Imam, fled to Hajjah and from there mobilised the tribes against Sana'a. The prince won over a large number of warriors by promising them the city of Sana'a if they were victorious. And so it came about that Sana'a was violently plundered for the last time by the tribes in 1948. The tribespeople were so greedy that they even took doors and window frames with them. Imam Ahmed then set up residence, not in Sana'a but back in Ta'izz.

However, the resistance against the Imamate was by no means broken. There were more and more attacks on Imam Ahmed. When the Imam finally

Flooding the market–mass-produced goods from India and China.

died in 1962 from the after-effects of his wounds, his son Mohammed Badr proclaimed himself the new Imam. He in his turn promised reforms. The resistance movement, which was now more and more in the hands of the military, was already determined, however, to dispose of the Imamate once and for all and to establish a modern republic.

Exactly a week after Ahmed's death, on 26 September 1962, tank units led by Abdulla as-Salal, the future first president of the republic, fired on the royal palace. At the same time the new republic was proclaimed over the radio. Imam Badr was allowed to flee the country, and he continued to fight a bitter civil war against the Republicans.

The year 1967 was a particularly critical year for the young republic. Gamal Abdul Nasser, president of Egypt at the time, who had supported the Republicans from the beginning, withdrew his troops from Yemen. The Royalists saw their chance and prepared for a large-scale attack on the capital Sana'a. For 70 days the city was besieged by Royalists and bombarded almost daily with heavy artillery. The long siege ended unsuccessfully on 8 February 1968, and the republic had withstood its baptism of fire. Every year on this day the end of the siege is commemorated with ceremonies and speeches.

The civil war, however, was not to end until 1970, when Royalists and Republicans met during a conference of foreign ministers of Arab states in Jeddah and agreed on a compromise which excluded the royal family of Hamid ad-Din. As a result of this a permanent constituition, recognising the fundamental rights of the people, was declared in 1970. For Sana'a, this meant the start of the long-awaited peace and the beginning of a remarkably rapid development into a modern 20th-century city. Today Sana'a has just emerged from a long drawn-out struggle to preserve her national goal which is peace and a governemnt by consent as well as economic and social development.

Men among men–a comfortable gathering in the _mafradsh_.

Architecture and lifestyles: The unique architectural style of the old city of Sana'a fascinates the eye of the beholder again and again. Whether you walk through the narrow, shady alleys and let your glance run up the façades of the houses or whether you are looking down from one of the houses with several floors onto a lower building, it is the spontaneity and light-hearted variety of the styles of building which make each house into a unique work of art. The houses are built close together and are partially linked one to another in what sometimes looks really creative. As the area within the city walls was limited, every scrap of ground had to be used in the best possible way, and the houses had to expand upwards. The basic ground plan of the town might just as well date from the 15th or 16th century. In fact, some of the houses are rarely older than 100 or 200 years. The upper storeys with their high-rise reception room, the *mafradsh*, usually date from this century.

Beautiful ornamental bands of geometric patterns, formed by bricks protruding in a relief-like manner, mark the boundaries between the floors or playfully surround the windows. When these ornaments have been whitewashed, which house owners usually do once a year, the houses look especially fresh and clean.

Typical of the houses are the arches above the windows filled with coloured glass. Floral or geometric patterns are marked with compasses and ruler in the still damp plaster and cut out with a knife. Once the openings have been filled with coloured glass, another layer of liquid plaster is poured over the window arch. The craftsman then has to cut exactly the same patterns out of the new layer of plaster. Wealthy houses are distinguished by double window arches, with the decorations of the outer arch being made of plain window glass, but in a different pattern. If you look closely through a double window a third pattern will be formed where the plaster

ornaments overlap. At night, when the electric light in the rooms can be seen from outside through the arches, you can get something of the feeling for the medieval Islamic world, as it is so brilliantly described in the stories of the "Arabian Nights."

These semi-circular fan lights, however, have only been in existence for about 150 years. When Carsten Niebuhr visited the city in 1763 only very few houses had window glass: "The fine palaces are also praiseworthy. In one I saw glass panes in the window openings. The others have shuttered windows, which are open in good weather and closed in bad. In the houses of the Imam and of his ministers I saw coloured glass panes which had come from Venice." The oldest houses are distinguished by their circular window lights, with two being placed one above the other. Thin plaques of polished alabaster were used as panes–alabaster was quarried in Yemen until a few decades ago. They give an unusual warm and

Men predominate in the streets of the city–a Sana'ani.

milky light to the rooms.

The foundations of the houses are not very deep and consist of roughly hewn basalt blocks. The outer walls of the ground floor consist of natural coloured limestone and tufa, which alternate in geometric patterns along the door and small window frames. Only the outside faces of the stones are smoothed off. The inside walls are made smooth with a mixture of stone splinters and clay.

A steep staircase, sometimes with unusually high steps, leads up and around a square stone pillar. This pillar, known as the "mother of the house", gives, as name suggests, stability to the building. An old rule of thumb states that repairs can only be made to a building as long as the stone pillar is undamaged. If the pillar shows cracks or is damaged, it is better to rebuild the house from the foundation upwards.

There is no doubt that the old city of Sana'a is a masterpiece of Islamic architecture. The sudden opening up of the country, especially after the end of the civil war in 1970, brought with it a wave of modernisation which has also brought previously unknown dangers for the physical and social structure of the old city centre.

It is not surprising, therefore, that international organisations such as UNESCO have shown an interest in the preservation of the unique old city. In the mid-1970s Sana'a was declared one of the the most endangered cities in the world. On the occasion of a conference of Islamic foreign ministers in Sana'a in 1984 a campaign for preserving the old city was introduced by the Yemeni government together with UNESCO. A high-ranking committee in charge of renovating the old city was appointed, and its executive organ, the "Bureau for the Preservation of the Old City of Sana'a", given the responsibility of organising and supervising the work. Under the direction of this Bureau streets have been paved, caravanserais restored, and consideration has been given to ways of preventing the youthful population from moving out into modern districts of the city. A further task is the preservation of the stylistic features of the buildings, which is intended to prevent the city being disfigured by modern building methods and materials.

Around Tahrir Square: The Midan at-Tahrir is indisputably the centre of the modern capital. All day long the central park is full of people who come to watch the water of the fountain or be photographed in front of the monument in honour of the revolution. The tank right next to the monument is supposed to have fired the first shots at the Imam's palace in 1962. If you stand in front of the entrance to the **Main Post Office**, **Abdul Moghni Street** runs off to your right in the direction of **Zubayri Street**, and to the left, in a westerly direction, is **Gamal Abdul Nasser Street**. Diagonally opposite, in a northeasterly direction, is the former city gate of **Bab as-Sabah**, now a lively market and the entrance to the old city.

Pumpkin dealer on the way to market.

158

Abdul Moghni Street and Gamal Abdul Nasser Street are the main business streets of the city. The shops mainly sell gold and luxury articles. Gamal Abdul Nasser Street leads to another square, **Midan al-Qa'**, to the west of which lies the former Jewish quarter, **Qa' al-Yahud**. In the early 1950s the majority of Yemeni Jews emigrated to Israel, and only a small Jewish minority remains in the north of the country. It is worth your while taking a walk through this quarter. The alleys are very narrow and twisting. The original houses were not permitted to be higher than two floors and are distinguished by a central courtyard surrounded by living accommodation. There the families could carry out their religious observances undisturbed. Deep cellars, which served as storage space, were dug under many houses.

On Gamal Abdul Nasser Street, still on Tahrir Square, is the **Military Museum**. It is easy to find due to the two howitzers and the torpedo outside. The museum mostly records the history of the civil war and the development of the modern Yemeni army.

The Airport Road leads from Tahrir Square in a northerly direction. From the post office you cross the square and its park, passing the **Mutawakkil Mosque**, and then follow the **Airport Road**, until after about 150 metres (495 feet) you come to the **Dar as-Sa'ada** ("Palace of Good Fortune"). This building, within the grounds of the royal palace, was built by Imam Yahya and served as his residence. This multi-storey building is now the home of the **National Museum**.

You enter the museum through several arches and the first things you see on the ground floor are the enormous statues of the Himyar kings Dhamar Ali and his son Ta'ran. Along the sides of the entrance hall are fragments of those statues whose copies can be seen in the Römisch-Germanisches Museum in West Germany.

On the first floor you can see finds dating from the Neolithic period and a large collection of figures, fragments of stone, and inscriptions from the South Arabian frankincense route kingdoms. The Islamic history of Yemen up until the Hamid ad-Din dynasty is recorded on the second floor. The ethnographic section of the third floor displays models of houses from different regions of the country, various traditional costumes, pieces of craft work and old agricultural implements. On the fourth floor official state gifts to the Yemeni president are on display.

If you want to go from Tahrir Square to Bab al-Yemen, you can either go in one of the multi-passenger taxis or walk along Abdul Moghni Street in a southerly direction. After passing the **Sheba Hotel** on your right, turn left into **Zubayri Street** and keep walking towards Djebel Nuqum. Cross the bridge over the Saila, from which point you will have a wonderful **view of the old city**. From there, just follow the line of the old city wall until you arrive at the

Modern architecture–the high-rise office block of Yemen.

Bab al-Yemen located in the background on your left.

From the Sheba Hotel to Al Qasr: This route across the city from west to east begins with a little alley which runs east, parallel to Zubayri Street. You can see it clearly from the entrance to the Sheba Hotel: on the other side of Abdul Moghni Street on the left, past the Central Bank. Soon you will see on your left the **remains of the old city wall**. If you are adventurous enough, don't hesitate to get up onto these mud brick remains. From the top you will see a wonderful view of the old city. To the east, Djebel Nuqum towers above the city. At the point where there is a break in the city wall the Saila runs through from south to north. To the north there is a large open space by the Saila, at the end of which lie the dome and the minaret of the **Qubbat al-Mahdi Mosque**. The whole area is known as **Bustan as-Sultan** after the Ayyubid sultans, who settled here with their armies in the early 12th century and thus founded a new district of the city.

Once you reach the Saila, keep to the left, until you see on your right a broad street paved with dressed stone, leading east again towards Djebel Nuqum. To your left is the little **Barum Mosque**. Here your way leads past a **maqshama**, one of the typical gardens that can be found all over the old city.

The paved road narrows and then leads into **Midan al-Qasimi**. At the end of the square, to the left, a paved way leads to **Dar al-Dshadid**. Keep to the right here and go up a few steps until you can see on your left the tall Dar al-Dshadid. This houses the **Bureau for the Renovation of the Old City**, where Yemeni and foreign experts work together in their offices on the various floors. On the top floor there is a spacious *mafradsh*, from which you can get a magnificent view of the old city. If you want to visit Dar al-Dshadid, make necessary arrangements with the official department first.

Back in Qasimi Square, the main way

Rain and Ramadan have emptied Midan at-Tahrir.

160

leads past the minaret of the **Abhar Mosque** directly into the spacious **Midan Abhar**. This square was paved in the early 1970s by development workers for the United Nations and serves as a model for the paving of other alleys which is taking place at present. To the left on the pavement is a memorial plaque which says that the Yemeni Prime Minister and the Secretary of State of the Italian Foreign Ministry laid the foundation stone for the renovation of the old city on this spot on 6 April 1988. The paved alley to the right is **Bahr Radshradsh** and leads past the **sesame mills**, which are powered by camels, to the inner side of the **Bab al-Yemen**. To the left the alley, which is not paved yet, continues to wind through the tall houses until the massive walls of the **Djamal al-Kabir** can be seen on the right. This great mosque was founded during the lifetime of the Prophet and, from that time until the 20th century, it has been the religious centre of the city. Together with the mosque of Al Janad, it can claim to be the oldest mosque in Yemen. It is built in the old Kufic style. This means that the basic plan consists of four roofed galleries of pillars, which surround an open inner courtyard.

Various parts of the mosque buildings reflect the entire history of the city, even as far back as pre-Islamic times. Especially interesting are the pillars which come from pre-Islamic buildings and have been re-used. Some of the pillars still clearly bear visible Abyssinian crosses, thus it is assumed that they originally came from the cathedral of Al Qalis.

Many Islamic rulers have contributed over the centuries to the extension and reinforcement of the mosque's buildings. In some places on the inner walls calligraphic inscriptions cut in stone commemorate the generous donors and governors who have contributed to the building of the mosque.

During renovation work on the west wall of the mosque in 1972 a real treas-

Evening on Az Zubayri Street.

ure was discovered, in the form of ancient fragments of the Koran and other manuscripts, which are now being restored in the **House of Manuscripts** on the southern side of the mosque. The project was originally financed by funds from West German cultural aid and comprises some 15,000 fragments belonging to some 800 to 1,000 different copies of the Koran. Because of the dry climate of Sana'a the ancient pieces of parchment, some over a thousand years old, have fortunately been preserved almost undamaged. The oldest pieces of writing, in the so-called Hidshazi script, date back to the first century of Islam.

The pride of the exhibition which was mounted in the House of Manuscripts on the occasion of the conference of Islamic foreign ministers in 1984 are two pages of a very large copy of the Koran dating from the Ummayyid period. On these the elevation and ground plans for two different types of mosque can be seen. The exact detail of the drawings and the variety of colours probably make them unique in the Islamic world. Unfortunately the Great Mosque and the House of Manuscripts are not yet prepared for visitors, so it is extremely difficult to gain entrance to either of the two buildings.

Carry on walking straight on from the north side of the Great Mosque towards Djebel Nuqum. In the small shops on your left there are still a few traditional **bookbinders** at work. You then pass the southern **market centre** and go past the short minaret (on your right) of the **Madhab Mosque**. At the end of the market centre you pass the **Suq al-Chobs**, where food is prepared all day long.

Shortly before you get to **Midan al-Laqiya** a little alley leads off to the right to the remains of the Ethiopian **Al Qalis Cathedral**. The English architect Ronald Lewcock believes that he has discovered the crypt of the cathedral in the circular foundations still visible today. The size of the block of houses

This garden in Saila is the starting point for many tours of the old city.

162

which adjoins it on the west side is more or less identical with the recorded dimension of the length and breadth of the cathedral. At the western end of the block of houses, in a star-like pattern, four roads meet which could have once led to the main entrance of the cathedral. Back on the original route, carry on towards Djebel Nuqum, until you reach **Midan al-Laqiya**. Right behind it rise the walls of the **Al Qasr fortifications**. The fortress now belongs to the military and may not be entered (or photographed). Before you get to Al Qasr you will come to an asphalt road, which runs to the left of the **domed mosque of Al Bakiriya** to **Bab Sha'ub** in the north of the city. Turning to the right, you will come to **Bab as-Salam** (both gates no longer exist) and continue along the outside, so to speak, of the former city walls to Bab al-Yemen.

Bab al-Yemen, Suq al-Milh and Bab Sha'ub: Continuing straight on from Bab al-Yemen towards the centre of town, you will eventually come right into the centre of the **Suq al-Milh**, the market of Sana'a. A confusing labyrinth of little alleys opens up before you. Just a little to the right is the shortest way through the market, leading past the **corn market** and the **spice market**. The latter is impossible to miss. The strong smell of freshly ground pepper, coriander and cumin mingles with the scent of the piles of cinnamon, cardamom and cloves. These are the same spices which were carried northwards thousands of years ago by the Sabaeans on the gold and frankincense routes to the centres of the great Mediterranean civilisations.

If you'd like to spend a little more time in the market, don't take the route just to your right, but keep a bit more to the left. Here lies the former **copper market**. Items required by the religious classes of the qadi and the sadaah are sold here: hand-embroidered *imamas* (special headgear for religious scholars), belts with fine gold and silver threads woven into them, and the most

Typical houses in the endangered old city of Sana'a.

expensive *djambias* are on sale here, together with walking sticks and large books of religious writings.

Carry on walking and you will pass the **Samsarat Mohammed bin Hassan**, the largest and tallest caravanserai in the market. Today there are still more than thirty of these *samsaras* in the suq, mostly used as warehouses for dried foods. In earlier years the caravanserai served as an inn for travelling merchants. People and animals could spend one or several nights there. The lower rooms were used as stables and storage while the merchants slept on the upper floors. The merchants leave only after their goods had been sold.

To the left is the Suq al-Dshanabi, where the traditional curved daggers or *djambia* are still made. Over the centuries four different crafts have been developed in order to produce this status symbol. The smiths make the blades of high quality steel. A second craftsman polishes the blades until they shine like mirrors. It is then passed on to another craftsman who is specialised in manufacturing the hilts, which are made of cattle horn or of expensive rhinoceros horn smuggled in from Africa. A fourth group makes nothing but scabbards and belts. The price of a *djambia* ranges from a mere US$20 to a hefty US$2,000, according to age and the patina of the hilt.

To your left you can hear the click-clack of falling hammers, providing the beat for the rhythmic singing of the smiths in the **Suq al-Hadadin**. Sparks fly everywhere through the air, especially when the bellows are puffed vigorously into the forge. When a large piece of iron is being worked, the smith calls his neighbours to help him, and they quickly come running up with their hammers ready to oblige.

The cap market–**Suq al-Qawafi**–is followed by the narrow alley of the narghile makers–**Suq al-Qasib**. The wooden pipe, more than a yard long, is glued with hot resin to the round water container. White clouds of smoke rise

Djerras or roasted locusts are a delicacy in Yemen.

up, with the scent of incense. Further east lies an open square space, the **Suq al-Mibsata**. Here anyone can try his luck and sell his watch, his cassette recorder, his *djambia* or other treasures.

The silver market–**Suq al-Fidda**–which adjoins the Suq al-Mibsata to the east is probably the quarter most visited by foreigners. Finely worked necklaces, bracelets, rings set with red carbuncle stones are offered for sale, together with ancient muzzle-loaders and oil lamps. Many pieces of silver workmanship are still skillfully made by Jewish silversmiths. Every little shop holds a treasure trove of silver jewellery and antique weapons.

From the silver market you can enter the **Samsarat al-Mizan**–the caravanserai of the scales. In earlier times all newly arrived goods had to be brought into this caravanserai. There they were weighed, the customs duty was determined and everything was recorded by the head scribe in an enormous register. Only then were the goods allowed to be taken by bearers to other warehouses. The great scales are still in use today for weighing bales of tobacco and sacks of coffee.

Back in the Suq al-Mibsata, follow the street to the north in the direction of Bab Sha'ub. After first making a turn to the left and then again to the right, you come to a long shopping street, the **Suq al-Zumur**. Easily recognisable structure on your left is the **Az-Zumur Mosque**. The street, somewhat wider now, eventually leads to the former city gate of **Bab Sha'ub**, of which absolutely nothing can be seen today.

The Ring Road around Sana'a: If you want to get a good view of the capital by car, drive around Sana'a on the Ring Road. From the Airport Road going north, turn off right onto the Inner Ring Road and then drive in an easterly direction towards Djebel Nuqum. Soon you will cross the **river bed of the Saila**, which is dry for the greater part of the year. Only during the two rainy seasons are dirty brown waters to be found flow-

A little salesman in the raisin market.

ing northwards in the bed of the wadi. If it has been raining particularly heavily, it could happen that it is just not possible for you to cross the bed of the wadi on the Ring Road.

The next crossing takes you across the **Sa'adah Road**, which starts at Bab Sha'ub. Then you drive across **Sheich Za'id Road**, named after the president of the United Arab Emirates, who presented Yemen with this asphalt road which runs as far as Ma'rib. It then climbs the foothills of Djebel Nuqum; just to your left is the Omar al-Muchtar high school and farther up the road is the **Sheraton Hotel**.

The road then bends to the right and leads past a slope planted with trees. This area is known as **Duhr Himyar**. A little farther, on your right, there is even a car park. Behind it lies a new park with a restaurant. From the western edge of this park you can get a beautiful view of the entire city.

You can enjoy yet another beautiful view of the old city if you drive on along the Ring Road, which then begins to go downhill and passes just above the market of **Suq Nuqum**, this market was originally a market for *qat*. Over the years it has developed into a large market for domestic animals and building materials. You can watch the busy life of the market in the mornings quite well from the edge of the road.

After this, you will be driving through the district of **Lakamat az-Zabib**, until the road bends to the right and carries on in a westerly direction. At the second crossroads you can either keep going straight on the **Inner Ring Road**, or you can follow the **Ta'izz Road** southwards. If you stay on the Inner Ring Road, you will cross the Saila once more and drive right through the district of **As-Safia**. At the next crossroads you turn left into the **Old Airport Road**, and then keep going south towards the Haddah Mountains.

After another crossroad, you will come to a broad **parade ground**, which used to be the original airport of Sana'a

during the rule of Imam Ahmed. It is now known as "70 Day Square", a reminder of the 70 day siege of Sana'a by the Royalists. A big military parade is held here every year on the national holiday (26 September). On the left-hand side are the "TV tower" and the grandstands, while on the right is a park, bordering the road. The six pillars of the monument in the park symbolise the six principles of the September revolution, and the two bent structures on both sides of the pillars represent the Arab numeral 26 (26 September).

At the end of the parade ground you come to the **Outer Ring Road** and turn right into it. The next road you cross is the Haddah Road. The Outer Ring Road is also known as Sixty Road, as it is intended to be 60 metres (179 feet) wide in the future. To the right are the houses of university professors, while a little later, on the left, you can drive up to the **Fadsh 'Attan Garden**s. In this very new park there is even a swimming pool, which can be seen from the restaurant. From this point you also have a very good view of the capital, looking east this time.

The Ring Road then crosses **Zubayri Street**, into which you turn left in the direction of Hudaydah and drive up as far as the edge of the Sana'a Basin. More places from which you can get a good view are the memorial to the Egyptian dead of the civil war and, farther up, the Chinese cemetery with the little temples which seem rather strange in this Arab cultural context. You can also drive right up to the edge of the basin and from there you can get the best view of the whole valley.

Return to the Outer Ring Road, and drive towards a northerly direction until the road finally leads you into **Wadi Dahr Road**. From there you drive past the teaching buildings and faculties of the new university till you come to the crossroads with the Inner Ring Road. If you turn left into the latter, you will come once again, after another right-hand turn, onto the Airport Road.

After the 1962 revolution Sana'a became the capital of the new republic. Work was already beginning during the civil war on alterations and expansion to turn the city into a modern centre of administration. The narrow streets of the old city, with their packed houses, were not attractive either for commercial or administrative use. For this reason, the historic core of Sana'a was spared the more far-reaching changes of the turbulent post-revolutionary times. This

lack of interest made it possible for the Madinah to survive, but also led to the situation that no measures were taken to preserve the old buildings for many years. The image of the city today is essentially determined by the busy life of the streets as well as by the everyday work carried on in the old city. Most important are the little shops and workshops in the market, but the more imposing buildings and the evidence of the long tradition of Sana'a as a trading centre–the big warehouses and inns or *samsarah* around the edge of the main market of Suq al-Milh–are also significant.

The Madinah derives its unique style from the large vegetable gardens or *maqshamah*. The traders and craftsmen make up the colourful life of the suq. The work of the women in the vegetable gardens preserves the green oases in the stone desert of the city. Children playing in the alleys, women swathed in black cloth, qadis or legal scholars, sadaah, members of the religious aristocracy in their traditional clothes, and also the camels which keep the oil presses moving in dark rooms, as well as whole herds of sheep and goats, all found in the middle of this very big diverse city.

By now it is clear that the matter is not merely one of repairing old houses and freshening up façades. The old city has to be seen as a very complex structure made up of varied elements. This structure came out of balance due to the social upheaval after the revolution; many of the elements of the architectural and the social structures no longer match with modern expectations. For instance, the Sana'anis would like to drive up to their houses in the old city. The traditional houses of the old city are very picturesque, but the endless climbing of stairs in the tower houses is quite exhausting.

It is not surprising that many families are attracted by the idea of their own bungalow. But even those families who have decided to remain in the old city and have modernised their houses accordingly have not necessarily made a contribution to the preservation of the old city. Poor sanitary installations have meant that many buildings suffer from damage to the wooden ceilings and to the walls of the bathrooms, as well as to the foundations: burst water pipes have already led to the collapse of these houses.

Businesses in the old city are also at a disadvantage because very few businesses have opportunities for expansion, and the use of modern machinery is often not possible. Many customers with cars prefer shops with a car park outside, which is impossible in the suq. In earlier years the different trades and crafts had their own alliances whose rules were binding for all. Nowadays, these guilds have practically no influence. All these factors influence the viability of businesses in the old city; diminishing profits will not permit further investment. The citizens used to administer their own areas, but these organisations are losing importance. At the same time, responsibilities are growing–such as rubbish collection, street cleaning and the re-organisation of traffic–which cannot be carried out

so that it matches with modern expectations of living and working conditions.

For the first phase of this project, therefore, the bureau is concentrating on the less contentious activities such as water supply, sewers, and paving the streets and the squares. Apart from these programmes to improve the technical infrastructure, the following points will be central to any future work: the restoration and if necessary change the use of historic buildings, the

by the central administration without the support of those living in the affected areas.

Any programme to preserve the Madinah, has to take into account many problems. The main aim is to make living in the old city and working there attractive once more. The bureau responsible for the old city, which is housed in one of the former palaces, has to perform this impossible trick of preserving what exists and at the same time changing it

Left, the monsoon rains put many streets under water. Above, part of the programme for renovation work is the paving of the streets.

expansion of social and cultural facilities and the support of the tradesmen and craftsmen of the Madinah. In order to accomplish these aims, Yemen has to rely on foreign aid. For this reason, UNESCO is conducting an international campaign to save the old city of Sana'a. Friendly countries are, though not always entirely selflessly, contributing to this campaign by taking on the costs for individual projects, such as financing the paving of streets or restoring an important building. Even so, the preservation of the Madinah remains a difficult and perhaps unsolvable problem.

AROUND SANA'A

Around Sana'a there are a number of interesting towns and sights which are well worth a visit even if time is short. The most important thing, though, is to obtain a *tassarir* right away if you are not travelling with a tour arranged by one of the two big hotels or by a travel agent based in Sana'a. This is a permit in which the official departments list the towns which you intend to visit.

Bear in mind that Sana'a is bounded in the north and east by Saudi Arabia. On the south by Aden and on the east by the Red Sea. But Sana'a's eastern border with Saudi Arabia (known as the Empty Quarter) remains undemarcated. Thus making it impossible to determine the actual size of Sana'a.

The Tourist Office of the Yemen Tourist Corporation is situated at the western end of Midan at-Tahrir. Apart from a shop selling crafts and souvenirs from all over Yemen, postcards, posters and maps, the ground floor of this building dating from the second Turkish occupation houses the tourist office. Tell them which towns or regions you want to visit, fill in the required forms and you will be told straight away whether this is possible or not.

It is not unusual for the more isolated regions in particular to be prohibited from time to time because of tribal feuds or for other reasons. There is no need to worry about problems in the vicinity of Sana'a, however, though you still have to equip yourself with this piece of paper and have sufficient copies made in the photocopying shops, even for short day trips.

Palacial treat: One of the most visited and most accessible places for an excursion is the summer palace of Imam Yahya at **Wadi Dhar**. This is a group of palaces which is particularly famous for its delightful situation on a steep rock

and its beautiful gypsum ornaments in the Sana'a style. The palace, built in the 1930s, has its own wells inside, dug through the underlying rock, which make the building independent of outside water supplies. At the moment it is not clear how the building is to be used in future–whether as a museum or as a hotel. Both have been under discussion but have not been put into practice over the last few years. Part of the group of palaces, which incidentally look quite different when viewed from the side of the village than they do on the ubiquitous photo and postcard view, can be visited. It depends, though, on the mood of the doorkeeper at the time. On Fridays, the Islamic holy day, the palace is completely closed.

It is also worth while taking a walk through the garden town of **Suq al-Dhar** which surrounds the palace. There are a number of beautiful houses here, as well as gardens which are defi-

Preceding pages: ba'ra dancers in Wadi Dhar. **Left**, the palace on the rock of Wadi Dhar. **Right**, Dhulla, on the road to Shibam.

nitely worth stopping for a visit. The town is particularly busy on Fridays, when the Sana'anis take a trip out to the palace. Not far from the town, on the edge of the wadi, is a **prehistoric temple site**. Chiselled into the rock are leopards, goats and a six-foot (two-metre) high statue of a divinity. Not far away sacrificial basins and steps cut into the rock can be seen, together with little caves which served as homes 6,000 years ago.

Before the road from Sana'a goes downhill into the wadi there is a rocky plateau on the right-hand side, which offers a good view of the whole of the Wadi Dahr. On Fridays wedding guests meet at this plateau with musicians, relatives and friends, in order to celebrate thoroughly once more on the last day of the wedding festivities. Here you will have the opportunity of watching one of the many Yemeni dances, such as the ba'ra. The men dance among themselves, and the women have their own meeting places a little to one side. At the

climax of these ceremonies all the men fire their guns with enthusiasm at the rock opposite, which is showing some signs of damage due to these high-spirited signs of rejoicing.

On the way to the airport lies the garden town of **Ar Rawdah**. It is a small town but an inviting place to take a walk, especially in the evening, through the streets with their fine houses and gardens. Many of the old houses still have the wonderful alabaster windows, through which the sun shines through. Less elaborate is the **Ar Rawdah Palace Hotel**, which is housed in the former palace of the Imam. It is run-down and grubby. However, you can take a look at the inside of the building in order to get an impression of the interior of a Yemeni stone house. Right next door is the **Ahmed Ibn al-Qasim Mosque** with its square inner courtyard. The strong and unpleasant smell which hangs over Ar Rawdah when the winds are unfavourable comes from the collected sewage of Sana'a which is sim-

A beautiful view from the other side: the palace of the Imam.

174

ply deposited outside Ar Rawdah.

Gardens galore: Another garden town and a favourite place for picnics for Sana'anis is the little town of **Haddah**. The gardens with their old walnut trees are inviting places to walk or to stop for a rest. On the western side of Djebel Haddah is the little mountain town of **Bayt Baus**, which is surrounded by a town wall and can only be entered through a single gate. Even nowadays the inhabitants still have to get their drinking water from springs which lie outside the town. Because of the isolation and the lack of modern conveniences more and more families are moving to Sana'a, so that the town itself is gradually becoming derelict.

In the direction of Ma'rib lies the **Wadi Mahdi**, which offers the opportunity of a hike lasting several hours through picture-postcard scenery. If this is too strenuous, you can walk through the grape-growing area of **Beni Husheich**, which is as famous for its warriors as for its delicious grapes. Not far away lies **Hosn Husheich**, the fort belonging to the town.

Other places nearby which are popular for excursions are the two towns of **Shibam** and **Thula**, which are described in a separate chapter. On the way there you pass the small town of **Huth**, which dates back to pre-Islamic times. In this town you immediately notice the ancient Himyar inscriptions, as the white inscription stones and the remains of pillars contrast with the black stone of the houses. Huth is also interesting for those who have visited a few Yemeni towns already, as it is different in many ways from other towns and villages.

Also in Huth are the ruins of an ancient Himyar fort, where according to the townspeople no-one has discovered to this day where the entrance might have been. The excavations of recent years have not led to any new discoveries about the matter. From here you can also get a beautiful view of the **Chinese Temple** or of **Suq Nuqum** at sunset.

Enjoying the view of the valley–a favourite Yemeni pastime.

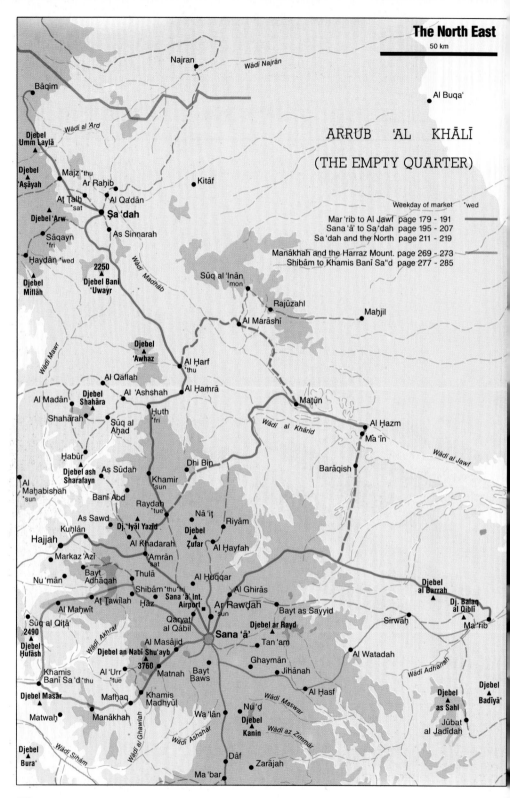

Najran

Wādī Najrān

Al Buqa'

Bāqim

ARRUB 'AL KHĀLĪ

(THE EMPTY QUARTER)

Wādī al 'Ard

Djebel
Umm Laylā ▲

Kitāf

Djebel
'Aṣāyah ▲

Majz *thu
Ar Raḥib

Weekday of market *wed

At Ṭalḥ *sat

Al Qa'dān

Ṣa'dah

Mar'rib to Al Jawf page 179 - 191
Sana'ā' to Ṣa'dah page 195 - 207
Ṣa'dah and the North page 211 - 219

Djebel 'Arw ▲

As Sinnarah

Manākhah and the Harraz Mount. page 269 - 273
Shibām to Khamis Banī Sa"d page 277 - 285

Sāqayn *fri

Haydān *wed

2250

Sūq al 'Inān *mon

Djebel
Miflāh ▲

Djebel Banī 'Uwayr ▲

Rajūzahl

Maḥjil

Wādī Madhāb

Al Marāshī

Djebel
'Awhaz ▲

Al Ḥarf *thu

Wādī Mawr

Al Qaflah

Al 'Ashshah

Al Ḥamrā

Maṭūn

Al Madān

Djebel
Shahāra ▲

Wādī al Khārid

Al Ḥazm

Shahārah

Sūq al Aḥad

Huth *fri

Ma'īn

Wādī al Jawf

Ḥabūr

Dhi Bin

Barāqish

Djebel ash
Sharafayn ▲

As Sūdah

Al
Maḥabishah *sun

Khamir *sun

Banī Abd

Raydah *tue

Nā'iṭ

As Sawd

Riyām

Kuḥlān

Dj. Iyāl Yazīd

Hajjah

Djebel
Zufar ▲

Markaz 'Azī

Al Khadarah

Al Ḥayfah

Nu'mān

Bayt
Adhāqah

'Amrān *sat

Al Ḥuqqar

Thulā

Djebel
al Barrah ▲

At Ṭawīlah

Shibām *thu *fri

Al Ghirās

Dj. Balaq
al Qiblī ▲

Al Maḥwīt

Ḥāz

Sana'ā' Int.
Airport

Ar Rawḍah *sun

Sirwāḥ

Ma'rib

Sūq al Qiṭā'

Qaryat
al Qābil

Bayt as Sayyid

2490

Sana'ā'

Djebel
Ḥufāsh ▲

Wādī Akhraf

Al Masājid

Djebel ar Rayd ▲

Al Watadah

Djebel an Nabi Shu'ayb ▲

Tan'am

Wādī Adhanah

Khamis
Banī Sa'd *thu

Al 'Urr *tue

3760

Matnah

Ghaymān

Djebel Masār ▲

Mafḥaq

Bayt
Baws

Jihānah

Djebel
Badīyā' ▲

Matwaḥ

Manākhah

Khamis
Madhyūl

Wa'lān

Al Ḥasf

Wādī al Ghawiah

Nu'd

Wādī Maswar

Djebel
as Sahl ▲

Djebel
Bura' ▲

Wādī Sihām

Djebel
Kanin ▲

Wādī az Zimmār

Jūbat
al Jadīdah

Dāf

Ma'bar

Zarājah

Wādī Ashshār

MA'RIB AND AL JAWF

The drive to Ma'rib is part of the standard itinerary of any tour of Yemen. Most visitors, however, are probably less fascinated by the archaeologically interesting sights than by the magic and myth which surround the city. It is stories of the Queen of Sheba, that legendary figure, which have appeared for thousands of years in the tales of East and West. Countless legends, stories, anecdotes and fairy tales surround this mythical character.

The Queen of Sheba is depicted in art forms ranging from Islamic miniatures to medieval altar panels, from church windows to modern comic strips, and as far as such cinematic offerings as Gina Lollobrigida portraying the Queen of Sheba in the bath.

Sabaeans and Minaeans, a breath of the ancient frankincense route that once led through those kingdoms, all this can be felt in Ma'rib. Even if you are only visiting what was once a minor resting post on the long route that led from the frankincense fields of Oman right up as far as Gaza–with a little imagination, maybe even the ancient caravans will turn up again.

Ma'rib is also the gateway to the great Arabian desert, the **Rub al-Khali**, which is mostly translated as the Empty Quarter. Long before you get to Ma'rib the first yellow sand dunes can be seen, covered with the little wave patterns of windblown sand, their intensive yellow contrasting with the geologically black volcanic rock make a spectacular scenery. Here too, in the great Arabian desert black gold has been discovered. Camel caravans have moved into the background, new concrete buildings are replacing the old mud brick ones, large newly-built hotels are firmly in the hands of the employees and managers of oil companies.

From Sana'a to Ma'rib: If you happen to have enough time on your hands, a visit to Ma'rib should begin with a short trip to the National Museum in Midan at-Tahrir. Even if you cannot spend as much time browsing around as you would like, looking at the finds on display, the individual representations and also the photographs of less accessible places such as Sirwah or Ma'in give a good general impression of the area and put the complexity of the structure of the town of Ma'rib into an even more impressive context for the interested traveller.

You leave Sana'a along the Ma'rib Road and at first you pass the inevitable petrol stations and garages which decorate the roads leading out of Sana'a. After only a few miles, though, you will come to a number of smaller settlements with tall tower houses and beautiful fields of grapes and *qat*. This is the territory of the **Beni Husheich**, a fa-

Preceding pages: the monolithic pillars of the Awwam temple in Ma'rib. **Right,** the temple of the moon god in Ma'in.

mous Yemeni tribe, very conscious of their traditions, who founded several smaller settlements such as Hosn Husheich. The grapes which are sold at the roadside here during the summer are by far the best tasting in the whole of Yemen, and the Beni Husheich are famous for this particular fruit. A walk through the scenery and the gardens– with the appropriate permit, of course– has its unique charms.

The tribe of Beni Husheich played a decisive role towards the end of the civil war. The lieutenant general of the Royalists, Qasem Munassar, changed sides in the late summer of 1968 with his tribe of Beni Husheich and 60,00 tribal warriors. This meant that the Royalists lost the necessary strength of numbers in order to win.

When you leave the tribal territory of the Beni Husheich, the road continues on for a few miles across the plateau of Sana'a. A little way beyond Beni Husheich you will see **Djebel Marmar**, on the summit of which lie the ruins of a city more than 1,000 years old. After some 19 miles (30 km) you leave the plain of Sana'a. The road winds upwards in a number of steep bends to **Naqil Bin Ghaylan** (7,546 feet/2,300 metres), which is the first pass along the route to Ma'rib. The road is very often busy with traffic, and the heavily laden tankers of the oil companies in Yemen, whose drivers rest in the shade of the rocks for their regular *qat* breaks, which do not have a very calming effect on one's nerves.

Once you have crossed the high point of the pass a wide valley opens up right before you, with its wadi stretching away northwards, where it later meets with the Wadi Al Jawf. Apart from a couple of small settlements and farms with a few fields, the landscape is arid and can be quite monotonous. The rock of the mountains has split because of many years of erosion and weathering and the hilly landscape has deteriorated into a desert of stones.

Beware the wild east: Before you reach

Bedouin women at the edge of Rub al-Khali.

Naqil al-Fardah, the second pass, at a height of 7,218 feet (2,200 metres) above sea level, you will pass two police stations which will check your *tassarir* most carefully. This is the point where the "Wild East" of Yemen definitely begins. Heavily armed men with cartridge belts around their hips, Kalashnikovs over their shoulders, *djambias* and pistols in their belts, stand around in vigorous discussion at the occasional isolated petrol station. The inhabitants of these regions–Ma'rib, Al Jawf, Al Barat–are not always on the best terms with the central government in Sana'a. There are also recurring disagreements among the tribes themselves in this area.

The jeeps and vehicles of the Yemen Hunt Oil Company are often fired upon by the warriors. The warlike equipment of the *gabilis* is not just for decorative purposes, but it is actually used from time to time. The direct route to Ma'rib is secure and not very dangerous, but if you should plan to make an excursion to the left or right of the road, it would be as well to take these circumstances into consideration.

After crossing **Naqil al-Fardah** and following the deeply cloven valley of the **Wadi Fardah** for a few miles farther (it leads directly to Baraqish, where ancient mummies have been discovered which are now on display in the Natural History Museum of Sana'a), you will, if the weather is good, see before you a grand view of the great Arabian desert, the **Rub al-Khali**. You have now crossed the last ridge of the central range, and the way downhill runs in steep curves to the level desert. Just before the road goes into the plain a simple inn on the left-hand side is an invitation to stop and take a break, and this inn is not only for truck drivers. If you like genuine Yemeni food, *selter*, take a break here.

After a few miles the track to **Baraqish** branches off to the left. Today it is easily recognisable thanks to a huge building site. The asphalt road soon leads you away from **Fardah** via

Silver belts worn with the earth-coloured traditional clothes.

Baraqish as far as **Al Hazm**. The road is being built with a loan of six million dollars from an Arab bank.

The asphalt road to Ma'rib continues along the edge of the desert. Again and again you cross dried-up wadis, which have water running in them during the rainy season. To the left and right of the road there are more and more plantations, watered by irrigation systems and pipelines from the new dam. Forty-nine miles (78 km) beyond the place where the track to Baraqish leads off, you arrive at Ma'rib.

MA'RIB

Once you have passed the police station and sufficiently admired the burnt-out plane of the Yemenia on the runway to the left of the road, you can now drive through the modern town of Ma'rib. This town, which has shot up out of the ground over the last few years after the bombardment of the old city during the civil war, has nothing interesting to offer the tourist. However, there are two hotels, among them the four-star Bilqis, which give the traveller the opportunity to stay and rest for the night. The new town of Ma'rib has nothing else to offer except the rough and ready charm of an oil town.

14. A sign there was to Saba in their dwelling places: two gardens, the one on the right hand and the other on the left. "Eat ye of your Lord's supplies, and give thanks to him: goodly is the country, and gracious is the Lord!"

15. But they turned aside: so we sent upon them the flood of Irem; and we changed them their gardens into two gardens of bitter fruit and tamarisks and some few jujube trees.

This is how the 34th sura of the Koran describes the bursting of the dam at Ma'rib. It was not the first dam to burst in the Sabaean kingdom, but it marked the beginning of the decline of the city. The remains of ancient Sabaean culture which can still be seen in Ma'rib today

The new dam of Ma'rib in the Wadi Adhana.

182

give us an impression of the high degree of civilisation at the time, even after 3,000 years.

Ma'rib was not the first capital of the Sabaean kingdom–that was **Sirwah**, 25 miles (40 km) away, which can be reached from Ma'rib or along a difficult track from Sana'a. The beginnings of Sabaean civilisation can be dated to about 1,200 years B.C.

Wealth of the Sabaeans: The rule of the Sabaeans (from about the ninth century to 115 B.C.) established itself first in Sirwah and later on in Maryab (Ma'rib). Their wealth was based less on agricultural success, through building of the dam and the highly evolved techniques of irrigation, than on customs duties and tolls which were levied on the caravans passing along the frankincense route. Ma'rib was founded in 1,200 B.C. and by the fifth century at the latest it was strongly fortified with a city wall, as the pre-eminence of the Sabaeans had been shaken by the establishment of the Minaean city states in

the northeast and Qhataban in the south.

Ma'rib was besieged unsuccessfully by the Roman general Aelius Gallus in 24 B.C. From about A.D. 100 on the Himyar laid claim to Ma'rib and then styled themselves kings of Ma'rib and Zafar (located near the town of Yarim). Once the capital had been moved to Zafar and shipping routes had been opened for trade, Ma'rib finally lost its former importance.

This also led to the slackening of maintenance of the dam and the irrigation system. It is recorded that the dam broke in the years 100 B.C., A.D. 370, 449 and 450. In 525 the Christian Abyssinians conquered Ma'rib, had a victory inscription made and built a church. Under Negus Kaleb in 542 the dam burst again. The dam broke again in 570 in the so-called Year of the Elephant and it brought about the end of the oasis of Ma'rib. (See also the "Elephant" sura in the Koran for other significant events that had happened.)

The dam: You reach the dam–the an-

Bedouin women decorate their hands with henna patterns.

cient one and the new one–by driving along six miles (10 km) of asphalt road which runs from the new Ma'rib in the direction of Wadi Adhana. Here you cross an area where the old ruins of wellhouses still point to the original technique of irrigation. In this area today agricultural crops such as citrus plantations or grain fields follow one after the other in rapid succession, irrigated by diesel-driven water pumps. More than 300 additional wells have been dug over the last few years. The irrigation system ranges from the normal flooding of whole fields to the carefully directed irrigation of parts of fields by means of hoses. However, the fields are irrigated with water from underground and not by the stored water of the artificial lake.

The **ancient dam** lies in the desert at the end of the **Wadi Adhana**. Only the north and the south sluice and some parts of the dam in the north sluice survived. Work on the dam began as early as c. 800 B.C. The first dam was proba-

bly only a piled-up earth wall, and was not reinforced with stone until much later. You can still see how accurate the work of the stonemasons was when you look at the two sluices. The stones fit without a gap.

They were further strengthened with metal bolts. The facing stones are surrounded with a band of decoration, and the pattern can also be found on re-used stones in the houses of ancient Ma'rib. On the **north sluice** a series of inscriptions can be seen which give information about the work on the dam. A large part of the ruined dam still has its original plastering on the inside–it is the original plaster even if it doesn't look like it. Higher up by the northern sluice the remains of one of the houses of the dam guardians has survived. If you stand on the sluice you can clearly make out the small ellipse which the length of the dam once followed. Directly in front of the northern sluice the ancient dam has a sharp bend. Here you can also clearly see the collection of eroded

The most frequently photographed people–the children of Ma'rib.

material in front of the sluices and the line of the original dam.

There is even more of the great skill of the Sabaean masterbuilders to be admired at the **south sluice** than at the north. The sluice has been preserved almost at its former height and therefore gives more concrete insights into the system of water distribution. Behind the sluice a channel cut into the rock let the water run into the appropriate distribution cisterns. The mechanism of the sluice gates and the overflow can be easily traced. If you climb the slope of the neighbouring hill you will have a fine view over the entire wadi and can get a fairly good impression of the size and extent of the dam. The dam, after all, was 1,969 feet (600 metres) long. The access to the south sluice is at times blocked by the Wadi Adhana, which lies right below the sluice.

The ancient dam irrigated an area of about 2,471 acres (1,000 hectares) of farmland. Now that plantations and fields have returned to the wadi bed,

you can imagine what the "two gardens" of Saba must have looked like in the past. This image of a rich and fruitful oasis is the one the government uses when they report on the new dam of Ma'rib on television. This former dusty and deserted dump is intended to become a major regional capital over the next few years. Speculative plans for the size of the new population is targetted at 500,000. Oil and the dam are to be the two main financial support for this future development.

Only a few miles up the wadi is the **new dam** of Ma'rib. This dam is a 75 million dollar present from Sheikh Zaid bin Sultan of the Arab Emirates, who traces his family back to Sabaean origins. Work on the dam began in 1984. The surrounding rock walls were made waterproof with concrete and a reinforced concrete wall that is 180 feet (55 metres) deep, based on a rubble wall, was built across the valley. The new dam is 131 feet (40 metres) high and 2,297 feet (700 metres) long. The dam

It is rare for Bedouin women to allow strangers to approach so closely.

was completed in April 1986.

The stored water is not used for agriculture at present, as the distribution system has not yet been completed. The Wadi Adhana has a catchment area of nearly 3,860 sq miles (10,000 sq km), and the lake can hold around 14,126 million cubic feet (400 million cubic metres) of rainwater.

The Moon Temple and the Bilqis Temple: Back on the main asphalt road, which still runs a short distance as far as Bayhan, you get to the so-called Moon or **Almaqah Temple**. At the moment nothing much can be seen except for the five monolithic pillars, but field research has been able to bring a couple of interesting items to light. The temple site is also known as **Arsh Bilqis**, the Throne of Bilqis. The children who climb up the pillars in the classical manner before sliding rapidly back down again are probably the most photographed people in the whole of Yemen.

A better impression can be gained from the so-called Bilqis Temple,

Mahram Bilqis. This is an oval temple, partially excavated in 1952 by the famous Wendell Phillips expedition. Although the major part of the temple has been covered over and over again by drifting sand, you can get an impression of the size and the construction of the building. Here, too, you will find the monolithic pillars, which once supported the monolithic roof construction. The site is believed to have been a sanctuary (with "mahram" status). According to legend, anyone who hid in this temple to escape his pursuers was protected from his enemies by the holy place as long as he stayed within the confines of the temple walls. The temple was built some time around the eighth century B.C. A little way away from the pillars in the sand lies a large stone with fine Sabaean inscriptions.

Wendell Phillips and his team spent nine months on the excavations in Ma'rib from 1951 to 1952. The work was hindered from the very beginning by the Bedouin of the area and particu-

The houses in Al Jawf are brightly painted.

186

larly by the soldiers of the Imam, who resisted and constantly interrupted the archaeological work. After countless squabbles the team had to leave the country in a great hurry on 12 February 1952. Most of the finds that remained behind was unprotected.

Ancient Ma'rib: Ancient Ma'rib, built on a hill of sediment, is unfortunately nothing but a town of ruins today, with only a few houses being lived in. After the bombardment of this fortress of troops loyal to the Imam by Egyptian planes during the civil war the inhabitants left the town and have settled a few miles away in new Ma'rib. A walk through the old city is still extremely interesting, however. In Ma'rib, for instance, you have an excellent chance to study the techniques of mud building still in use there. Some houses are still firm enough so that you can, with a bit of care and a flashlight, climb up onto the roof. From there you will also get a beautiful view of the entire area as far as Wadi Adhana.

However, if you enter a house, watch out not only for the state of the floors and stairs and the stability of the building but also for *hanesh* or puff adders, who prefer to withdraw into shady places of this sort. In the fabric of the houses you can also discover countless spoils of the individual temples and of the ancient dam–bands of ornament, friezes and carved stones. This makes a walk through it an interesting archaeological experience, and the few children who remain in the town will be glad to act as your guide.

Outside the town is a Turkish-style fortress–the residence of the Imam in Ma'rib. The old **mosque** is worth special attention. Sabaean pillars support the old wooden beamed ceiling. Along the rear wall you can also see monoliths which probably came from one of the two temples. Even though the mosque is deteriorating and is no longer used, it still has its own charm.

From Ma'rib to Al Haz: Some time ago the government in Sana'a opened up

Sentry guarding a village in the valley of the Al Jawf.

what is probably the most imposing ruined city in Yemen to visitors. The building of the asphalt road probably made it much easier, as it brought about an improved infrastructure and greater security for travellers.

The road to Baraqish branches off at the main road from Sana'a to Ma'rib at Fardah and, in those places where the the road has not yet been asphalted, it is an unspeakably dusty drive along the feet of the central mountains and the Wadi Fardah. You pass several small farms until after some 16 miles (25 km) you see the massive ruined city of Baraqish with its city wall studded with many fortified towers rising majestically on the horizon.

BARAQISH

The ancient city of Baraqish, or Yathul as it was known to the Minaeans, boasts a genuine fortified city wall dating from Minaean times. It is by far the best preserved pre-Islamic ruin in the whole of Yemen.

The city, still inhabited in Islamic times, was surrounded and protected by more than 50 fortified towers. The former city gate which, is today blocked up with stones, was the entrance through the southwestern part of the walls. Next to it, inscriptions and snakes carved in the stone can be seen. If you climb up into the old city you can get a good impression of the former city, even if it is just by admiring the ruins. Most of the buildings, which can now only be guessed by their foundations, date from the Islamic period. The one roofed structure with the typical large stone pillars, which also make up the horizontal links, is clearly Minaean. Lying almost exactly in the centre of the city are the remains of the mosque with its domed roof, and next to it is a deep well and a small round tower.

In 400 B.C. Baraqish was for a short time the capital of the Minaean kingdom, until the city of Qarnawu or Ma'in was built a few years later. The city walls in Baraqish, up to 46 feet (14

The Wadi Al Jawf after rain has fallen in the highlands.

metres) high, were built less for protection than for ostentation. The wealth gained from trade was intended to be visible from far away. At this time the kingdom of the Minaeans was one of the most urbanised states found in the Arabian peninsula.

Baraqish is usually the final stop for tourists. The Tourist Office in Sana'a will only approve a *tassarir* for places in Al Jawf under special circumstances. The journey through the Wadi Al Jawf is somewhat difficult and, most importantly, dangerous, even today. As long as the situation in Al Jawf remains unchanged you should not visit this particular region.

MA'IN

To get to the second Minaean city of Ma'in you have to branch off the track to Al Hazm and find a way through the tributaries of the Wadi Al Jawf. It is relatively easy to find Baraqish, but for Ma'in you really must take an experienced guide with you, as it lies in an area where shots will be fired if you go too close to a house or to one of the many nomadic tents.

According to the estimates of some French archaeologists, Ma'in was built between the 4th and 2nd centuries B.C. Only a few sections of its great city wall survive, especially on the eastern side. Of particular interest within the city wall is the roof construction of a small shrine. It is still completely intact except for a few collapsed beams. The remaining buildings are all ruined.

The **Athar Temple**, outside the gates of the city, is of great architectural beauty, outstanding because of its aesthetic form as well as its intricate and simple construction. The many stones decorated with friezes of stone blocks which can be found around the temple are also very impressive. When looking at the Minaean towns in Al Jawf you should remember that the climate of those days was definitely much more favourable. There was more rain, and the fields were fertile enough to feed

relatively large towns.

No *tassarir* is usually issued by the appropriate departments for visits to the Minaean ruined cities of Al Bayda and As Sawda.

Through the Wadi Al Jawf: Some 12 miles (20 km) away from the ruined city of Baraqish is the little town of **Al Hazm**. The name means "fortress." Al Hazm al-Jawf is a dusty little town, its few mud brick houses are falling apart. To make up for this, there has been busy building activity around the town, creating a number of mostly very unattractive buildings.

A track runs from Al Hazm which later joins the asphalt road from Sana'a to Sa'dah at Al Mathun, also known as Al Matarnah. A drive through Al Jawf should only be undertaken with a knowledgeable local guide. A sandy track runs through the river valley, which is several miles wide. Farmers draw up the plentiful underground water supplies with the aid of diesel pumps, turning the wadi landscape

Kept in the family for generations— the *djambia*.

green and making large-scale agriculture possible.

The impressive sights on this trip are the farms and little villages lying off the road. The houses are mud buildings several stories high, with a square enclosure surrounded by a mud wall. The steel gates, blue or red, are mostly barred, and only rarely can you see inside the compound. On the top of the walls there are thorn bushes or broken bottles, protection against unwanted strangers. Only the upper floors have any windows, often framed with white or red paint. The houses of Al Jawf are fortresses in themselves. The men you see on the way also leave a very warlike impression. No-one around here leaves the house without a machine gun, and they wear well-filled cartridge belts over their shoulders. A cartridge costs ten rial, a Kalshnikov several thousand. Around Al Hazm in particular you often see the tents and camps of the nomads with their herds of goats and camels. However, most nomads no longer make use of camels for transport. They have gone over to modern Toyota pickup trucks and drive around in those, without number plates, of course, and often in vehicles studded with bullet holes in the bodywork.

The track continues past more ruined Minaean sites, the two cities of **As Sawda** and **As Bayda** with its 4,921 feet (1,500 metres) long, excellently preserved city wall. After a dusty drive lasting several hours you eventually draw near to the town of Al Mathun, where the tracks divide. The southern branches runs past another town with the name of Al Hazm (this one has a large army barracks) and on to Dhi Bin and eventually to Raydah. The northern branch goes to Al Marashi via some small hot springs.

The northern route: If you choose to take the northern route, you will pass a military post just beyond Al Mathun. Then you follow the Wadi Madhab and at its upper end you will come to the hot springs of **Hammam al-Wagarah**. The region between Al Mathun and Al Marashi is extremely sparesely populated. You will come across only a few houses and some nomads. Later, after crossing a small river valley, you will see the divided peak of **Djebel Mafluq** in the distance. Crossing a high plateau littered with broken rocks you slowly draw closer to Al Marashi.

This little market town has the appearance of a typical desert oasis. The town, with its fine, well preserved mud-built houses, lies among huge date palms and fields of alfalfa. From Al Marashi a track leads north through Wadi Charab to Suq al-Inan, 19 miles (30 km) away, also known simply as **Al Barat** named after the local province. At first the road runs north following an arid and almost uninhabited river valley. At the end of the valley a steep road winds upwards in precipitous curves to the high plateau of Al Barat. On this desert plateau you will see the fortified mud houses of Suq al-Inan. These houses reflect the wealth of the town.

The cistern of the mosque of Dhi Bin.

Packed close together, they stand side by side and are reminiscent of the skyline of Shibam in Wadi Hadramaut. Suq al-Inan owes the greater part of its wealth to, among other things, the busy "trade" in luxury goods from the Najran province of Saudi Arabia, only a few miles away. A further track runs from Suq al-Inan, eventually reaching Sa'dah. You will need about three hours for the 25 miles (40 km) journey from Al Marashi to Al Harf.

The southern route: If you choose the southern and busier route to Raydah, you will come after a time to the valley of the Wadi Kharid, the course of which can be followed almost as far as Sana'a. On the way you will pass the residence of an important sheikh, secured by barbed wire and electrified fences. The sheikh is not only the proud owner of this Arab equivalent of Fort Knox, but also of huge plantations of citrus fruit which fill the whole valley.

This route is also sparsely populated, and it seems all the more surprising to come across a big military camp in Al Hazm. From here a newly-laid track runs to Sana'a over a distance of just under 60 miles (100 km) via Hayfah.

Again and again you will see burned-out tanks at the roadside, remains from the time of the civil war. Just beyond the military camp you will come to the great flood of lava which once poured from a crater near Raydah and reached this far. After about nine miles (15 km) on this extremely trying lava track the road forks again, and you will see the ruins of **Dhi Bin** before you.

The three ruined cities of Dhi Bin, all picturesquely situated on the summit of the hill, and the tomb and mosque of the Imam Abd Allah ib Hamza, a Zaidi Imam who ruled Yemen from 1187-1218, are among the finest sites of historical interest after Ma'rib and the Minaean city of Baraqish. It is about a two-hour walk from the small town of Dhi Bin with its beautiful mosque, similar to the one in Yafrus, to the ruined cities on the hill.

Children playing in the ruins of Zafar-Dhi Bin.

FROM SANA'A TO SA'DAH

The 155 miles (250 km) which separate Sana'a from Sa'dah might as well be a journey into another world. The horizon takes on a peculiar colouring which is a typical feature of the desert. Rain clouds pile up in the high central mountains, so that the wadis are filled with nothing but sand. The rocks of the mountains are bare due to erosion, and only a few sheltered slopes are terraced.

The starkness of the landscape is similar to the character of the people. No intruder in this region has ever succeeded in breaking the resistance of the Yemeni people, and even nowadays this pride is reflected in the attitudes of the warriors from the two major tribes, the Hashid and the Bakil. They were the last to join the republic after the deposition of the Imam in 1962, and are still very attached to their customs, which are similar to those of the nomadic Bedouin. Although most Yemenis are Muslims, they are further divided into two traditional Islamic sects, the Sunni and the Shi'ite. The first is represented by the Shafis the latter by the Zaidis and the Ismailis.

Most tourists use the asphalted road which leads from Sana'a to Sa'dah for a quick trip there and back. However, those who take a bit more time will experience the magic of the region, with its wonderful scenery and its ancient culture, which is expressed in an architecture unique in North Yemen.

AMRAN

If you leave Sana'a in a northerly direction, you will pass the airport of Al Rawdah on your left and through the last few villages of Sana'a's hinterland. Soon there are no more signs of agriculture, and the ground takes on a black colour from the volcanic rock. At an altitude of 8,530 feet (2,600 metres) above sea level you will come to a small pass among the peaks of ancient volcanoes. To your left you have a fine view of the steep rock walls of the Djebel Kawkaban and of Thula with its magnificent fortress. On the way downhill from the crown of the pass the view is already changing to one of a broad and fruitful plain, with the busy town of Amran nestled in its centre.

The new town lies to the right of the road to Sana'a and is divided by the road to Hajjah. When you catch sight of the fortifications on your right-hand side, you should stop the car. The old town is worth a visit on foot, and you begin by entering it through the old gate. The foundation of the walls are made of stone, the upper part of beaten earth. The walls enclose a complete self-sufficient town with houses all built in the same style and completely surrounded by the walls. Amran is the first town to

Preceding pages: swarms of locusts descend on the country more and more frequently. *Left*, the older men usually wear skilfully draped headcloths. *Right*, Turkish window grilles.

have mud houses–with the exception of a few scattered farms which can be seen on the way to Sa'dah.

The appearance of the town is architecturally very harmonious, as the lack of space has simply banished all the more recent buildings to sites outside the walls. The streets are too narrow for cars, so that within the old town–in complete contrast to the new–an air of peace and calm reigns, often broken only by the laughter of children playing. There are no shops apart from the tiny stalls with their countless delicacies, where small girls play at being shopkeepers. The houses have several floors but are often very narrow compared to Sa'dah. The soft lines of smoothed mud are accentuated by an often very restrained decoration using white gypsum. The windows, mostly small and of rounded shape, often still have alabaster panes. The asymmetrical placing of the windows gives the smooth façades a quaint appearance.

The city wall is accessible in several places. The steps which lead up also serve as access for several houses at a time. From the top you have a clear view of the broad fields which cover the plateau. Leaning against the northern part of the wall is the mosque with its minaret, remarkable for its crooked position and fine decoration. You can enter the fortress through the main gate. When leaving it again, you will see on your left a stone set into the wall which is engraved with Sabaean inscriptions, a sign of the great age of the town.

There is a row of shops pressed up close against the town walls, under a roof supported by pillars. They are shut except on Saturdays, the day of the weekly market. The market in Amran is very lively and is visited by people from the many villages around this plateau. Here you can find carpets made of black and white goat hair, which is also woven into the small, elegant waistcoats of the mountain people. When it gets cold (the surrounding mountains are over 9,800 feet/3,000 metres-high) the peasants

The Kalashnikov is always kept handy–even at the wheel.

wear sheepskin coats.

Even when there is no market, you can find a lot of shops around the square which lies just inside the main town gate and on the main street of the new town. Many glassworks make use of the gypsum which is found in the area.

RAYDAH AND KHAMIR

After Amran, the road crosses a fertile high plateau, with fields of crops large enough to allow mechanised agriculture and irrigated by many pumping stations. After 11 miles (18 km) you reach the large market town of Raydah. It is particularly interesting to visit the town on Tuesdays, market day, when the peasants from the surrounding area all come to sell their produce. In earlier years, before most of the Yemeni Jews emigrated, the Suq al-ahud or Jewish Market was held in Raydah. Even nowadays you can still occasionally see a few Jews in Raydah or in the neighbouring town.

The difficult track to the village of

Many of the Imams fled to Shaharah.

Dhi Bin with its famous 13th-century mosque also branches off from Raydah. The track then continues into the valley of the Al Jawf.

A few miles beyond Raydah the road rises to a recently opened pass at 8,530 feet (2,600 metres). Encircled by the surrounding mountains, the plateau of Amran shimmers either fresh green or harvest gold, according to the season. From the crown of the pass, however, the landscape changes abruptly and you find yourself in a bare and arid mountain range. The grey rock has innumerable cracks and splits. These, smoothed by wind and water, turn the scenery into a sea of stone. Only the countless cacti, peering from the cracks like little soldiers on sentry duty, find any nourishment here.

The town of **Khamir** with its imposing white stone houses, the façades decorated with black lines of volcanic rock, turns up unexpectedly on the horizon. Khamir is an important centre of trade and administration, and also, ac-

cording to ancient tradition, gives right of sanctuary to the Hashid tribe.

Khamir dominates a valley in which generations of peasants have managed to terrace the land despite their hostile environment. The old town lies a little way away from the shops along the roadside. On Sundays you occasionally meet Yemeni Jews here, their side locks showing under their turbans. Like the Jews in Raydah, they are part of a small community of Jews still living in and around Yemen.

HUTH

The landscape hardly changes at all beyond Khamir. The road follows the folds of the hills and the region remains barren, but not without its usual charm. Even the smallest patch of earth among the rocks is cultivated, nothing is left to waste. Farms, single or grouped in small settlements, are scattered across the hills. The houses have hardly any windows and they look more like fortresses. Many are shaped like great towers and look as if they are ready to repel any attack. Other towers, narrow and tall, guard the more isolated fields. Nowadays the farmers use them to store their tools and their produce. However, if you get too close to to one of the towers near a *qat* field in the evening as dusk is falling, you might encounter a suspicious farmer pointing a gun at you. Such precautions may be surprising in a country where theft is very uncommon– after all, according to Islamic law or sharia, theft is punishable by cutting off a finger or a hand.

However, in this area people still speak of the depredations of the Bedouin raiders who once invaded the country just as if they were about to reappear at any moment. This impression is increased by the somewhat mournful appearance of the farmers. **Huth** lies some 19 miles (30 km) beyond Khamir. It is a pleasant place to end one stage of your journey, as it offers weary travellers restaurants and a *funduk*. Behind the rows of shops lies a

Carefully smoothed mud façade in the town of Amram.

charming town, built in the same style as Khamir. There are a few well-designed houses here, and the mosque has black garland patterns around the windows and between each floor, which accentuate the effect of the earth-coloured stone. You can also see two neighbouring houses joined by a bridge.

For many years Huth was the site of an important religious school, where Zaidi doctrine was taught and interpreted. It is said that the Zaidis have valuable manuscripts in the library at Huth. Just before reaching town a track branches off which leads in a westerly direction to Djebel Shaharah.

Al Harf and the "desert balconies": Al Harf is only 22 miles (36 km) away from Huth. You cross the last slopes of the mountains and at first drive through some wadis that is overgrown with thorny shrub. The first nomad camps can be seen in the valleys of the wadis. You cross one final pass with a height of 5,577 feet (1,700 metres), and then you finally leave the mountain massif

of central Yemen.

At first sight, the market town of **Al Harf** displays the same row of shops and workshops as everywhere else–just a bit more dusty, perhaps. But a little way away from these recently built houses lie the tall mud buildings. They have only a few windows, decorated with brightly-painted shutters. The doors to the narrow streets are also framed with packed mud surrounding it, which seem to keep the houses upright. The effective use of brown colour emphasises the beauty of these entrances. Here you can get a taste of the architectural specialities of the valley of **Al Jawf**, which begins just on the other side of the mountain. The track to Al Marashi branches off right behind the exit from the village. Thursday is market day in Al Harf.

From Al Harf the road becomes fairly straight and crosses fields of millet and sorghum. Between the fields lie scattered groups of trees, the beautiful Judas trees being the most noticeable. There

An old tin bucket provides an alternative to wooden screens.

are many villages lying at the feet of **Djebel Awhaz** seeking its protection. This mountain marks the end of the plain to the west. All villages are built in the most beautiful style using mud brick, which allows the buildings to merge with the surrounding soil. If you drive along the road in the early afternoon you can see the unforgettable sight of sand storms moving over the plain.

After another 19 miles (30 km) the horizon widens and the land becomes more of a wilderness. There are no more farms on the stony plateau, and the thorny growths congregate at the bottom of the wadis, which give the black earth a striped pattern with their long sandy beds. Thorny shrubs are the only growth present in huge quantity in this area, and the nomads have become specialists in collecting firewood from these shrubs. Traders along the roadside offer their huge piles of bundles for sale. Buyers come from as far away as Sana'a to buy this fuel, essential for cooking and especially for baking bread. If you are curious, ask how much wood you can get for 100 rials. The answer will help you to understand the triumph of the gas stove–even though the flavour of the bread or *chops* suffers very much from it. However, at least the gas stoves are helping to preserve one of the few wooded regions of Yemen.

On the right of this barren landscape, the high basalt peak of Djebel Mafluq (7,513 feet/2,290 metres) rises up. The divided peak can be seen from quite a distance and is useful for determining direction. The road starts to climb once more and crosses a pass, 6,234 feet (1,900 metres) high and guarded by police. In the distance a few high altitude villages can be seen against the pinkish walls of the rock.

The sun is reflected in a few corrugated iron huts at the roadside. This is **Al Ahmar**. On Tuesdays an interesting market is held here. Hundreds of Toyotas bring in the peasants and the Bedouin, with their Kalashnikovs and ancient muzzle loaders hanging over their

Many small cacti grow in the area around Huth.

shoulders. In the shade of the cars they offer the produce they have brought with them for sale: tomatoes, onions, and especially *enab*, the juicy grapes–fresh or dried. There are also craftsmen who will repair *djambias* or belts. The butchers here have a peculiar trick of winding the intestines of the animal around the hand like a length of wool. One single chop with a *djambia* is enough to cut off the portion required by the customers and let it slide into a plastic bag. However, your greatest surprise is likely to come when you discover the weapon stall. Apart from a few rifles laid out on old cloths, the boxes hold a regular arsenal: revolvers, bullets of all calibres and sometimes even hand grenades.

Just beyond the market and a little to one side, to the right of the road alongside a rocky spur of the mountain, lie the houses of the village of **Al Ryam**. The finest are those of smoothed mud which have fine relief patterns around the doors and windows. From up in the

The beautiful euphorbias flower in the tropical climate of Wadi Lissan.

village you have a fine view of the plateau and the vineyards which cluster at its foot. The vines, held by narrow posts struck into stones, grow between mudbrick walls. In the corners, under the shade of the watchtowers, pomegranate trees grow. In earlier years little boys stood here to scare the birds away from the ripe grapes by clapping switches of goatskin together. Nowadays coloured nylon nets are spread over the vines.

From this point on the countryside is densely populated once more, and the silhouettes of the tall fortified houses can be seen against a magnificent background of rocks rounded by many years of erosion. Many of these villages are worth a visit, especially in the early hours of the afternoon or evening, when the sun bathes them in a soft, golden light. To the right of the road, just before the short rise that marks the boundary of the plateau, lies the village of **Farwah**, one of the many villages in Yemen, which can easily be reached

along a track under shady trees, known to be hundreds of years old. In the mornings men and women work in the fields and the silence is interrupted with calls and laughter. The climate here allows several harvests a year. The tomato plantations are protected from the very low temperatures of the winter nights by improvised greenhouses made of large plastic sheets.

A village high on a hill towers over the valley. It is built entirely in one single architectural style. The truncated pyramids of the houses are crowned with a frieze of mudbrick, into which the ends of the ceiling beams are set. The buildings look like fortresses, and this impression is increased by the arrow slits in the lower storeys.

Following the asphalt road, after one final hill you get to the **Wadi Haf**. Here the farms are almost hidden behind huge trees and hedges of tamarisk. However, after a few miles the valley widens, and the first modern buildings line both sides of the road. A row of shops, banks and hotels follows, until you reach an open gate in a mud brick city wall: **Sa'dah**.

SHAHARAH

A visit to Shaharah is bound to be one of the most impressive excursions that you can make to the heart of Yemen. However, you will have to put up with a great deal of discomfort and have to accept the most primitive overnight accommodation available, even after a journey that could be described as more than strenuous. This trip is recommended for travellers who have at least two days to spare and a considerable amount of courage at their disposal. Those who want to drive will find the Djebel Shaharah an ideal location and one which is impossible to miss.

The fortress is known as an impregnable place where the Zaidi Imams had always found refuge and from which they fought many courageous campaigns, especially against the occupation by the Turks. The Imam Mansour

Women at the roadside selling valuable firewood.

al-Qasim used the fortress as the base for his campaigns and forced the Turks to withdraw in 1636. Also from Shaharah, Imam Yahya conducted the reconquest of Yemen at the end of the second Turkish occupation during the early 20th century, in order to make Yemen into a unified state. Not until the air attacks of the Egyptians did the defenders of this proud citadel run into real difficulties, when the fortress was being used as a refuge for the Royalists in their struggle against the Republicans in the 1960s.

From Huth you can reach the other side of the mountain range to the west by means of a good gravel track. After 11 miles (18 km) you get to the little village of **Al Ashshah**, where the road divides. To the right it runs to **Al Qaflah** and further on to **Al Madan**, a little village in the north of Djebel Shaharah. The road proper, however, is the left branch, which follows the **Wadi Lissan**. Several tracks make their way through the lush vegetation. These are

Ritual cleansing basin in a small mosque in Djebel Shaharah.

all tracks left by cars which have tried to dodge the many places where bumps and potholes line up one after another to turn your journey into a painful torture. Wicked little climbs can only be achieved at a crawl, for the road is nothing more than a heap of piled-up gravel. It is not surprising, therefore, that you need a whole hour to travel eight miles (12 km) to **Suq al-Ahad** (named after its Sunday market). However, you can comfort yourself by admiring the wonderful adenium obesium or "bottle trees" which bear their beautiful pink blossoms at the upper end of their thick stems. Other tropical plants, too, profit by the intensive sun here at this altitude of 3,609 feet (1,100 metres), and the vegetation is similar to that at the edge of the Tihama. If not for its Sunday market Suq al-Ahad is a deserted little village for the rest of the time which has nothing in it but the school which is used by the children of the valley. The houses are single-storeyed and are more like the huts of the Tihama. The dark-skinned women protect themselves from the blazing sun with amusing straw hats which are worn over a headscarf.

You can clearly see the town of Shaharah on the peak of the mountain, which lies some 4,920 feet (1,500 metres) away from where you are now. However, you still have to manage another nine miles (15 km) or so up to the village of **Al Gabei** before you can start out on the six-hour climb along a bad road and steep paths.

Those who want to climb Djebel Shaharah on foot have to stay the night in Al Gabei before setting out next morning on a hike lasting five to six hours. One of the village houses serves as a *funduk*, but you can also camp in the wadi below the village. Basic provisions can be bought in a small shop, and on Tuesday, market day, the mountain dwellers, armed to the teeth, arrive to make their purchases.

Taxi drivers usually refuse to drive you any further. However, the inhabitants of Al Gabei will gladly offer (with a price of course) to drive you up the steep mountain in one of their four-wheel drive Toyotas, which have room for at least ten or more people. The asking price of five to eight hundred rials may seem extortionate at first, but you will come to understand it better during the hair-raising journey, which takes about an hour and a half. The track in fact has the steepest stretches that are still possible for a vehicle to drive up. Rain has eroded it in an unpredictable fashion. In other places, where the road is covered with huge slabs of stone, you are thrown several feet up in the air. A drive up the mountain is therefore by no means relaxing and is also not one of the best ways to enjoy the unique view the country has to offer.

Those on foot follow the same track as the cars at first. It runs past the first small settlement to the village of **Arhaba**, where food shops sell fresh drinks. From this point you can already clearly make out the gorge with the

famous bridge. Now you leave the main track, which goes around the mountain to the left, and carry on walking on the right side towards a pool. Directly above the pool a small spring and a rest hut mark the starting point of the former mule track. This is paved for much of the way and leaves the *qat* fields to wind its way up among thistles and euphorbia plants. The steepest parts are provided with steps, and if you leave yourself time the ascent is pleasant and easy. While walking you can thoroughly enjoy the peace and quiet and the wonderful view, which stretches far out beyond the Wadi Lissan. From this point, looking across the terraced slopes which fall vertically downwards, you can see the central massif of North Yemen with Hajjah and the Djebel Masar.

When the path reaches the vertical wall of rock which surrounds the peak you will suddenly come to a fortified gate in a crack of the rock. This used to prevent anyone coming up any further. The heavy nail-studded gates still have their old locks. The climb gradually becomes less steep as you approach the broad terraces of the flat land where sorghum is cultivated. On the peak there are only a few farms near the first cistern. Turn right on the same level as the small mosque and you will emerge above the stone bridge. This crosses the vertiginous ravine that divides the two peaks of Djebel Shaharah. This daring work was built in the early 17th century by the architect **Salah al-Yamani**.

Three arches span the rocky ravine, which is several hundred feet deep, one above the other. In the walls of the ravine you can still see traces of the lower arches, which supported the bridge during its construction. From here you reach the centre of Shaharah in just under a quarter of an hour. Before you get there, you pass several of the huge cisterns which collect rainwater and have made it possible for the inhabitants to withstand all sieges. Even today Yemeni women still come out two or three times a day to draw water for the

household. The biggest cistern is situated among the houses in town. A little way away from it, the three white domes of the mosque can be seen against the dark background of the surrounding houses. The façades of these four to five storeyed houses are decorated with intricate inlaid patterns shaped like tree branches and plain white borders around the windows. Above each of the main window openings, a small projecting arch encloses a series of two or three smaller window panes.

You can find all the necessities in the shops–there is even a small pharmacy. The *funduk* which takes in strangers is right opposite the entrance to the mosque. It is the house of a man of importance in the town and accordingly has plenty of space to offer. The salon with its beautiful old stucco walls is roomy and offers enough space for at least 15 guests to spend the night. The house offers more than a roof, simple but delicious food is served in a family-like atmosphere. The price of 100 rials for a night's stay should be treated as a minor detail. The greatest pleasure can be gained by strolling through the town in the evening or in the early morning, when light casts its illuminating shadow across the rows of peaks and the villages on the Djebel Ahnum opposite seem to float above the clouds.

HAJJAH

Administratively, Shaharah belongs to the province of Hajjah, which covers the northwest of the country as far as the Red Sea. It is extremely difficult to cross the mountain ranges and the only road leading to the provincial capital goes through Amran. The route, some 40 miles (65 km) long, was built in co-operation with the People's Republic of China, and represents a great achievement considering the difficult ground it had to cover.

Broad grain fields lie at the edge of the village of Amran, following without a break after an industrial and business zone. One of the few cement factories in

Yemen is situated here. Villagers throng this fertile basin, using earth and stone for their buildings in an astonishing variety of styles. The vernacular rural architecture integrates wonderfully well with the landscape. To your right lies a deep ravine, cutting into **Djebel Hadur** (11,810 feet/3,600 metres). To the south a cascade of villages covers the peak of **Djebel Masar**, its shape completely determined by terracing. Halfway between Amran and Hajjah, after passing a place where you can stop to see the view, you come to where the road forks to Kuhlan. This pretty village offers a spectacular view of the curves of the road and of the **Wadi Sharis** lying below. After a few miles, at a height of about 3,280 feet (1,000 metres), you enter another world. A market, **Suq al-Sharis**, is held on Sundays in the wadi under banana and papaya trees.

If you have had enough of long drives along twisting roads, you have the opportunity to vary your journey now with a little walking. Follow the Wadi Hajjah, which runs parallel to the road, after the intersection of the Wadi Hajjah and the Wadi Sharis. The walk leads you through little oases where cypress and coffee grow.

The road climbs up just as steeply as it led down into the wadi, and it follows the tiny stream. Coffee plants are cultivated among the thick vegetation that lives off this water. Soon **Hajjah** appears, up on the mountain. This town has developed rapidly and offers all sorts of modern comforts. Its tourist attractions are limited, but it is a pleasant place to stop between the mountains and the Tihama. The town was once fought over vigorously because of its strategic position. The fortress which towers above it dates from the time of the Turks. In the fortress the Imams kept the sons of sheikhs as hostage because they wanted to be assured of the sheikh's loyalty. Several government departments are today housed in the former palace of the Imam.

Right, in Yemen, too, children are the pride of the family.

SA'DAH AND THE NORTH

The town of Sa'dah lies in a fertile basin, into which the valleys of the surrounding mountain massif run, and which opens out towards the **Wadi Najran**. Sa'dah has always been important as the way into the great desert of Arabia, the Rub al-Khali. It was a suitable staging post for the caravans along the frankincense route from the Indian Ocean to the countries of the Mediterranean. The town must have developed before the coming of Islam, although there are no traces of pre-Islamic events worth mentioning. The famous historian Al Hamdani described its splendour and wealth in the 10th century. It was the city from which Zaidism developed and spread, and for this reason it remains to the present day for Yemenis a sacred place with a proud history.

As late as the early 1970s, before the road had reached this far, arriving in Sa'dah was an unforgettable experience. A belt of mudbrick fortifications rose from the fields, and all the buildings were packed closely together within it. Vehicles had to remain outside the fortifications; you entered the town through one of the two gates. Today Sa'dah has become the administrative centre of the province and the border station between Yemen and Saudi Arabia and has undergone rapid development. Trucks and taxis drive between the shops and offices which lie along the asphalt road to Sana'a in the up and coming suburbs. There are a few more or less comfortable hotels and restaurants outside the Bab al-Yemen, the south gate of the old town. The town centre itself, apart from a few "modernisations", still preserves the unity of its remarkable architecture. An observant visitor will find numerous interesting things to see.

The first Zaidi capital: The inhabitants of the Sa'dah region belong to the Kawhlan tribal alliance; the town is *hijra de Shuhar*, i.e. it offers sanctuary. Every member of the tribe can find sanctuary there or, in the case of a dispute or disagreement, turn to the traditional tribal courts. As disputes frequently do arise among the tribes and often–even nowadays– develop into warlike conflict, the aim is to save the honour of the members of a community from the enemy and not to destroy the latter. The tribes are also allied by treaty to aid one another against any common enemy from outside.

In order to decide disputes among the tribes, their members approach a neighbouring tribal leader, whose decision both parties agree to honour. Usually, such a judgement entails the payment of *diyah* by the guilty party, i.e. the price for blood spilt or for insult, a payment sufficient to remove the insult from the injured party. Some sheikhs who are known for their cleverness have great influence which goes far beyond the borders of their tribal territory. If, on the other hand, there is a tendency to put personal family interests above the demands of the office for instance if one party in the dispute is a relative, the rule is that the holder of that office should approach the most respected tribal representative. A new candidate can still try and get the tribe to support him, if he is eligible for the office.

The move of *Al Hadi Yahya ibn al-Hussein* to Yemen in 898 came about through the pronouncement of judgements within this system of tribal law and custom. He came from Medina and had been called in to decide conflicts among the tribes of the region. He gained so much respect that he was able to rely upon the support of the majority of tribes and have himself recognised as Imam. He was a descendant of Ali, the Prophet's son-in-law, of the line of Zaid ibn Ali, who initiated the revolt against the Umayyids of Damascus in 740. The Umayyids were a largely merchant family of the Quraysh tribe centred at Mecca. Originally opponents of Mohammed, they converted to Islam in 627 and became prominent administrators. They also became Mohammed's immediate successors. The movement of **Zaidism** dates from the time of this revolt, and Al Hadi based his claims on it. This was the foundation of the Zaidi Imamate, which was to endure until 26 September 1962. Power within this system was handed according to rules which were very similar to that of the tribal system, with the additional qualification that the candidate had to be a descendant of Ali and his wife Fatima, daughter of Mohammed and also a religious scholar. The latter still form the aristocracy of the saadah with its 50,000 or so members.

Zaidi doctrine, which is closer to that of Sunni Islam than to the teachings of other Shi'ite sects, is surrounded by very little superstition and gives great importance to divine justice and the individual responsibilities of the faithful. Many Imams were also concerned with the interpretation of religious texts, among them Al Hadi. The latter ruled over the town of Sa'dah and a small part of the north until 911. His three successors also resided in Sa'dah. Then the Imams expanded their rule, mainly into the mountainous regions of Yemen, and established capitals in various places (Shaharah, Kawkaban, Thula). However, their support was based on the Zaidi tribes of the Sa'dah region, just like Mansour al-Qasim they had to fight the Turkish occupation before eventually extending their power over the whole of Yemen and making Sana'a their capital.

Mudbrick architecture: The great attraction of Sa'dah and the surrounding area for the visitor is based on the mudbrick architecture. This style of building is excellently suited to local conditions, has no need of stone and also provides good insulation against

Houses built in the traditional *sabur* style in Sa'dah.

heat. The houses are built within walled villages on the edge of the cultivated land. If you are lucky, you might have the chance to watch a mud house being built in Sa'dah. The walls are composed of a mixture of mud and straw which is mixed on site. Matching their action to the rhythm of a song, the workers throw little balls of this mixture to the master builder, who puts them together so that big rolls, about 16 inches (40 cm) high, are formed.

The whole is formed by hand, and each layer is usually bent to form the corners. Each layer is allowed to dry before the next one is placed on top. Each new layer is set slightly inside the previous one, so that the whole building is given a tapering pyramidical shape, which gives greater stability. This style of building is known as *sabur* technique. In Sa'dah the division between the layers is usually left visible. The spaces for openings, such as windows, doors or arrow slits, are decided on during the building. There are very few windows on the ground floor, and in the upper storeys they are often set in pairs, surrounded by white paint. Little wooden shutters and projecting roofs protect the windows. A strip of gypsum may surround the roof, the corners of which are elongated to form points. The wealthiest houses have roof ridges completely covered with jagged white ornaments. Even so, the proportions of these large buildings are extremely well balanced, and they are given an airy appearance by clever use of dependent structures.

Through the town: Even though it is no longer possible to walk all the way around the mudbrick town walls, large parts of the fortifications are made accessible. The most beautiful gate is the **Bab Najran.** You can readily imagine what difficulties an enemy must have faced when trying to take this complicated obstacle. From the Bab you can see the Zaidi cemetery which lies between the two roads to Sana'a and to Saudi Arabia. In earlier years it lay

The few remaining Jewish families live mainly in the north.

outside the gates of the town and was surrounded by its own mighty wall. The tombstones, facing Mecca, have wonderful calligraphy and inscriptions, and a few half-ruined domes rise above the tombs of former dignitaries of the Zaidi kingdom.

It is not hard to find the **Great Mosque**, which lies on the left next to **Bab al-Yemen**. Built in the 12th century, it houses the tombs of the first Imam al-Hadi Yahya as well as those of eleven further Zaidi rulers. Non-Muslim visitors are not allowed to enter the mosque and therefore may not see the chiselled stone sarcophagus. However, even if you have to stay outside, you can at least admire the wonderful traditional architecture of the mosque from the outside. Numerous domes, whitewashed with lime, rise above the building, which is a mixture of brick and stone. Another old mosque, the **Al Nisari Mosque**, lies a little further towards the centre of the town.

The produce market: The market be-gins in the main square and continues along the adjoining streets. It is a big Sunday market, but the shops are open every day, and many gardeners sell their produce: tomatoes, courgettes, root vegetables or grapes from the walled gardens just outside the town. The cultivation of citrus fruits is a new development in Yemen, so these can be fairly expensive. Among the stock of the usual tradesmen, who deal in cloth, foodstuffs and modern goods smuggled in from Saudi Arabia or legally imported, you can find some local products such as the *maqla saadim*. These are bowls cut from a single piece of stone, which are used almost all over Yemen for cooking the popular dish of *selter*. Less frequently, you can find beautiful basketware, died and woven by women, who–in contrast to the women of Djebel Sabir in Ta'izz–do not themselves come to market in town.

In the early 1980s you could still find numerous money changers who would change silver Maria Theresia talers

From the city wall you can get a fine view of the old town.

(coins named after an 18th-century Austrian empress) for Saudi or Yemeni rials. At their stalls you could not only change money but also buy ammunition for automatic weapons, often essential for life or for survival in this region. Today, with the rise of banking and tougher controls on the arms trade, the money changers have gone and can only be found in the village markets.

A few traders offer jewellery and daggers for sale to tourists. The very best pieces, though, can be found at the Jewish jewellers who have settled right at the entrance to the town of Bab al-Yemen. Apart from many different kinds of necklaces, they also sell old weapons, *djambias* and the old flint-locks once used by the Bedouin–all cheaper than you can find them in Sana'a. With a bit of luck you may even find a *sahiba*–kind of dagger and a longer version of the *djambia*–once the weapon of the Bedouin.

Jews in Yemen: There are still Jews, particularly in the Sa'dah area, living scattered among the villages of the province. Even if the visit of the Queen of Sheba to Solomon, as reported in the Bible and referred to in the Koran, was only a legend, relations between South Arabia and the Hebrews undoubtedly go back to ancient times. They were maintained by trade in spices and frankincense, which had its main markets in the north of the Arabian peninsula. There is evidence for a Jewish presence in Yemen from the second century onwards, and Judaism was once so widespread that Dhu Nuwa, the last of the Himyar kings, even converted to Judaism. He then came into conflict with the Christian communities in Yemen, and the Koran reports massacres of Christians and Jews in the Najran province during pre-Islamic times. Once the troops of the Prophet had conquered Yemen, the Jews enjoyed a "protected" status which allowed them to practise their religion freely as long as they submitted politically and paid taxes. These conditions were confirmed by the

Domes of the mosque and tomb of the first Zaidi Imam.

first Zaidi Imam, Al Hadi.

Some Jews had to agree to specific limitations. For instance, they were not allowed to build houses taller than Muslims or to bear weapons, they had to wear black and were not permitted to own musical instruments. However, these conditions were probably not more repressive than many laid upon certain classes of Muslim society. The Jewish community flourished over the centuries, with periods of repression and discrimination alternating with those in which respected and educated Jews rose to high office. The Jews had an important place in society, particularly in the practice of crafts and trade, where they specialised in certain fields, for example in gold and silversmith work, in which they had a near monopoly in Sana'a. The decline of Jewish crafts in competition with modern products undoubtedly played a part in the return to Palestine. About 50,000 Jews, a large part of the Jewish population left Yemen in a massive wave of emigration, permitted by Imam Ahmed on the occasion of the founding of the state of Israel in 1949. Only a few communities remained in the north, in the area around Sa'dah and Raydah.

The Jews of Yemen had learned how to keep their own culture in a country ruled by Islam. But they also took on the customs and the language of the Yemenis. In Sa'dah they wear Saudi garments like the majority of the population, and can only be distinguished by the two long side locks which frame their faces. In the villages around you may be invited home by Jewish families, who will be proud to show you their books, written in Hebrew. However, you should not enter this region without a permit, as the government is very sensitive about such matters.

SA'DAH

Strangers only rarely go into the mountains to the west of Sa'dah or into the desert regions, through which runs the poorly defined border with Saudi

The vineyards outside the gates of the town are surrounded by mud walls.

Arabia. However, it must be said in this context that until a few years ago the area was by no means safe and was crisscrossed by the Toyotas of the Bedouin, who were not at all shy about extorting "tolls" from tourists. Without accurate maps and a local guide, the area is in any case a difficult one for those unfamiliar with the Arabic language and the local customs.

It is still possible to visit one of the villages around Sa'dah, though, in order to enjoy the atmosphere of the north, where people are more reserved than in the rest of Yemen. Such visits are particularly worth while on market days. The most famous suq is on Saturdays in **At Talh**, six miles (10 km) to the north of Sa'dah. Trucks bring in goods imported from Saudi Arabia. However, the market is known for its trade in arms. In the 1970s you could buy anything from the weapons dealers in At Talh from a rifle bullet to flak. Whilst trade has become a bit more discreet nowadays, customers still like to show off their Kalashnikovs and crossed cartridge belts.

If you like walking, you can make your way round the plains looking for prehistoric rock carvings. They date from the Neolithic period, and their perfect lines depict animals (usually moufflon sheep), sometimes accompanied by human figures. More recent carvings, using a dot technique, have been superimposed above these pictures. The rock carvings closest to Sa'dah can be found four miles (six km) to the north, and also in the surrounding mountains, where you can also discover other relics of the past, such as Himyar inscriptions in caves under the rocks, for instance in the **Saqayn** area, to the west of Sa'dah. In order to be sure of finding the carvings, you should take a local person with you.

DJEBEL UMM LAYLA

This is the most northerly excursion you could make within Yemen. Djebel Umm Layla is 37 miles (60 km) from Sa'dah, just before the Saudi Arabian border. The mountain is only recommended for very experienced and fit hikers, as there is no easy way up. However, just the asphalt road which leads to Umm Layla itself provides enough good opportunities for sightseeing. At the moment it is the most modern road found in the whole of Yemen, for it is not only well aligned but also the only road with regular signposts giving the names of towns and the distance in kilometres, not just in Arabic but also in English. Vehicles with unbelievably heavy loads, which are often piled higher than the car itself, drive skilfully along the road in the direction of Sana'a. These are taxis hired by Yemeni workers coming home from the building sites of Saudi Arabia bringing with them their purchases.

After leaving Sa'dah, you drive first through little villages and single isolated farms along the roadside. You will see some splendid estates with enclosed gardens and huge houses whose white-

The most northerly point of a tour of Yemen: the deserted fortress of Umm Layla.

washed roofs contrast with the blue of the sky. Sixteen miles (25 km) outside Sa'dah the plain ends, and the last important village is **Majz**. To the left of the road, at the foot of a little wall of rock, there are attractive groups of mudbrick houses. Here market day is on Thursdays. Behind the village a pretty, green wadi has dug a canyon which can be followed into the mountains. It is inhabited by peasants, distinctive bedus. They have kept their sense of tradition, and a hiker can end up facing a wild-looking man, wrapped in a cloth with a black and white checked pattern, who without a word will offer you a bowl of milk from his goats. If you thank him, the Bedouin will reply that it was a gift from God.

The road now leads you into a sandstone massif, crisscrossed by wild-looking landscape formations left by erosion. The area is completely desert-like, though basins of rock in the valleys have retained some unexpected pools of water. You have to drive for another 12

miles (20 km) before you reach the village of **Rougafah**. From here you can see the majestic outflung mass of **Djebel Umm Layla**, which towers above the neighbouring peaks. At the foot of the mountain a small oasis supports a few fields and impoverished houses. You can very easily make out the ruins of the citadel which once defended the peak (some 8,202 feet/2,500 metres-high). In order to climb the mountain you have to continue on to the end of the ridge which is an extension of the mountain to the north. From this point, the climb will last about an hour. A difficult section at the end of the old mule track will give you access to the fortress. This huge side covers the whole peak to the south. Your first discovery will be three beautifully preserved cisterns, one placed above the other. Well-preserved steps lead down to the floors of the basins. If you turn your attention back to the buildings, you will discover old granaries which look more like imposing caves or grottos. They were made by human hands and have only a simple hole instead of a door to give access.

A broad staircase leads to the living accommodation at the peak, past an overhanging rock with a Himyar inscription. This is one of the earliest inscriptions in the Arabic language. Written in an ancient script, it dates back to the period of the Islamic conquest. Behind the gate you will discover more recent houses, mostly in a dilapidated condition. On the ground you will find plenty of spent cartridges, a sign that this place was the site of war and conflict not so very long ago, probably at the time of the civil war. A very fine mosque in the Ottoman style presents its many white domes and large, well-preserved baths. There are more cisterns and storage buildings scattered all over the entire site, and you can easily imagine the number of people who must have garrisoned the fortress when it defended the entrance to the valleys from the desert.

Left, to stabilise the mud houses, the corners are raised. **Right**, mud house in the evening sunshine.

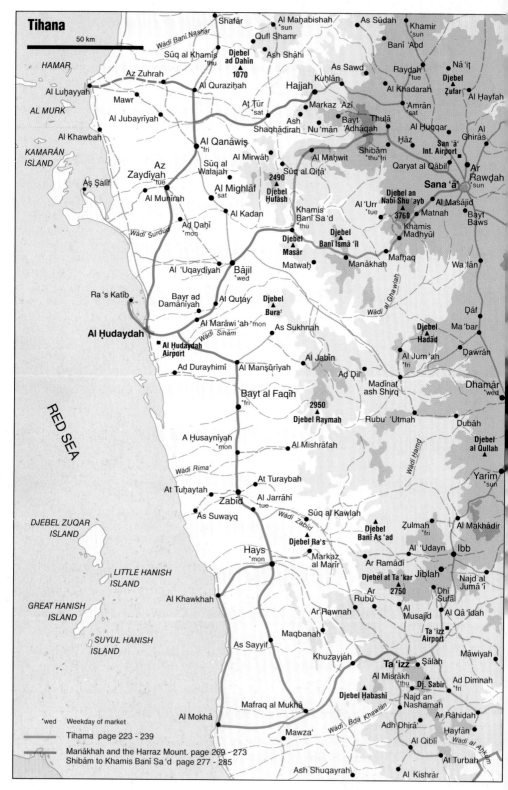

Tihana

50 km

HAMAR

AL MURK

AL MURK

KAMARĀN
ISLAND

RED SEA

DJEBEL ZUQAR
ISLAND

LITTLE HANISH
ISLAND

GREAT HANISH
ISLAND

SUYUL HANISH
ISLAND

Shafār
Al Maḥabishah *sun
Qufl Shamr
As Sūdah
Khamir *sun
Banī ʿAbd
Sūq al Khamīs *thu
Djebel ad Dahīn *
1070
Ash Shāhī
As Sawd
Kuḥlān
Raydah *tue
Nā ʿiṭ
Djebel Zufar *
Al Ḥayfah
Az Zuhrah
Al Qurazīḥah
Hajjah
Al Khadarah
ʿAmrān *sat
Al Luḥayyah
Mawr
Aṭ Ṭūr *sat
Markaz ʿAzī
Ash Shaqhādirah
Nu ʿmān
Bayt ʿAdḥaqah
Thulā
Al Ḥuqqar
Al Ghirās
Al Jubayrīyah
Al Khawbah
Al Qanāwiṣ *fri
Al Mirwāḥ
Al Maḥwit
Shibām *thu *fri
Ḥāz
San ʿāʾ Int. Airport
Ar Rawḍah
Aṣ Ṣalīf
Az Zaydīyah *tue
Sūq al Walajah
Sūq al Qiṭāʿ
Qaryat al Qābil
Sana ʿāʾ *sun
Al Munīrah
Al Mighlāf *sat
2490
Djebel Ḥufāsh
Khamis Banī Saʿd *thu
Al ʿUrr *tue
Djebel an Nabī Shuʿayb 3760
Al Masājid
Matnah
Bayt Baws
Ad Daḥī *mon
Al Kadan
Djebel Masār
Djebel Banī Ismāʿīl
Khamis Madhyūl
Mafḥaq
Wa ʿlān
Wādī Surdūd
Al ʿUqaydīyah
Bājil *wed
Matwaḥ
Manākhah
Ra ʾs Katīb
Bayr ad Damānīyah
Al Quṭay
Djebel Buraʿ
Wādī al Ghawlah
Dāf
Al Marāwi ʿah *mon
As Sukhnah
Djebel Hadād
Maʿbar
Al Ḥudaydah
Al Ḥudaydah Airport
Wādī Sihām
Al Jabīn
Al Jumʿah *fri
Dawrān
Ad Durayhimī
Al Manṣūrīyah
Aḍ Ḍilʿ
Madīnat ash Shirq
Dhamār *wed
Bayt al Faqīh *fri
2950
Djebel Raymah
Rubuʿ ʿUtmah
Dubāh
Djebel al Qullah
A Ḥusaynīyah *mon
Al Mishrāfah
Wādī Ḥamd
Yarīm *sun
Wādī Rimaʿ
At Turaybah
At Tuḥaytah
Zabīd *tue
Al Jarrāhī
Sūq al Kawlah
Zulmah *fri
Al Makhādir
As Suwayq
Wādī Zabīd
Djebel Banī Asʿad
Al ʿUdayn
Ibb
Djebel Raʿs
Hays *mon
Markaz al Marīr
Ar Ramādī
Djebel at Taʿkar
Jiblah
Najd al Jumāʿī
Al Khawkhah
Ar Rubuʿ
Ar 2750
Dhī Sufāl
Al Qāʿidah
Ar Rawnah
Al Musajīd
Taʿizz Airport
Maqbanah
As Sayyif
Khuzayjah
Ta ʿizz
Ṣalāh
Māwiyah
Al Misrākh *thu
Dj. Sabir
Ad Dimnah *fri
Djebel Ḥabashī
Najd an Nashamah
Mafraq al Mukhā
Ar Rāhidah
Adh Dhirāʿ
Ḥayfān
Al Mokhā
Mawzaʿ
Wādī Bdaʿ Khawlān
Al Qiblī
Wādī al Aḥkum
At Turbah
Ash Shuqayrah
Al Kishrār

*wed   Weekday of market

——   Tihana page 223 - 239

——   Manākhah and the Harraz Mount. page 269 - 273
       Shibām to Khamis Banī Saʿd page 277 - 285

THE TIHAMA

The Tihama is a hot, sandy coastal strip that separates the Red Sea from Bab al-Mandab, or the "Gate of Tears", up to as far as Saudi Arabia. In English, Tihama means "hot earth", and it certainly lives up to its name. Temperatures along the coast can reach as high as 50° C in the humid summer months, with a humidity of 85 percent. Even in the so-called "cool" winter months you can feel overdressed in a T-shirt.

The Tihama is different from the other regions of Yemen, and not only in its temperatures. In contrast to Ma'rib or the Sana'a-Ta'izz line there are hardly any traces of South Arabian culture to be found here. The people of this coastal strip and the mountains bordering it are darker. Traces of African ancestry are clearly visible in many of them. Their houses and huts are more like African kraals than the castles and towers of the mountains of Yemen. In contrast to most of the tribes and regions of central and eastern Yemen the inhabitants of the Tihama are not Zaidis but belong to the Sunni and Shi'ite branches of Islam. The women are often not veiled, especially women in the countryside, and some mosques are even open to foreigners.

Sea Port: About a third of the population of North Yemen live in the Tihama. Hudaydah, the second largest city in Yemen, is considered a model modern town for other towns to follow. For a long time it was the only harbour in Yemen that could take deep sea shipping, and therefore played a central role in supplying the country. The Yemen Navigation Company runs passenger and cargo shipping services to many ports in the Red Sea as well as on the east coast of Africa. Smaller companies with cargo boats mainly ply between Al Hudaydah, Djibouti and Aden.

Zabid, founded in 800 by an Abassid governor, was for a long time the centre of the entire region. Bayt al-Faqih and Zabid both harbour important Koran colleges. The dark-skinned warriors of the Zaraniqs around Bayt al-Faqih were famous for their courage. During the Turkish occupation the struggle of the powerful Tihami tribe determined the fate of the region, ending with a revolt taking the form of a declaration of war on Imam Yahya and a demand made to the UN for recognition of a separate Zaraniqi state with its capital at Al Hudaydah. The ruins of the former busy and famous port of Al Mokha are a reminder of the town's former role as the centre of the coffee trade. Its fame, however, now survives only in the drink of the same name.

The landscape of the Tihama is not as varied as that of the mountainous regions of Yemen. In December 1982 a severe earthquake hit the Tihama region

Preceding pages: only a shadow remains of its former glory–Al Mokha. **Right,** in the market of Bajil.

leaving a trail of disasters behind–more than 3,000 people were killed and roads, bridges, power and water supplies, and agricultural works were destroyed. However, little coastal strips between Al Kawkhah and Al Mokha have retained their charms. The northern coast is covered in mangrove swamps. The tides here flood the levels and leave wide salt flats behind at low tide. Beaches, therefore, are only to be found at Al Kawkhah. Little sand deserts such as those at Bayt al-Faqih often run as far as the sea.

In the hinterland of the coast and in the bordering mountain ranges there are broad fields growing millet and, if there is sufficient rainfall or irrigation, other grain crops are also grown. The greatest amount of rainfall has been recorded in the south, central, and western highlands. The mountainous Tihama are particularly well irrigated by flooding of the fields. The rainfall allows the water in the wadis to rise rapidly, and it is then distributed as far as is humanly possible. Monsoon season occurs in April and May which alternates with a heavier monsoon in July and August. The valleys are covered with banana and papaya plantations. The transition area between the high mountain massif of central Yemen and its final outcrops in the Tihama display the same picture from north to south: a desert of stones with very little vegetation.

Only very few travellers are likely to arrive in the port of Al Hudaydah by ship from Djibouti. However, as the wild and rugged mountains of Yemen barely permit passage through them, the coast is difficult to reach from the mountains.

MANAKHAH TO AL HUDAYDAH ▬▬

The road from Sana'a to Al Hudaydah is the most important communications artery in the whole of Yemen. Nearly all the goods off-loaded in Al Hudaydah are transported along this twisting road. In Al Maghrabah the asphalt road crosses the last major ridge

African-looking round straw huts in the Tihama.

of the central massif. From the top of the pass you already have a view far into the valleys of the foothills. The road winds down towards the valley in countless loops, passing the last fortified settlements of Djebel Harraz and Djebel Masar. High above, villages such as Al Hajjarah cling to the rock like eagles' eyries. By the time you reach the floor of the Wadi Siham, which will be your constant campanion from now on, the temperature will have risen considerably. The few people who have settled beside the wadi depend on the little banana and papaya plantations for their livelihoods, the crops are watered by means of irrigation channels. The euphorbias with their pink blossoms are often the only vegetation.

It is all the more surprising, therefore, when you come to a small waterfall after some 12 miles (20 km). Hidden behind a large rocky outcrop precious water splashes over the rock even in the dry winter months. In the pool below live a great number of trout and frogs.

Lack of water is often a problem in the Tihama.

The scenery remains the same for the next 16 miles (25 km) as far as Khamis Bani Sa'd. Bare rocks and only a few signs of human habitation are all that is to be seen. In the wadi, however, where the amount of water increases steadily, various kinds of heron wade through the muddy water.

A visit to **Khamis Bani Sa'd** is particularly worth while early on a Thursday morning, when the weekly market takes place, winding its way among the trees to the wadi. Large cloths stretched between the few houses act as awnings. From livestock to spices, from agricultural tools to posies of fresh flowers which the women wear behind their ears, the lively suq has everything to offer that the Yemenis need. Teashops, several small restaurants and a number of small shops provide opportunities for refreshment.

After the meeting of the Wadi Siham and the Wadi Surdud the valley widens. The river has dug a deep bed in the gravelly plain, on which the first

Tihama villages can be seen. Wooden huts, thatched with grass and reeds, are divided one from another by fences of thornbush. At the roadside, tradesmen who have cut wood in the isolated side valleys sell their wares to passers-by. The road soon leaves the mountains and meets the barren and arid plain of the Tihama. The humid air draws a veil of haze over everything. The first large town of the Tihama lies a mere 22 miles (35 km) beyond Khamis Bani Sa'd.

From the roadside, **Bajil** does not give a particularly inviting impression. The road which crosses the newly built quarter is lined with restaurants and petrol stations. In the afternoons men meet outside the restaurants and coffee houses with their beds made of water pipes strung with nylon ropes and chew *qat*. To the right of the main road the weekly market takes place on Wednesdays, including a large livestock market. From the main road a side road branches off left to a permanent suq and into the old town. The crowded and very lively suq offers the same goods which are available everywhere else. However, the charm of the suq in Bajil lies perhaps in the fact that it is still very authentic and genuine.

It is 34 miles (55 km) from Bajil to the provincial capital of Al Hudaydah. The road crosses well-organised steppes of pure sand or large fields of millet. The landscape is divided by white markers into different sites. During the last two decades, property speculation along the good roads has become quite a normal occurrence in Yemen. The prices for pieces of land could multiply several times over in the space of a few years, particularly since oil has been discovered in many parts of Yemen.

AL HUDAYDAH

This city, with its population of 200,000, is the second largest and most modern in Yemen. Only a few houses and mosques remain as a reminder of the fact that Hudaydah was once the most important Turkish port in the Red

The Red Sea still guarantees a good catch.

Sea. During the period of competition between the colonial powers Hudaydah was intended to rival the British-held city of Aden. Twenty years before the first Turkish invasion, Hudaydah was occupied in 1515 by the Egyptian sultan, but at that time it was overshadowed by Al Mokha, which had better mooring places for ships. From 1849 on it was under Turkish occupation for the second time and formed the end of the line of supply from Hudaydah via Manakhah to Sana'a. It developed into a port in competition with Aden, after the port of Mokha had lost its importance due to the loss of the coffee trade. The sparse remains of the railway built at the time are no longer in use today.

The two German explorers of Yemen, Carl Rathjens and Hermann von Wissimann, described in their book *Landeskundliche Ergebnisse*, published in 1934, the colourful mixture of peoples in the port, which has by now lost much of its former importance. Apart from the usual Arab and Indian businessmen, Greeks, Italians, Russians and Jews are also mentioned. It is obvious that slavery was still common usage at the time of their stay: "The great mass of working people is composed of workers from the Tihama, much mingled here with negroes and Hamites. You can see representatives of almost all the East African races as slaves, both male and female."

Today Al Hudaydah presents the traveller with the opportunity of gaining an impression of a modernisation effort by a modern state. Even though Al Hudaydah does not match up with the image of a picturesque and medieval Yemen, familiar scenes from travel brochures, it is a better reflection of the modern, progressively orientated state of Yemen than any other town or city in the country. It is the busiest of all the three Yemeni ports, with a turnover of goods of some 180,000 tonnes.

Hudaydah has little to offer by way of sightseeing. It is worth while taking a walk through the old **Turkish Quarter**,

Dried fish can be bought in any Suq.

departing from the shore road. Most of the former offices, warehouses, settlements and palaces are now derelict. With a bit of luck, though, you will find the odd finely carved oriel window with female figures, or an entrance portal, but these will, because of the inhospitable climate, by now have the consistency of papier maché. Hudaydah has a fine suq in the old city behind the former Turkish citadel. Nowadays the citadel houses a police station. By the **Bab Mishrif** and along the road in front of it stalls sell spices, cloth, and especially fruit in great quantity. The vegetable market and the *qat* market next to it form an exquisite picture, especially in the evening against the light of the gas lamps. A spicy, smoked fresh cheese can be found in the suq, in three different flavours: without salt, with little salt and salted to the point of inedibilty.

If you want to eat fish in the true Yemeni style, visit the **food stalls** around Bab Mishrif. The most varied fish dishes are bubbling away in countless pots, and the customer can choose among them, freshly caught Red Sea fish for grilling comes straight from the icebox. A meal of freshly grilled fish served with oven-fresh *chops* washed down with a bottle of Shamlan water is a delicacy not to be missed. The restaurants, though, are not that luxurious. You eat on the floor and off little stools which you place in front of you. After you have eaten, all the leftovers end up in one big bowl, and finally the "waiter" turns up and wipes your eating place clean with a cloth that looks as if it dates from the last century.

The boats and the trucks arrive in the fish market, the **Suq al-Zamek**, from seven in the morning on. The market is somewhat out of the way, along the coast road in a southerly direction. In the market you can see all the wealth of fish in the Red Sea. From sharks to big mantas, from perch to lobster–the whole great variety is laid out for you to admire. A few little snack bars at the entrance to the fish market sell very

Living room inside a round hut in the northern Tihama.

tasty freshly fried fish, which is, of course, eaten with your hands. The fish market is in an enclosed area around Hudaydah and can only be visited with a *tassarir*. Taking photographs and videofilming are usually forbidden, but are sometimes tolerated if there are not too many tourists about.

Hudaydah unfortunately has no beaches to offer. However, in front of the gates of the city lies the great peninsula of Ras al-Khatib, where the container ships and oil tankers pass by on their way to the harbour entrance. On this peninsula some dilapidated beach cabins offer shade to the few visitors. In the background you can see huge tankers moored for loading oil.

HUDAYDAH TO AL MOKHA

Hudaydah is 34 miles (55 km) away from Bayt al-Faqih. After some nine miles (15 km) in the direction of Manakhah, just behind the military post and a fruit juice factory, the road branches off onto the Hudaydah-Ta'izz route. The road leads through an area that is partly desert, occasionally broken by plantations. Every possible form of irrigation is used here in order to wrest a crop from the sandy soil. A series of typical Tihama villages, with their thorn hedges, appear at the side of the road. But the road has little to offer apart from a few sand dunes, petrol stations and, with a bit of luck, the odd passing camel.

Some 18 miles (29 km) after branching off from the Manakhah route you pass the town of **Al Mansouryah**, from which a track leads to **Djebel Raymah**, which later meets with the Madinat ash-Shirq-Bajil link. If you like walking, you will find varied scenery near **As Sukhnah**, here too, you can visit the palace belonging to the Imam's family complete with hot springs and baths.

BAYT AL-FAQIH

The next major town is the old trading city of Bayt al-Faqih. Although the rapid changes in Yemen over the last

Weaving according to traditional methods by the men of Bayt al-Faqih.

few years have not passed this place by without making some changes, it has still kept some of its old tradition to this day, such as its Friday market. Apart from basket wares, it is mainly the handwoven cloths, *futah*, which arouse the interest of not only tourists.

A dusty sand track leads off from the main road into the old town centre. Thousands of colourful plastic bags have got caught in the thorn hedges and if the plastic catches the light, it glows like magical flowers. Seeing this pollution it is easy for visitors from the so-called developed industrial nations to complain of a lack of environmental awareness in Yemen. However, it is impossible for a nation to move from an almost medieval society to an environment-conscious and environmentally responsible state within a few years. The rubbish which piles up in Bayt al-Faqih and elsewhere in Yemen doesn't come out of the blue. It is of no use just to put out rubbish bins. A change to deep-rooted attitudes in the thinking of the Yemenis would be necessary—and in that of tourists, for plastic was unknown here until a few years ago, and products made of natural materials could without further thought have been dumped outside the front door or in the garden. It is debatable, anyway, whether Western industrial nations treat the environment in a more responsible fashion.

The town was founded in the early 18th century by the scholar Sheikh Ahmed ibn Musa. The literal translation of the name is "House of the Scholar." Bayt al-Faqih was a waystation for the entire coffee trade on its way to Al Mokha. This is where the merchants and tradesmen met. Later the town was fortified with a Turkish citadel. However, Bayt al-Faqih's present fame is mainly due to the weavers who work in a few shelters and huts in the middle of the town and make the long, dyed wrap-around cloths. Apart from silver jewellery and basket ware, this is one of the few genuine Yemeni craft products.

Back on the asphalt road, after 12

Whole families and clans live together in one hut village.

miles (20 km) the road leads across the Wadi Rihma, the course of which extends almost as far up as Dhamar. If you drive along the road Ma'bar-Madinat ash Shirq, you will already have followed parts of this wadi just before ash Shirq. Eleven miles (17 km) further on lies the town of Zabid.

ZABID

Zabid is by far the most interesting of all the towns of the Tihama. You would probably have no difficulty spending a whole day in Zabid, as the suq and the whole atmosphere of the town invite you to stay: to stroll around, to relax and to make discoveries.

Zabid was founded in 819 by an Abassid governor, Mohammed ibn Ziyad, who founded a new branch of his family. The Beni Ziyad dynasty held power for two centuries. From Zabid Ibn Ziyad ruled large parts of Yemen. He achieved a notable degree of independence and was able to loosen the ties to Baghdad and remove a good deal of

Men meet to chew *qat* in the Tihama too.

its influence. During this period Zabid became the centre of the Shafi'a doctrine, which spread far beyond the borders of Yemen. The **University of Zabid** enjoyed great respect and had great influence within Yemen and outside the country. It lost none of this respect and importance even after the end of the Ziyadites. Under the Rasulids in the 14th century Zabid held a more important position than Sana'a. It signalled the end of Zabid when the Turkish general Suleiman Pasha landed in Mokha in 1538. The city lost its position to Al Mokha, after the harbour of Zabid, Ghulayfiqa, silted up more and more.

The city wall with its gates, the citadel, 80 Koran schools and mosques remain as vivid reminders of the city's famous past. It is usual to start your tour of Zabid in the **Town Square** in front of the **Turkish Citadel**, as little streets and alleys lead off from here to all parts of the city. The Town Square is in fact a large oval space, somewhat unusual for Yemen. In its centre there is a little tree-

grown "garden cafe", with a fountain playing quietly to itself. On the one side the citadel with its massive gate rises majestically. On another, a gate in the fortress points a way out through the city walls.

The corners of the fortress have massive fortified towers. Inside the fortress, which has a very squat appearance, is the **Iskandria Mosque** (Alexandria Mosque) with its minaret forming one of the corner towers of the fortress. Like most of the mosques in the Tihama, it displays mainly Egyptian and Turkish features. The minaret was probably built around 1530, but the rest of the mosque dates from a much earlier period–according to estimates, from the time of the Rasulids. Similarities in the ground plan and in building technique with other Rasulid mosques point to such a date. In the Iskandria Mosque the building styles of the whole Islamic age in the Tihama are mingled with the new styles. At certain times you can climb the minaret of the Iskandria.

Excavations around the mosque have confirmed the assumption that another building previously stood on this site. A great basin has been found, which points to a palace or a precursor of the mosque. Immediately next to the mosque, few implements point to some early manufacturing industries, potteries or coin mints.

The **city wall** is more recent and dates from the 19th century. Carsten Niebuhr noted in 1763 that the structure of the walls were extremely dilapidated. On Turkish instructions the wall was rebuilt in the 19th century. The second "destruction" began in the 1960s, when the stones were used for building new houses as part of the economic changes throughout Yemen.

The core of the city of Zabid and its Shafi'a scholarship is the **Al Asha'ria Mosque**, also known as the Great Mosque. Your way to the mosque leads through the beautiful and authentic suq. The narrow alleys are protected from the blazing sun by canvas awnings and

The Turkish warehouses in Hudaydah are all derelict.

232

reed mats. A little way away from the main suq street there is a fine **sesame mill**, still worked by camel power. The entrance to the Great Mosque lies about three feet (one metre) below street level. Over the centuries all kinds of deposits have collected here. The shop next door will inform you about all the opening times. The first things you notice in the interior are the new asymmetrical purification basins. The green water, bathed in sunlight, makes a wonderful contrast to the whitewashed walls.

Schools of thought: The plain mosque, with its painted beamed ceiling, is fascinating because of the very beautiful and genius use of pillars in the construction. Several rows of pillars surround a longish inner courtyard, which provides light for the entire mosque. In front of the wooden chancel or minbar and next to the prayer niche or mihrab is a great wooden balcony. In earlier times this was where the callers sat, their job was to relay the imam's preaching to the back of the building. A plaque with in-

scriptions in Arabic gives some information about the founding of the mosque. Sometimes the imam will allow access to the roof, which gives a fine view of the "garden city" of Zabid. Narrow stairs pass by the former study rooms, in which students still meet today to study the religious scriptures.

It is worth while taking the trouble to find one of the 80 **Koran schools** of Zabid. Even if you are not allowed to enter the building, it is worth taking a close look at the often magnificent decoration of the outer walls. Usually of stucco ornaments in the Egyptian or Turkish style, complemented by the decorative brickwork in the typical Tihama style of the surrounding façades, can frequently be seen.

In earlier times the city of Zabid must have been very much larger than the present city walls would indicate. Excavations have uncovered remains of buildings, cemeteries, and other finds to substantiate this assumption. Discoveries of early potteries also point to settle-

Cheap tin plates have replaced pottery as decoration inside the huts.

ment in Zabid during pre-Islamic times. In the surrounding fields large paved areas have been discovered, which could possibly have belonged to a former palace. Bricks from such ruins would probably have been used for the typical **Tihama style** of decorative brickwork. The excavations of the Royal Ontario Museum concentrated mainly on potteries, but have also provided important information on the history and origin of Zabid.

Situated outside the present city centre are the well-preserved fortified gates dating from Turkish times and the **Mustapha Pasha Mosque** on the road from Zabid to Ta'izz. It is named after the first Turkish governor after the conquest of the Tihama in 1539.

The road continues through the landscape of the Wadi Zabid in the direction of Ta'izz. In the town of Suq al-Jarrahi there is a weekly market on Tuesdays. A good 12 miles (20 km) further on lies the ancient town of **Hays**, especially famous for its pottery. The ancient town centre, about half a mile (one km) away from the road, is particularly beautiful, like that of Zabid.

Just like those in Bayt al-Faqih or Zabid, the houses here are of a very unusual design. A house consists of several small rooms surrounding one or more courtyards in which the kitchens and toilets are placed. The façades of the main rooms have very fine stucco reliefs. The family house is surrounded by a fairly high wall with a wooden gate, mostly of two doors. The angled construction of the entrance usually prevents an observer from seeing inside, even if the gate is open. This is where two worlds meet: the private, almost sacred life of the family and the profane outside world.

After 44 miles (70 km) the asphalt road reaches the small village of **Mafraq**, which in English means crossroads. The sole building at this point is a petrol station. From here it is 28 miles (45 km) to Al Mokha and another 39 (62 km) to Ta'izz.

Bajil has one of the largest livestock markets in the Tihama.

AL MOKHA VIA AL KHAWKHAH

If you are not in a hurry, take this road along the coast in the dry months. A track, some 19 miles (30 km) long, which will probably be asphalted in the next few years, leads to the little town of Al Khawkah.

The coastal strip of **Al Khawkhah** offers the only possibility of sea bathing in beautiful surroundings. Groves of palm trees separate the desert-like hinterland from the level coastal strip. Coral reefs, which can be recognised by white patches of foam dotted along the sea, allow you to swim without fear of sharks. However, you should take care, as the flatter ray fish do sometimes come right in to the shore. To the north of Al Khawkhah, the romantic palm groves offer a simple place to spend the night. You sleep in the open air on typical Tihama beds.

The town of Al Khawkhah depends on fishing, and there is a small fish hall just below the town by the beach. Apart from the fine houses, Al Khawkhah also has a suq to offer, with a number of typical coffee houses and tea rooms in the open air. The track to **Al Mokha** first goes through Al Khawkhah and then after a few miles runs directly along the beach. Before the beach you pass a little tomb, Mu'scheich Ali. The star of David above the entrance is not necessarily a sign of Jewish use. Such elements of decoration can be found even in the mosques.

After this small marabout the track carries on through the wet sand of the Red Sea to **Wadi al-Mulkh**. In front of a dense grove of palm trees lies yet another beautiful bay, inviting you to swim. In the hinterland of the coastal strip there are great flocks of flamingoes wading in the pools of brackish water. Behind the fishing and smuggling village of **Yathul** the tropical splendour is over once more, and the road runs along a salt track directly towards the power station of Al Mokha. This drive is only recommended in the dry season. Thick mud often lies under

The camel is still often used as a work animal.

the hard salt crust of the wadi bed. Once you have broken through, it is almost impossible for your vehicle to get out under its own power. The drive towards the power station, the desolate sands, the stormy gusts of wind which fling sand into your face and the heavy, humid air all prepare you for the ghost town of Al Mokha.

AL MOKHA

The name is all that remains of the fame of Al Mokha. The disappointment of travellers hoping to find something left over from past glories is often very great. Apart from the **Al Shadi Mosque**, the remains of the great minaret in front of it, and a few sorry ruins of the former **warehouses and offices**, there is little to be seen and admired in Mokha. The unfavourable climatic conditions–the humid, hot air and occasional sand storms in the mornings– soon drive most tourists out of town after a few minutes.

The town of Mokha owes its found-

ing to Sheikh Ali Shadili, who is supposed to have settled here in 1430. The town was known as a harbour as early as the Himyar period. The ancient harbour was filled in, and there are no remains of buildings dating from this time. According to legend, though, Shadili is supposed to have been a great lover of coffee, recently imported by the Arabs from Ethiopia.

Indian merchants carried coffee from those shores, and so it set out on its triumphal progress through the world. This, however, is only one of the legends surrounding coffee. From the 16th century on Al Mokha enjoyed its status as *the* port which exported coffee that was cultivated in the mountains of Yemen and transported by camel caravan via Bayt al-Faqih.

In 1616 the Dutchman van der Broeke came to Al Mokha and reported that goods from Venice and Nuremberg could be found in the markets. Just under a hundred years later the Dutch and the English founded the first trade settlements. Gradually other nations joined them. In 1803 an American ship entered the harbour for the first time. And 17 years later a British gunboat fired on the town and occupied it. After the taking of Aden by the British and the decline of the coffee trade Mokha sank into insignificance, and the harbour silted up. Today, new and better docks are being built once more. Just as in Hudaydah, some industrial firms have settled in Mokha too. From Mokha the asphalt road runs on to **Al Mafraq**, where it meets the main road from Hudaydah to Ta'izz once more.

NORTHERN TIHAMA

Only a few tourists take the trouble to get to know the northern Tihama, i.e. the coastal strip between Al Hudaydah and the Saudi Arabian border. The appearance of the north, both in the landscape and in the structure of its villages, is very different from that of the south. In order to get there, the most beautiful, although not necessarily the easiest,

Strict geometrical lines: the ritual cleansing basin in the mosque in Zabid.

236

route crosses the mountains of central Yemen and goes through the provincial capital of Hajjah.

HAJJAH TO AL LUHAYYAH

From Hajjah itself, just as from Al Maghrabah on the Hudaydah-Sana'a road, you get a marvellous view of the valleys of the Tihama mountains. However, even in the early hours of the morning, thick clouds rise up along the steep ridge of the mountains from the humid Tihama. The road, by now an unpaved track, winds in a number of curves down into the valley of the **Wadi al-Aman**, which later leads on to the **Wadi Mawr**. Here, too, the scenery is monotonous and grey to begin with, and only a welcome view of the upland town of Hajja makes some recompense for the dusty rigours of the journey. But after only a few miles along the floor of the wadi valley the vegetation changes to subtropical plants such as euphorbias, papayas and bananas. Occasionally old, ruined tanks and tracked ve-

hicles may be seen by the roadside. After the flight of Imam Badr from Sana'a, Hajjah was one of the centres of the Royalist tribes.

The attractions of the highland Tihama lie in the gentle shapes of the hills and in the lush vegetation of the deep wadis. It is not far to the first hut settlements–such as the village of **Aman**–with their typical "straw hats." In contrast to the southern region, these villages seem to be more compact, more unspoiled and less covered with plastic rubbish. Just under 25 miles (40 km) the road comes to the town of **Suq at-Tur**. The suq here sells excellent *qat* and *shami*. With this particular variety not only the young leaves but also whole shoots can be used. The price is correspondingly higher.

After a further seven miles (11 km) a road branches off to Al Mahwit. The main track, though, runs straight on for about another 12 miles (20 km) through a gentle and beautiful landscape with rocks of a deep black colour. A few

Once a famous Islamic university: Zabid.

miles before reaching the asphalt road the plain opens out, and at **Dayr Duknah** the track meets the well-built main road from Hudaydah to Jizan (in Saudi Arabia).

To the north the road crosses the Wadi Mawr, having followed the right bank this far. After eight miles (12 km) it branches off in **Al Ma'ras** towards Al Luhayyah. The road now runs directly into the huge wadi basin and through an intensively cultivated region. Scattered through this broad and gently rolling landscape are villages of huts or whole small towns such as **Az Zuhrah**. The many fortifications, towers and town gates in the Turkish style are notable. Around the dominant fortress, low huts of the African type are grouped.

In these hut villages with their cheerful "straw hat" roofs an entire extended family could live in a kraal or in several family buildings. The head of the family owns the most magnificent hut, and the smaller huts of the brothers and sons surround it. The women have their own huts too. Apart from a communal kitchen, every family has its own cooking space as well. A specially separated area acts as a toilet, and behind a mud-brick wall lies the communal bath.

The round huts consist of a wooden frame which is roofed with various materials such as reeds. The whole is arranged so that it looks like a pointed hat. The hut is plastered with mud and painted inside and outside, and the walls are decorated with coloured plaques. The huts can be closed by means of doors, some of which are finely carved. Wooden couches, *qa'dah*, and wooden beds, *sarir*, serve as reclining places for chewing *qat* and as beds for sleeping. They are strung with a kind of sisal grass. Some of the door frames are painted, and the space in front of the door is raised a little above normal ground level and painstakingly kept clean. The domestic animals of the family are kept in little stables within the small kraal. Apart from the round huts, however, a number of other kinds

Straight along the beach is often the quickest way.

238

of housing are noticeable, such as the long huts which have roofs decorated with little flags and other decorations. This type of building is to be found particularly near the coasts and around Al Luhayyah. The region along the road to Al Luhayyah is relatively densely settled and little patches of woodland appear from time to time–quite an unusual scenery for Yemen. The long salt track to Al Luhayyah runs directly beside the sea and passes four sizeable hills, fortified with small Turkish forts dating from the 19th century. The hills are called **Djebel al-Milh**, the Salt Hills. From this point the salt track runs through an area partially flooded by tides. Long-legged grey herons wade through the shallow water among the mangrove trees. Agriculture and cultivation disappear once you have passed the Djebel al-Milh; the countryside has a desolate and unattractive aspect.

Al Luhayyah: The road leads straight to the Turkish fort of Al Luhayyah, which dates from the 19th century. Only a few hundred yards farther on the town itself begins. Its foundation dates back to Sheikh Saleh in the 15th century. People gradually settled in this area and probably made their first home in simple round huts. Al Luhayyah began to flourish with the rise in coffee trade. Stones had to be brought great distances in order to build warehouses and settlements. Large blocks of coral from the sea lightened the structures of the building. Al Luhayyah also became an important port for pilgrims to Mecca, and many began their pilgrimage from this point. Carsten Niebuhr and his Danish expedition also visited Al Luhayyah. During the second Turkish occupation, the area around Al Luhayyah secured Turkish interests in the Red Sea.

The **tomb and mosque** of the founder of Al Luhayyah, Sheikh Saleh, has 14 small domes. The old houses and warehouses are mostly derelict now. Among them the typical Tihama huts have made a come back. The harbour, long since silted up, has a thick belt of mangrove trees crossing it, which is a paradise for water fowl. If you want to gain an impression of a really typically medieval Arab fishing village, you will find what you are looking for in Al Luhayyah. Tourist attractions, however, are hardly worth mentioning.

AL LUHAYYAH TO HUDAYDAH

For the route to Hudaydah, you have to go back to the asphalt Hudaydah-Jizan road. The track along the coast is not open to traffic, as it passes too close to the oil depots, the end of the pipeline from Ma'rib, in Salif, and also to some military installations just before the **island of Kamaran**. The town of **Al Khawbhah** with its large fish market is also in the restricted area. The road runs past the old towns of **Al Qanawis** and **Az Zaydiyah**. The latter is famous for the manufacture of the *thuma*, the curved daggers worn by nobility and the qadis. Travel for another 40 miles (64 km) past Az Zaydiyah, and you will arrive at Al Hudaydah.

Coffee grower from the highland Tihama.

The South

50 km

Amrān 'sat
Al Ḥayfah
Wādī al Khārid
Thulā
Al Ḥuqqar
Al Ghirās
Ḥāz
Sana 'ā' Int.
Airport
Ar Rawḍah 'sun
Bayt as Sayyid
Sirwāḥ
Djebel al Barrah
Djebel Balaq al Qiblī
Ma 'rib
Qaryat al Qābil
Sana 'ā'
Tan 'am
Al Masājid
Matnah
Bayt Baws
Ghaymān
Jihānah
Al Watadah
Wādī Adhanah
Khamîs Madhyūl
Mafḥaq
Nu 'd
Al Ḥasf
Djebel as Sahl
Djebel Badīya '
Jūbat al Jadidah
Wa 'lān
Wādī 'Ashshár
Wādī az Zimmār
Harib
An Nuqub
Wādī al Ghawlah
Dāf
Zarājah
YEMEN
Bayḥān al Qaṣāb
Djebel Ḥadād
Ma 'bar
Al Jum 'ah 'fri
Dawrān
ARAB
Madinat ash Shirq
Dhamār 'wed
3190
REPUBLIC
Rubu 'Utmah
Dubāh
Abāsir
Djebel Isbīl
Ad Dar 'ah
Radā 'a
Wādī Ḥamd
Djebel al Qullah
Dj. Mathuwah
Mawkal
As Sawwādīyah
Aṭ Ṭaffah
Arām
Djebel Riyām
Wādī Zabid
Yarīm 'sun
Ar Raḍmah
Ẓulmah 'fri
As Saddah
Damt
Djebel Mudīr ad Dār
Al Munqaṭi'
Al Bayḍā'
'Uwayn
Al 'Udayn
Al Makhādir
An Nādirah
Az Ẓāhir
Mukayrās
Djebel Nu 'mān
Ibb
Ar Raḍā 'ī
Naqīl Zubar
Juban
Mirarah
Djebel al Maḍraḥ
Jiblah
Djebel at Ta 'kar
Dhī Sufāl
Najd al Jumā 'ī
Qa 'tabah
Djebel Kisād
Lawdar
2750
Al Musajid
Dj. ad Dāmigh
Ar Rubū'
Al Qā 'idah
2790
Ta 'izz Airport
Djebel Sawraq
Māwiyah
Wādī Banā
Ta 'izz
Dj. Sabir
Al Misrākh 'thu
Ad Dimnah 'fri
Musaymir
PEOPLE'S
Shuqrā
Najd an Nashamah
Ar Rāḥidah
Adh Dhirā'
Djebel aṣ Salw
Ḥayfān
Al Faqarah
Wādī Tuban
At Turbah
Al Kishrār
DEMOCRATIC REP. OF
Zinjibār
GULF OF ADEN
YEMEN
Al Manṣūrah
Shaykh 'Uthmān
Little Aden
Aden
Ra 's al 'Ārah
Dār am 'Umayrah

Weekday of market   'wed

Sana 'ā' to Ta 'izz page 243 - 254
Ta 'izz and the South page 259 - 265

Aden and into the Wadi Hardramaut page 288 - 294

242

FROM SANA'A TO TA'IZZ

A good asphalt road, built with technical aid from West Germany, ensures that the 159 miles (256 km) journey from the Bab al-Yemen in Sana'a to Ta'izz takes no more than just over five hours. Right outside Sana'a the road runs first of all through a recently built-up area which lies on the plateau of **Sanhan** and shows how much the capital has expanded over the past few years. Shortly before the end of the city one of the big *qat* markets is held. Farmers from the area sell the popular fresh branches and shoots of the *qat* plants from sheds, little tents or just off the backs of their Toyotas.

A distance of 25 miles (40 km) beyond Sana'a, all along to the 9,816 feet (2,800 metre) high **Naqil Yislah** (Yislah Pass), the scenery remains fairly monotonous. At the crown of the pass above the plateau of **Ma'bar** there is a majestic Turkish fort. Despite its sinister military architectural style, it blends completely with the landscape. This fortress guards a point that has always been of strategic importance: everyone who travelled along the north-south route from Sana'a to Ta'izz had to pass through this place which can be seen from all sides.

The plain of Ma'bar is a fertile region which is intensively cultivated. The fertility of the volcanic soil, the broad extent of the shallow basin and the all-important level of the water table permit mechanised, large-scale agriculture. Many farms, traditionally run as well as modern, mechanised ones, line the road. The village of **Ma'bar** itself is a small peasant village, its mudbrick architecture reminiscent of the farms and buildings of the north. To everyone's surprise, the mudbrick buildings of Ma'bar survived the earthquake of 1982 relatively unscathed, in contrast to the fate of stone buildings.

Earthquake zone: The many new buildings in this area are very noticeable. Cubic in shape and with only one floor, these concrete boxes are hardly suited to the traditional Yemeni way of life. These houses, which conform to anti-seismic standards, were built after the 1982 earthquake, financed by friendly Gulf states and erected with technical aid from Japan.

The earthquake claimed more than 2,000 victims and completely or partially destroyed 180 villages. The Dhamar region in particular was badly damaged and suffered great loss of life. Before 1982, Yemen had not been considered an especially endangered earthquake zone and had therefore not been equipped with seismic recording stations. However, the whole length of the country borders the eastern coast of the Red Sea, which is still in a stage of geomorphological development. As a result, Yemen suffers from the consequences of this instability. The 1982 earthquake was not the first. As early as 1941, two earthquakes were recorded in the region. In addition, a chain of volcanoes crosses the region. One of them, Mount Haras, erupted in 1937, and three more in the Damt region and around Djebel Zufar near Raydah were active in the first century A.D.

Westwards from Ma'bar: The road that links Ma'bar to the Tihama was completed only a few years ago by the Koreans. It winds its way through a mountainous region of volcanic origin, where pillars of basalt have been eroded into fantastic shapes and vertigo-inducing crevices. There are places to stop along the road and admire the view of this moon-like landscape. At Kilometre 15 you will come to **Dawran**, which has often served as a refuge for members of the Zaidi royal family. The mosque here is remarkable, resembling that of Ar Rawdah near Sana'a and also built in the Turkish style with a minaret of terracotta bricks.

The pass at Djebel Dawran at Kilometre 50 marks a steep drop in the direction of **Madinat ash-Shirq**, a small and busy town which has also profited from the building of the asphalt road and is rapidly expanding more and more. In earlier times it was known as Madinat al-Abid (the Town of Slaves), as the name suggests, was mostly inhabited by the descendants of slaves. During a visit by President Ibrahim al-Hamdi the town was summarily renamed Madinat ash-Shirq (Town of the Orient). The asphalt road runs on through partially desert-like country to **Bajil** and into the Tihama.

A well-built track from Madinat ash-Shirq allows you to return to the Ta'izz-Sana'a route, which is not without interest for tourists. You pass the little thermal spa resort of **Hammam Ali**, where the Yemenis come to cure rheumatic and arthritic illnesses in the hot sulphuric springs. There are several small places offering accommodation, neatly divided into rooms for men and for women, which act as a spa hotel.

Southwards from Ma'bar: The Sana'a-Ta'izz route runs through the newly built areas of Dhamar; the old town, which is well worth seeing, lies off the road to the east. Dhamar is the highest town in Yemen with the exception of Yarim, and its founding can be traced back to pre-Islamic times. It is only a few miles away from what was the Himyar capital of Zafar, and is bound to have been an important trading centre.

As Dhamar dominated a wide area, it was frequently a place of refuge for the Zaidi Imams at various times in its history, and was also the seat of one of the major theological universities of the *madhab zayidit*, a Shi'ite sect. Numerous mosques house tombs of various Imams and their fine sarcophagi of stone or carved wood (Imam Yahya ibn-Hamza, 14th century; Imam al-Mutahar, 15th century; Imam al-Kacem, 16th century).

Artistic building in stone in medieval Jiblah.

The plain of Dhamar was once famous as the breeding ground for the best Arab horses (one good example is the Dhamar stud farms). Marco Polo once wrote that Yemen exported "a great number of good Arab battle horses, horses and stud stallions with two saddles" to India.

Dhamar is surrounded by a mudbrick wall, of which only the eastern section survives, and offers the greatest variety of building styles in the whole country. The styles, from stone houses in all sorts of colours to mudbrick towers, are similar to those found in Sana'a, but do not equal the magnificence and the fine detail of the façades to be found in the capital. In earlier years the town was divided into a Turkish, a Jewish and a Muslim quarter. The different faiths lived side by side and left behind a harmonious and homogenous architecture. Unfortunately, the earthquake of 1982 had destroyed a large part of the old town. Many of the families and businessmen affected had to leave their houses in the town centre and move outside the town walls to houses along the Sana'a-Ta'izz road.

Eastwards from Dhamar: From Dhamar the highland plateau extends further in an easterly direction as far as the two important towns of Rada'a and Al Bayda. A difficult track branches northwards off the same route near **Djebel Isbil** (10,466 feet/3,190 metres), leading to the ancient site of **Baynun**. As the former capital, Baynun was, before its destruction in 525 by the Abyssinians, one of the most beautiful cities of pre-Islamic South Arabia. Today only a huge area of ruins and the remains of an enormous irrigation system can be seen.

To the south of the ruined city, in the town of Al-Nunrah, inscriptions have survived above the entrance to a tunnel. The Yemeni chronicler Al Hamdani wrote: "Baynun was pierced..., so that a flow of water could be brought from the lands beyond to the region of Baynun." The massive tunnels through the mountain were once used to supply the neigh-

In Rada'a, on the edge of the desert, mudbrick buildings are common.

bouring valleys with water and are now used by the farmers of the area as pedestrian short cuts. There is definitely a need for large-scale field research in Baynun in order to produce excavations worthy of the whole complex of royal castle, historic town and mountain tunnels. The drive from Dhamar to Baynun can only be undertaken in an overland vehicle and with the appropriate permit. It covers a difficult stretch of track and takes about three hours.

RADA'A

This town, which is not much visited by tourists, dates back to pre-Islamic times, as is shown by a number of historic finds (ruins, stone blocks with South Arabian inscriptions, remains of ancient irrigation systems). The fortress or *hosn*, situated on a rocky mountain peak, houses a number of treasures from Himyar times: inscriptions, water cisterns, granaries, and pillars. Up until the last civil war the fortress of Rada'a has had to suffer repeated sieges and re-

building. Today it is a military installation and as such cannot be visited.

After the defeat of the Rasulid dynasty, the Tahirids (1454-1517) became rulers of Ta'izz, Zabid and Aden in south Yemen (al-Yaman al-Asfal). They then turned their attention towards the north, but had to be contented with making Rada'a their capital, after Imam Al-Nasir successfully blocked their way to Sana'a.

The Tahirids, who believed that they could trace their descent back to the Umayyids, actually belonged to the powerful confederation of the *madhedj*, mountain tribes of the Rada'a region. Their rule has left behind a number of mainly religious buildings, such as the mosque of Yafrus, the mosque of Rada'a and a few madressas in the Tihama. They contributed to the development of agriculture by building irrigation systems and walls of earth as a protection against erosion. The slow economic decline of Yemen which began towards the end of Rasulid rule

Inner courtyard of the mosque and tomb of Queen Arwa.

could not be stopped by the Tahirids. The country was much weakened politically and economically by the boycott of Indian ships, which no longer moored in the harbour of Aden.

Rada'a is famous for its mudbrick architecture. The tall houses with their pale colours (made from the type of mud found in this area) have foundations and ground floors built of blocks of stone. There are a few old houses around the market square which have upper storeys with terracotta bricks and façades with friezes in the Sana'a style, old alabaster window panes or finely carved wooden shutters. The heart of the old town is the market with its narrow streets and tiny shops, whose displays of spices, scents, grain and fruit contribute to the charm of the town.

The Al Amariyyah Mosque: Built under the rule of the emir Amir Abdel-Wahab Ibn Taher around the year 1512, the mosque is impressive mainly on account of its unique style. It has no minaret, but a marvellous dome with Indian influence. Also unique is its elevated position on a platform which has ground-level loggias opening towards the town. The space beneath is occupied by a tall caravanserai, a basin for ritual cleansing and a women's mosque which lies beneath the main mosque. Inside, the ceiling of the loggia and the dome of the prayer hall are adorned with splendid stucco decorations, which are equal in splendour to the Ashrafiya Mosque in Ta'izz. The whole complex, which has become very dilapidated in recent years, is now being restored as part of an international project.

AL BAYDA

The "white town" of Al Bayda lies 112 miles (180 km) away from Dhamar, on the undefined border to South Yemen, and is built in a baroque plaster style. The colourfully painted houses reflect the influence of southern Yemen, which is more visible here than in Ta'izz. From Al Bayda a road leads to **Mukairaz** at the other side of the old

Coloured glass panes have ousted the old alabaster windows.

border in former South Yemen. It then makes a breathtaking descent to the plateau of Lawdar (see chapter "Aden to the Wadi Hadramaut").

Southwards from Dhamar: After about half an hour's drive from Dhamar along the Sana'a-Ta'izz road you come to the town of Yarim. At an altitude of 8,858 feet (2,700 metres) above sea level it is the highest town in Yemen. But the earthquake of 1982 had destroyed most of the buildings. A few small restaurants at the roadside offer good Yemeni food: *hulba*, a kind of ragout of small vegetables, with a mousse of grain, mutton, beef and chicken, as well as *selter*, the well-seasoned favourite dish of Yemen, or vegetable dishes with rice.

Not far beyond Yarim you turn off eastwards and arrive at another important Himyar capital.

ZAFAR■■■■■

Not much remains of the once famous capital of the Himyar. Stones scattered across a hillside, used by the inhabitants for building their houses, and a few small stables cut into the rock; these miserable remains are all that is left of the successor to Saba. In the neighbouring village of **Bayt al-Ashwal** a small museum is responsible for the upkeep of the archaeological site as attempts are made to collect the wealth scattered over the countryside.

The Himyar, a highland tribe, profited by the decline of the states on the borders of the desert had built a new state with its capital at Zafar. After conquering Saba in 328, the Himyar king turned his attention to Hadramaut and Yamamat, the modern territory of both Yemeni states.

However, the main event of this period is the conversion to Judaism, a process which seemed to parallel the conversion of the Aksumitic kingdom under King Azena. This confirms the desire of the Himyar not to be drawn into depency on the Roman Empire, which was very active in the Red Sea at this time. The period in which the

Women are an important part of the agricultural workforce.

Himyar flourished was, however, short (4th to 6th centuries).

Once the sources of South Arabian wealth had dried up, the political situation worsened, the deterioration speeded by tensions between Jews and Christians. This finally led the ruler Ash'ar Yath'ar (518) to strengthen his commitment to Judaism by persecuting the Christians of South Arabia, having them massacred and carrying out a military campaign against the province of Najran, where Christianity was widespread. The Aksumite empire did not delay and began a campaign against the Himyar king, defeating him in 570. This happened in the so-called Elephant Year, in which two other events of great importance for Arabia occurred: the bursting of the Ma'rib dam and the birth of the Prophet Mohammed.

Euphorbias on the basalt slopes between Ibb and Ta'izz.

DAMT

Travelling some 29 miles (47 km) from Yara in a southwesterly direction on an easily accessible road lies the "spa" of Damt. This asphalt road runs through an impressive and beautiful mountainous landscape of volcanic origin, including the fertile strip of the **Wadi Bana**. The extinct crater above the town can be climbed without difficulty by means of an iron ladder. At the bottom is a small lake, fed by underground springs. From the edge of the crater you can get a beautiful view of the surrounding area and of the extinct volcanoes. The hot springs and the hammam at the foot of the volcano are popular with the local people because of their healing powers. Men bathe in the mornings, and the springs are reserved for women in the afternoons. From Damt you can get to two other places by means of a track: **Al Madrah** and **As Sadah**, which has a very lively weekly market on Mondays.

NAQIL SUMARAH

The Sumarah pass with its height of 9,186 feet (2,800 metres) offers one of the finest views in all of Yemen. You

can look out over terraced fields, scattered farms and villages, valleys and wadis. On the other side of the Naqil Sumarah lies the *Al-Yaman al akhdar*, Green Yemen. This region does in fact have some of the best climatic conditions of the entire Arabian peninsula: temperate and moist in summer, but relatively dry in the winter. The monsoons provide sufficient amounts of rain. This intensively cultivated region had already given Yemen the name "Arabia felix" in ancient times.

IBB

The city of Ibb, at an altitude of 7,546 feet (2,300 metres), is the capital of the province and the fourth largest city in Yemen. Built on two opposing hills, Ibb has the appearance of a young and expanding city. However, just a few steps away from the main street in an easterly direction are enough for you to discover the remains of the fortifications and the old city. The houses are built entirely of stone blocks, in the same style as in Jiblah, and the windows display the same gypsum motifs which are commonly used. In the suq a variety of agricultural produce is for sale, as are a few craft items.

JIBLAH

In order to get to Jiblah, you have to leave the asphalt road of Ibb-Ta'izz and drive for about five miles (eight km) along a track which is dusty in summer and extremely slippery in the rainy season. However, whatever the time of year, you will drive through a fertile and pleasant green region. The lush vegetation along the edges of the wadis and the valley bottoms consists of acacias, eucalyptus, carob trees, cacti and spurges is an excellent scenery.

The town of Jiblah appears, hugging the hillside, once you cross the mountain ridge. It lies on a large outcrop of basalt, and is the perfect example of a homogenous town. It is built on a supporting wall and bordered by the ravines of two wadis which join again just

In the strict Zaidi town of Jiblah even young girls are veiled.

outside the town by two remarkable stone bridges.

First female ruler: Capital of the Ismaelite Sulayid dynasty in the 11th and 12th centuries, Jiblah still preserves the memory of Queen Arwa, the second legendary female figure after Bilqis the Queen of Sheba. Queen Arwa was one of the few Muslim women to rule a people and decide the fate of a nation. For a short time she succeeded in uniting the tribes and imposing her authority on them.

In 1037 Ali Ibn Muhammad as-Sulayhi, one of Queen Arwa's predecessors, first conquered the capital of the Ziyadite dynasty, Zabid, and then marched on to Sana'a, where he established his centre of power. This was the beginning of the Sulayid dynasty, who, under the leadership of the Fatimids of Egypt, succeeded in creating and maintaining an unprecedented unity of wide areas of Yemen.

After the disappearance of Ali Ibn Muhammad as-Sulayhi his son Al Mukarram, who was a paraplegic, had to surrender his position to his wife Arwa. She immediately moved the capital from Sana'a to Jiblah, in order to escape from the warlike tribes of the north. This exceptionally intelligent woman also put into practice important building construction, especially the building of road links between the capital and neighbouring provinces as well as a series of religious buildings. The expansion of the mosque of Sana'a and the building of the mosque of Jiblah both date back to Queen Arwa.

With its population of around 6,000, the majority of them Shafi'ites, Jiblah is a large trading centre in the midst of an agriculturally rich area, which has plenty of rain in the months beginning from June through September.

Jiblah, which is considered one of the most picturesque towns in Yemen, has preserved the traditional features of its skilful architecture. Tall, five-storeyed houses of stone blocks are arranged in harmonious rows on the hill and seem to

Young Yemenis are often charming and very ready to help.

interconnect with each other. The windows are large and numerous and are surrounded by friezes with motifs in white gypsum, *guss*. If you make your way through the narrow alleys you will recognise the variety of different façades, the work of talented and highly-skilled Yemeni craftsmen. The skilfully carved doors have iron knockers in the middle and are decorated with inscriptions from versus of the Koran. If you follow the narrow alleys, you will come to the cemetery, which offers a fine view of the town.

The former capital is a fine example of the planning that lies behind an Islamic town: a centre, marked by the large Friday mosque; nearby lies the permanent market, suq, consisting of tiny shops and craft workshops. The craftsmen and traders are organised in guilds and all have their traditional places in the suq. The house of the governor is somewhat to one side. Around this ensemble lies the living accommodation, segregated according to social status, and the connecting roads which link the town gates with the centre. In Jiblah the two very beautiful stone bridges, marking the main entrances to the town, also fulfil this function. The **American Hospital** near one of the bridges is run by American missionaries and is an important medical institution for the whole region.

The Great Mosque: The Great Mosque of Jiblah, one of the oldest and most beautiful in Yemen, was built in 1088 on ancient ruins by Queen Arwa. The style of the building has been strongly influenced, particularly in its structure and decoration, by the Fatimids. You get to the mosque via one of four gates, which are to be found in different places in the town: from the great square via some stone steps which run between two anterooms up to a terrace leads to the access of the main courtyard; from the market via an outer courtyard, which can still be entered with your shoes on, and which has a door adorned with fine inscriptions and stucco bas-

Yarim Zafar, the former Himyar capital.

reliefs. The door leads directly into the hall of prayer in the direction of the qiblah, the wall which faces Mecca. This entrance crosses an alley in the market like a bridge. Finally, you can gain entrance to the mosque from the houses and homes of the town by going in the direction of the madressa, from which point you get to the inner courtyard or, going in a slightly roundabout way, pass the ritual cleansing basins.

At the southern corner of the mosque there are two minarets. The tower at the southwestern corner is the older, although it has only recently been rebuilt, dating from the 14th or 15th century. The second, more recent and taller, is decorated with bas-reliefs in stucco.

In the **main courtyard** there are arcades and galleries providing a welcome shade for prayers or Koran schools. A little fountain shaped like a dome and a water basin occupies the southern corner of the courtyard.

The **hall of prayer** has a high, vaulted central transom reaching from the courtyard to the qiblah wall. Several rows of arcades support the ceiling, which is still partly panelled with old wood, most likely of cedar wood. The minbar, or seat of prayer, to the right of the mirhab, the prayer niche, points towards Mecca.

In the western corner is the **tomb** of **Queen Sayed Arwa Bint Ahmed**, which is slightly hidden behind a high wall. It is adorned with magnificently carved inscriptions from the Koran, *kufikes*, in beautiful calligraphy. The mosque is one of the few that can be visited by non-Muslims, but only on condition that they remove their shoes, dress modestly, behave quietly and avoid the hours of prayer – especially on Fridays. Apart from the great Friday mosque, Jiblah also has two other important houses of prayer as well as a number of smaller mosques in the various quarters around town.

Like most small towns in Yemen, Jiblah, despite the large number of tourists, has no hotels but only two smallish

The road across Naqil Sumarah has now been asphalted.

funduks or guest houses which offer modest comforts.

Around Jiblah there are many opportunities for hiking, for instance in the direction of **Djebel at-Taker** (2,007 feet/3,230 metres). This region, with its picturesque villages and farms, is especially beautiful even in the rainy season, when cascade-like waterfalls fill the surrounding wadis. If you want to carry on in the direction of Ta'izz, it is worth while taking the old footpath to **Naqil as-Sayani** (8,202 feet/2,500 metres). This way you will come to the Ibb-Ta'izz road once more.

From the crown of the pass you can get to the large trading centre of **Al Qa'idah**, from which you can already see the mountains of Ta'izz, located in Yemen's southern highlands. Many tourist sites worth stopping for are found in Ta'izz. About eight miles (12 km) before Ta'izz, and before you get to the airport, the four-mile (six-km) long track to Al Janad branches off.

AL JANAD ▬▬▬▬

Al Janad's fame in Yemen and throughout the Islamic world is due to the glories of its past and to its mosque, which shares the honour of being the oldest mosque in Yemen with the Great Mosque in Sana'a. It was built in the 7th century by a companion and pupil of the Prophet, Mu'ad Ibn Jabal, the designated caliph of the province.

Al Janad was the most important of the three *miklaf*, administrative areas, which comprised South Arabia at the time of annexation to the great Arab caliphate at the beginning of the Islamic era. Unfortunately, nothing remains of the town today except for an uninteresting little village, as Al Janad lost its position to Ta'izz at the height of the Rasulid period.

Al-Hamdani, the great 10th-century historian of Yemen, claimed that Al Janad was the first mosque on Yemeni soil. This fact has not been definitely confirmed one way or the other to this day. None the less, the Al Janad mosque is the goal of many pilgrimages, which are considered almost as important as a visit to the holy places in Mecca. The clarity and strictness of its lines give the mosque an almost modern appearance. In the course of history it has suffered destruction several times during tribal wars and campaigns. It was therefore rebuilt in 981–1011 by a vizier of the royal court of the Zabid dynasty and again in 1105, this time completely in stone, by a minister of the Sulayid dynasty during the reign of Queen Arwa Bint Ahmed. After the mosque caught fire during an attack in 1130, suffering heavy damage, it was restored again in 1184. Since that time the mosque of Al Janad has undergone no noteworthy changes. The last restoration was done in 1973–74. But it was not done according to the high standards expected.

The mosque surrounds a large courtyard, framed by arcades which are carried by round, well-proportioned pillars. In the centre of the inner courtyard an upright little stone pillar serves as a sundial for the hours of prayer. A 230-foot (70-metre) high minaret towers above the mosque, with a stone bearing the name of Allah set into its foundations. This stone, together with the ritual cleansing basins, has withstood destruction and renewal better than the rest of the mosque.

The town of Al Janad itself is a popular stop for taxi drivers and bus parties, who take a break in one of the many grill restaurants.

The final drive of six miles (10 km) or so in the direction of Ta'izz goes through the collection of garages and car repair workshops common to all towns. Just before Ta'izz on the right-hand side you can see the Luna Park, which is visited by many Yemenis, particularly on the Islamic weekends. If you don't take the trouble to visit the park, it is enough to switch on the television in order to see it. Many programmes featuring Yemeni musicians are filmed in this park and broadcast in the early evening programme.

Impressive, but hard to get to: the tunnel at Baynun.

TA'IZZ AND THE SOUTH

Ta'izz is impressively located at 4,593 feet (1,400 metres) above sea level in a narrow valley at the base of the rugged **Djebel Sabir** mountains in Yemen's southern highlands, about 165 miles (265 km) south of Sana'a. Little is known about the founding and the history of the city prior to the Rasulid period (1229–1454), except that Turanshah, the brother of Salah-Eddine (1137–93), the famous Saladin of the crusaders) sought out this place because of its healthy climate and its abundant water resources. Ta'izz does indeed enjoy a temperate climate, a kind of eternal spring.

After Imam Ahmed allowed his warriors to plunder and burn Sana'a in 1948, Ta'izz served as his capital for 14 years, until the revolution of 1962. Once the second largest city in the former Yemen Arab Republic, today it has lost this position to the port city of Al Hudaydah on the Red Sea coast, and of course, since the unification of the country in 1990, to Aden. It remains to be seen just how far Ta'izz can maintain its importance in the united Yemen of today. But as it now provides a vital link on the road from Aden to Sana'a, it seems very likely that industry will continue to be located here in the future.

Ta'izz has undergone rapid development and urbanisation in recent years. The general appearance of the city reflects a modern and recently built urban area, even though it was the capital of the Beni Rasul dynasty from as early as the 13th to the 15th centuries. You can still see part of the former fortified walls which still exists around the old town, and the walls also surround the colourful and lively market. Within the city walls there are also a number of fine historic buildings to be found, among

them are the remains of the Rasulid period which are considered to be the most important historic buildings to be found in Yemen today.

The Rasulid dynasty: In 1171 Salah-Eddine, the first Ayyubid ruler, overthrew the Fatimids from Egypt and reintroduced Sunnism to the people. In order to strengthen the sovereignty of the Baghdad caliphate over all its predecessors and to exterminate all forms of Ismaelism, he sent his brother Turanshah to Arabia. He was to subjugate Yemen and unite the principalities which had arisen since the Sulayids. But his rule lasted only a short time.

When King Massaoud, the last governor of Yemen, died, a leader named Umar Ibn al-Rasul, descendant of a family in the diplomatic service under the Ayyubids, took power in 1229. He established his rule first over Zabid, then occupied Ta'izz and took Sana'a without meeting any resistance. He entrusted the administration of Sana'a to his nephew. Within a year he had become ruler of all Yemen and even had his own coinage minted. Word of Salah-Eddine's power expanded rapidly and soon reached from Aden to Mecca.

For many years under the rule of the Rasulids, Yemen experienced a period of peace and prosperity. There was a remarkable boom in urban building. The Rasulids, as great builders and architects particularly of religious buildings, have left historic buildings which can still be seen today in Zabid and Ta'izz.

Throughout the centuries Zabid has been the final stop for many travellers and merchants to Yemen. Coming from Mokha, they often had to wait in Ta'izz for months for word from the Imam, which in the end usually forbade the further journey to Sana'a anyway. But even as late as the 1970s Ta'izz was still the gateway to Yemen. The first groups of tourists came from Djibouti to Ta'izz. During the long years of the civil war and in the first months of the new republic, too, most foreign embassies were based in Ta'izz. The German ambassador at that time, Günther Pawelke, describes the arduous and at times dangerous journey to Sana'a across the Sumarah pass (without asphalt roads during that time) in his book *Jemen – das verbotene Land* ("Yemen – the Forbidden Country").

The old city: In earlier years the city of Ta'izz was surrounded by a thick city wall flanked by towers. Within the walls was the citadel Al Qahira, set on a hill 394 feet (120 metres) high and one of the residences of the Beni Rasul, dominated the city. This site has now been declared a historic monument after the discovery of armouries, secret passages and objects dating from the 13th to the 15th centuries. Ever since the military took over the building, which is now used as a barracks, visits have become very difficult but are still sometimes possible.

The suq: Smaller and more poorly organised than the market of Sana'a, the suq of Ta'izz lies on the road linking the the two former city gates of Bab al-Kabir and Bab Mussa. Here you can find textiles imported from Asia, old silver jewellery (sometimes much cheaper than those found in Sana'a), *djambias*, the curved daggers of the Yemenis, narghiles, spices, scents and much more.

The fruit, vegetable and meat market, which has been banished outside the city walls near the Bab Mussa, is very busy in the mornings when *qat*, honey and pastries made of dough and goat's cheese, a speciality of the region, are displayed for sale. In the suq of Ta'izz you will often see women doing the selling. The women of Djebel Sabir are famous for their independence, their self-sufficiency and their beauty.

If, when still in the old city, you take the first street to branch off from the market at a right angle, you will discover *hammam* (public baths) and *madressa* (Koran schools). Three

The Ashrafiya mosque with the remains of the old fortified wall.

mosques can also be seen, which are considered to be among the most beautiful and most respected by far in the whole of Yemen. Some of them can be visited by tourists, as long as you show appropriate respect for the sacred places, dress decently and avoid visits during the hours of prayer and on Friday afternoons.

The Al Muzaffar Mosque: Blinding white and of a perfect and complex architectural style, this is the oldest mosque in Ta'izz and dates as far back as the first half of the 13th century. Three great domes tower above it. The central one, above the mirhab or prayer niche, points towards Mecca, the other two cover the outer ends of the large hall of prayer. Inside, the domes are richly decorated with stucco reliefs, which display verses from the Koran in beautiful calligraphy together with decorative motifs. The mirhab is closed to the outside world except for a small open extension, the upper part of this extension is richly decorated with a geometric frieze right across the façade. The mosque had only one minaret, which was destroyed early this century and was never rebuilt.

The Al Ashrafiya Mosque: This mosque was built on a hill at the foot of Djebel Sabir and with its two white minarets is visible all over the city. The mosque, because of its situation, seems to grow out of the city. It was built in two stages, 1295–97 and 1376–1400, under the rule of two Rasulid sultans, Ashraf I and Ashraf II. From these kings it received its name, Al Ashrafiya. The mosque consists of a rectangular courtyard and a hall of prayer, roofed by eight small domes which surround a large central dome. The whole mosque is completely covered with beautiful decorative calligraphy.

The madressa which adjoins the courtyard and the ritual cleansing basins, which are equipped with an ingenious channeling and draining system, contribute greatly to the charm of the mosque. The state department of his-

Centre of pilgrimage in the south: the mosque of Yafrus.

toric monuments, working together with UNESCO, has emphasised the historic and cultural importance of the mosque and for this reason set up a project to restore the building and classify its features.

The Al Mu'tabiya Mosque: This is the third of the historically and artistically interesting mosques and is architecturally similar to the Al Ashrafiya Mosque, but it differs in one aspect–this mosque has only six elegant domes and one hall of prayer. An old Koran school borders the mosque, and a corridor leads to the beautiful basins for the ritual washing before prayers.

The former Imam's palace: Situated in the eastern part of the city, the former palace of the Imam is now a museum which enjoys worldwide respect. Built in beautiful Sana'a style of fired mudbrick, it was the residence of Imam Ahmed until his last days (1962). Even after the revolution the palace was left in its original condition. In the guard room on the ground floor there is an exhibit of photos showing martyrs of the revolution and scenes of public executions, intended to document the cruelty of the Imam. History books and archaeological finds which have recently been discovered in the citadel of Al Qahira complete the display.

The other rooms have not been changed since the last days of the Imam. They contain a great confusion of objects which resembles a flea market. A strange mixture of perfumes, gifts from various state guests, clocks and medals, clothing and plate, weapons and festive robes of the Imam, radios and household articles are on display in glass cases. On the ground floor is the Imam's own room filled with his most important and favourite possessions.

The museum is, in all respects, surprising, and is worthy of attention insofar as it reflects the life of an Arab monarch in the 20th century, apparently suffocated by the achievements of the Western world. In this strange museum, perhaps more than anywhere else, you

The women of the south are experienced dealers.

can get an impression of life in Yemen in the 1950s and '60s.

The Saleh Palace: The second palace of the Royal family, also located in the eastern part of Ta'izz, lies on a higher ground and offers a panaromic view over the whole city. This palace has also been turned into a museum, and apart from a few archaeological discoveries it houses a wide collection of coins, silver jewellery and an exhibition of Yemeni crafts. In the courtyard is the private zoo of the Imam where you can see the last survivor of his 10 lions.

AROUND TA'IZZ

With an altitude of 10,131 feet (3,070 metres), **Djebel Sabir** and its scattered villages tower above Ta'izz. The architecture of the settlements is simple and modest and displays no special features. Your reception at the hands of the people of Djebel Sabir will be warm and friendly. The women are unveiled and wear heavy gold jewellery. They are famous for their wealth and beauty.

Around Djebel Sabir, in contrast to the rest of Yemen, it is the women who carry out trade. There are theories that speak of a former matriarchy around Djebel Sabir. There is, however, no historical foundation for this claim. It can only be assumed that these women belong to an agricultural tribe which lives entirely on its own produce, and in which the women play an important part in economic and social life.

If you leave Ta'izz along the road to Mokha, a good asphalt road leaves it at Kilometre 5, running south through a very fertile region. In the peaceful mountain oases, fruitful and green, fields of grain alternate with papayas, mangos, guava and pomegranate. At harvest time, all this produce is sold by the women in the markets.

AL HUJJARIAH

Al Hujjariah has given its name to the whole region in this paradise of "Arabia felix". The majority of the population of this densely settled area live by agricul-

ture. Only about 10 percent of the men work abroad–in Aden, East Africa, England or the USA – a lower figure for other parts of Yemen. The economic wealth of the area is reflected, too, in the town of Al Hujjariah with its very fine and large buildings, where modern and traditional styles are for once favourably combined.

AT TURBAH

About 47 miles (75 km) away from Ta'izz, crowning the edge of the mountain range which runs through Yemen from north to south, lies At Turbah at a height of 5,905 feet (1,800 metres). Dominated by a rather grim-looking architectural style based on blocks of stone, it is the main town of the region with an important market serving the needs of the outlying communities.

At Turbah is situated just to the north of the former South Yemen border. But even after unification there are no plans for a better connection to the south as the impressive **Plateau of Maqatirah**

presents too much of an obstacle. The mild climate and the plentiful supply of water are in sharp contrast to the regions which lie beyond – some of the driest and hottest parts of the Arabian peninsula. In fine weather, when it is not too hazy, you can see the Gulf of Aden from the highest point of this plateau, as well as the Bab al Mandeb, the "gateway of tears" to the Red Sea. The straits got their name from the slave convoys that once passed through.

Suq Ad-Dabab: On the south side of Djebel Sabir is a series of villages surrounded by fields with lush vegetation. The Wadi Ad Dabab lies five miles (eight km) from Ta'izz. On Sundays the weekly market is held in the bed of the wadi. It offers a colourful range of local products for sale. At the edge of the market a big livestock market is held, selling dromedaries, cattle, sheep and goats. It is exciting and interesting to watch the dealing, even if you don't **Raisin seller** understand the language. The shouting **in the suq of** and the bargaining, the gestures and **Ta'izz.**

movements of the dealers are not only entertaining but also give a glimpse of daily Yemeni life. Also noticeable in the market are the women of Djebel Sabir, in colourful robes and with yellow make-up on their faces – they use a mixture based on curcuma and egg yolk, as a sun protection and also for reasons of vanity. Trade in the market is firmly in their hands.

YAFRUS

The town of Yafrus is famous for its gleaming white mosque, with its water basins still fed by a functioning aqueduct. The water comes from a spring located three miles away and first runs through the town in a system of underground channels. It then flows in a *segya*, an open-air channel which runs along an arcaded aqueduct, reflecting the architecture of the mosque.

The mosque was built in honour of the marabout or Islamic saint Ahmed Ibn Alwan, who was a scribe at the Rasulid court. He was weaned on Islamic studies and had also studied at a Sufi school, and he founded a Koran school in order to oppose the Shi'ite Zaidi branch of Islam in the north.

Honoured and respected by the Sunni population of the south, Ibn Alwan also received support from the Rasulid sultans who had recently come to power. Legend claims that he died at the age of 117, and he was buried in Yafrus. One of his pupils. Amer Ibn Abdul-Wahab, the last king of the Beni Tahar dynasty with their capital in Rada'a, built this mosque in Yafrus in the 16th century as a sign of gratitude, and the mosque is still one of the holiest places in Yemen.

Various religious festivals are celebrated here, for instance the birthday of the Prophet and Idd. During some ceremonies self-inflicted wounding and sacrifices take place. However, the practice of self-flagellation is becoming more and more of a tourist attraction, as fake penitents await the arrival of tourists in order to perform the ceremony for a few rials.

Young beauty in her Sunday best.

A distance of 72 miles (116 km) separate Ta'izz from the former port of Al Mokha. Road transportation in Yemen has been heavily financed by foreign aid. For example, the United States helped build the road from Ta'izz to Mokha. On the way you drive through a number of lively towns and villages, of which the permanent market in **Al-Barah** is the most interesting. Apart from the usual products, a number of traditional sesame and mustard seed mills can be seen and bought here. The oils are used for craft purposes (for instance in the working of leather) or for cosmetic uses. Al-Barah marks the end of the fertile mountain oases, and gradually you enter a desert-like, barren landscape, the beginnings of the Tihama.

Mafraq is a collection of petrol stations and corrugated iron huts, which offer the opportunity of buying smuggled alcohol at lower prices than in Sana'a. Don't forget that the purchase of alcohol is punishable by law.

MANAKHAH AND THE HARRAZ RANGE

Sana'a to Djebel Harraz: Leaving the main road from Sana'a, you come to the route to Al Hudaydah via the Az Zubayri road. From **Djebel Asr** you can get a good view of the whole of Sana'a. Here there are two **mausoleums**, right next to each other and in the smallest possible space. The first was built in memory of Egyptian soldiers who died in the civil war in Yemen (1962-67). The second mausoleum, in the form of a pagoda, is a reminder that the building of this road was by the Chinese, and those who died while building the road.

The impressive height (10,695 feet/ 3,260 metres) of the pass of Djebel Ayban rises in the midst of a wide mountainous landscape. From here you can see, on the right-hand side, the tallest mountain of the entire Middle East, **Djebel an-Nabi Shu'ayb** (12,368 feet/ 3,770 metres). The road is twisted and narrow, and a few of the curves are dangerous and surprising. It is very busy due to trucks driving from Hudaydah, the main port of the country, to Sana'a. Nearly all goods traffic uses this route, as there are no trains in Yemen. At Kilometre 50 you have a fine panoramic view of the valley of **Al Haymah** with its countless terraces and its little farms and villages clinging to the hillside. At Kilometre 80, at the level of the village of **Magrabah**, you leave the main route to turn off left in the direction of **Manakhah**, the capital of the province of Harraz.

DJEBEL HARRAZ

Djebel Harraz, 50 miles (80 km) away from Sana'a, gives its name to the whole surrounding region. Because of its position, which has always been of strategic importance, the area around Djebel Harraz has always occupied a key position in military matters. On every peak of Djebel Harraz a fortress guards this, the only possible way through from the Tihama to the capital of Sana'a: Hosn Bayh, Hosn Shibam, Hosn Masar, Hosn Saafan; check first as some of these forts are still used by the military today.

A former caravan station in Himyar times, this area was also a bastion of the Sulayids, a vassal dynasty of the Fatimids, who settled in Yemen from 1037 on. The area around Djebel Harraz and its centre of Manakhah was an important point for the realisation of Turkish interests in Yemen during the 18th and 19th centuries.

The fame of this area is based equally on the beauty of its mountain ranges and the unique nature of its villages, which cling to the peaks of the mountains in the most incredible and dangerous-looking positions. The architecture is splendid and impressive, an excellent

Preceding pages: evening light in the Harraz range. Left, early in the morning the clouds start to rise from the Tihama. Right, Al Hajjarah.

example of how to plan fortified housing and at the same time make the best possible use of the space available for cultivation. The villages are designed like fortresses, with the houses themselves acting as the walls. Pressed one against the other, they present an unconquerable bulwark to the outside world and blend completely with the landscape. It is often impossible to determine where the rock ends and the village begins. This harmony is due to the use of local building materials, especially stone (sandstone and basalt in shades of green, pink and grey), of which the Yemen masons make skilful use. They fit the stones together carefully and decorate the façades with chalk-white geometric patterns, in order to adorn the fronts of the houses to liven up the entrances.

The fashioning of terraces and the cultivation of the mountains in stepped fields has been carried out here in such a fine and impressive manner that you stand in admiration in front of this masterpiece, which has been maintained by farmers and masons and has survived for thousands of years.

In this centre of former coffee cultivation, which has not yet been quite abandoned, these terraces also grow a wealth of grain: millet, rye, wheat, barley, as well as lentils and beans.

MANAKHAH

In the heart of this majestic massif, Manakhah is a large market town whose houses line two or three hills and which reaches the other end of the valley. Just like other towns in Yemen, Manakhah has undergone economic and social changes since the revolution. It has become the most important town in the region and has sucked up the exodus of the surrounding villagers, who came to start small shops and businesses and to create a new town. Some recently erected buildings (e.g. the clinic, the bank, the school) have deliberately not been made too tall and therefore do not mar the skyline of the old town.

The rapidly expanding town of Manakhah is the centre of the Harraz region.

The oldest quarter is spread around the present large market square and stretches as far as the foot of Djebel Shibam. Narrow little alleys, lined by shops with finely carved wooden doors, lead to the suq, which lost its business to the larger shops around the market place. However, some of the small shops, such as those selling coffee, *qat* and groceries, have been able to keep their clients.

If you wind your way through the narrow alleys of the old town, you will see façades of beautiful houses of three to four storeys. The air-dried bricks in different colours have a wonderful decorative effect. The many narrow windows, surrounded by *guss* (a kind of gypsum), are mainly on the same level as the living accommodation. Some are covered by metal grids, bands of iron which function as *moucharabieh*. Many Yemeni Jews used to live in Manakhah, but left the Harraz area after the founding of the state of Israel.

Despite the fame of the Harraz region and the number of tourists, there is only one *funduk* in Manakhah which offers overnight accommodation and food. A new *funduk* is due to open soon, however. Manakhah also has a postal and telecommunications service, a small clinic and a pharmacy.

Around Manakhah: The eastern slopes of Djebel Harraz are scenically splendid. There are wonderful villages set on unconquerable peaks, in the midst of terraces planted with cereals, *qat* or coffee. Of special interest are the villages of **Al Khadi**, **Al Jabal**, **Beni Merrah and Kahil**, which is situated directly above Manakhah. However, **Al Houdaib** is particularly important.

Djebel Harraz is the **Ismaili** region of Yemen, and Houdaib is an important place of pilgrimage. The community of Ismailis, who came into being in Iran after the revolt of the Qarmats, was introduced into Yemen in the 12th century by the Sulayids. The Sulayids first reinforced their position in Djebel Harraz before going on to besiege Sana'a

The patterns are not just for decoration– they are supposed to turn evil away.

and finally settling in the region around Jiblah. The Ismaili community in Yemen is estimated at about 5,000 members–the Bohara's. The term comes from their *da'i* (preacher or imam), Muhammad Borhan-Eddin, the 52nd Ismaili Imam Dawdite now 76 years old lives in India. The Bohara's do not recognise the authority of the most respected spiritual head of the Ismailis, the Aga Khan. The community in Yemen, just like the one in India, follows a very esoteric doctrine whose main belief is that God is manifested more by emanation than by revelation.

Since they were persecuted for a long time by the Zaidi Imams, the Ismailis have gathered together in the almost unassailable villages of Djebel Harraz. They live, up to a certain point, in a community where property and work are shared, they marry within the community, and their women enjoy great independence. Their long history, linked with the Qarmats of Irak, has given them the reputation in the eyes of many a historian of being predecessors of socialism. Today the Ismailis have a good relationship with their Yemeni fellow citizens.

AL HOUDAIB

This little village, in the midst of a magnificent and majestic landscape, is about four miles (six km) away from Manakhah and can be reached by a track which winds its way through the mountainous massif. It has remained a small place of pilgrimage, which welcomes co-religionists from India, Sri Lanka, Singapore or Madagascar. A small mausoleum houses the tomb of the Yemeni *da'i* Hatem Ibn Ibrahim al-Hamdani, who lived during the 16th century. Stone steps lead up to the rock above Houdaib.

AL HAJJARAH

At a height of 7,546 feet (2,300 metres), about 30 minutes away from Manakhah on foot, lies the old fortified village of al Hajjarah. Since a few years

The whole village helps with the harvest.

ago there has been a track, bumpy and steep, leading up to the village, but you should only drive on it in dry weather. At first glance the village looks like a collection of houses packed tightly together, growing out of a huge block of rock. You should walk around this block in order to see for yourself that these houses really do cling to the rock without excavated foundations. Al Hajjarah is a fortified military settlement, and its foundation dates back to the Sulayids (12th century). It served as a fortress to protect respected people and dignitaries from attack. In the interior the inhabitants constructed several cisterns and granaries, so that Al Hajjarah (just like Thula or Kawkaban) could withstand a siege lasting several months without supply problems. A group of houses below the city wall were the homes of Jewish craftsmen, who made weapons for the Sulayids.

Al Hajjarah is undisputably one of the finest examples of mountain architecture in Yemen. The ochre stone houses are built in a harmonious style and have several floors (four or five), with the lower floors remaining windowless for defensive reasons. There are only little holes or *harr* which provide air circulation. Only the inhabited floors have openings, round or rectangular windows which have wooden shutters and alabaster panes. The white coloration or *guss*, which has come into use quite recently in Djebel Harraz, is the only decoration. Al Hajjarah has around 400 inhabitants today. A large part of the population has moved to Manakhah, almost certainly for reasons of convenience. Others have built new houses on a plateau next to the fortress which can be reached by car.

The western slopes of Djebel Harraz are just as varied and interesting as the eastern ones. There are several fortified villages scattered across this very craggy massif. It is possible to tour the nearby area from Al Hajjarah on foot or in a jeep. By car you can get to **Bayt al-Qanes** and **Bayt Shemran**, the most important villages at the foot of Djebel Masar, from which you have a splendid far-reaching view as far as Djebel Saafan. You can also follow the track from Al Hajjarah and visit **Argaz** as well as other small villages along the track. If you take the time to plan two or three days for your stay in Manakhah, you should spend the time on walks through what is probably the most beautiful scenery in Yemen. All the places mentioned in this article–Manakhah, Kahil, Houdaib, Argaz, Hajjarah–can be reached in two or three days. The area has by now been opened up sufficiently and is visited by so many groups that hikes can be undertaken on your own initiative without any worries. If you do not want to spend the night in a *funduk*, bring a tent. Your tours can be extended further than the hikes, just as you want. For instance, you could make the descent through the coffee plantations to the Manakhah-Hudaydah road. You should not take photographs without permission.

Individual farms near Harraz.

FROM SHIBAM TO KHAMIS BANI SA'D

The Wadi Dahr Road leaves the Sana'a basin in a westerly direction, it passes through the new university area and climbs over a small pass to a high plateau. On the right one can soon see the two marble domes of the medical faculty, glittering in the sunlight. They were a present from the Kuwaiti state to the people of Yemen.

Further on you pass the white walls of the Yemen Drug Company and finally see the blue building of the mineral water factory Shamlam. After about a mile and a half (two km) the road, which actually leads to the Wadi Dahr, forks off to the left in the direction of Shibam and follows the course of the **Wadi Dulla'** up the valley. Originally, the intensively irrigated Wadi was planted full of fruit trees. In recent years, however, *qat* plantations have spread and the expensive shrubs now line both sides of the road.

Dulla'i *qat* in fact commands the highest prices in the markets. One can see the big houses of the "Upper Dulla" location before the road takes a sharp right turn and climbs up the bank of the Wadi. Yemeni leaders like to stress that the biggest house once belonged to the former President, Hussein al-Ghashmi. The wadi banks offer a beautiful view.

The road then leads via a high plateau to the entrance of another valley. A small bridge crosses the emerging Wadi Dahr at Kilometre 18 before the road follows along a mountain chain. If you don't mind taking a hike lasting several hours, you can walk the entire Wadi Dahr from the Rock Palace to this bridge and then return to Sana'a with a collective taxi.

The road climbs up to another high plateau and leads on the left past the picturesque village of **Al Ghurza**, which is built on a rock. According to the inhabitants, it is of Himyarite origin. They will also tell you about caves which in pre-Islamic times apparently served as graves.

After coming to another high plateau, the road leads directly towards the long mountain ridge of **Djebel Kawkaban**. On the left side of the mountain irregularly shaped rocky peaks come into view which, in fact, are the houses of the town of Kawkaban which can be seen already although it is still a good 32 miles (20 km) away. To the right the peak of Djebel Thula appears, its square watchtower recognisable from afar. At the foot of the mountain is the town of the same name.

Before finally leaving the high plateau and driving into Shibam, which is further down, you should go and take a look at the village Hadshar Sa'd on the left. The literal translation of the name Hadshar Sa'd is "happy stone"; it lies on

the upper part of the small, intensively cultivated Wadi Askaran. Shortly before Shibam the tarmac road forks to the right to Thula.

THULA

For many visitors, Thula is the most beautiful small town in the region around Sana'a. The town, with its city walls in an almost completely preserved condition, is indeed a prime example of the Arab art of city construction using local stone. Houses three and four storeys high crowd the narrow streets, their stones supporting themselves without mortar. At most, clay was used as a binding material, since cement has only been available in recent years.

Finally, the asphalt road reaches the former city gate (now a modern building with an entrance resembling a gate) and comes to the main square of the town. The big house on the right belonged to the family of the Imam before the revolution and has been adapted into a *funduk* or guest house. If you can find the person in charge, you can climb up the many steps to the *mafradsh* (the best room), which is richly decorated with stucco ornaments, and have tea. A walk on the roof is rewarding, as it gives a lovely view of the entire town.

An impressive tour leads to the second city gate in the south-west, which has been preserved in its original state. On the way you come across some cisterns which collect rainwater and even today it still supply water for laundry and animals.

An especially rewarding excursion is a half-hour climb up to the fortification, which offers a wonderful panorama in all directions. In the 16th century, this was where the Zaidi Imam Mutahar Sharaf ad-Din barricaded himself against the Turkish armies. The history of the fort in fact goes even further into the past. Cisterns artfully constructed underground which supply crystal clear water, and rooms with niches serving as resting places which have been hewn into the rock, probably go back to **A fine view of the town from the fortress at Thula.**

Himyarite times. It is a pity that at this time, a visit is not possible for military and strategic reasons. The soldiers stationed there won't accept any visitors.

The previously mentioned asphalt road goes on to the left and ends at Kilometre 43 in Shibam. The roadworks that were begun in 1990 have left deep scars in both the Djebel Kawkaban and the Wadi Adshar, impairing the beauty of the region for years to come.

SHIBAM

Shibam, at the foot of Djebel Kawkaban, is already visible from a considerable distance. The car is best left in the empty space behind the first houses in the town. Shibam, with 3,861 inhabitants (1986 figures) is the second biggest town of Al Mahwit province. The market street leads to the old city which, on Friday mornings, market day, is particularly lively. Not until the end of the Suq Street do you come through the actual city gate and past the small shops of the old, inner suq. It is worth looking closely at the corner pillars of the city gate: they are visibly covered in small Sabaean writing. The stones are not, however, in their original place, but are spoils which were used when building the city gate to recall the pre-Islamic Himyarite history of the town. Similar relics of pre-Islamic times have also been worked into the arch of the gate.

Further on one passes the great mosque which is one of the oldest found in Yemen. It was built by Prince As'ad Bin Ya'fir in the 9th century. The Ya'firites, descendants of Himyarite nobility, were installed by the Abbasid caliphs, the dynasty that defeated the Umayyids in 750 and moved their capital to Baghdad, in Sana'a as the first Yemeni governors and created their own dynasty.

Shibam is mentioned by the Yemeni historian Muhammad Al Hassan al-Hamdani amongst others in his famous work *Al-Iklil*. The book, written in the 10th century, vividly describes the town as follows: "In Shibam Bayt Aqiam one

The arid plateau of Djebel Kawkaban.

can find pre-Islamic columns, which are called the 'columns of the hall' and which have pictures and symbols engraved on them. There are no other columns (in Yemen) that would surpass these in age and beauty."

KAWKABAN

An old footpath leads through Shibam to the rockface of Djebel Kawkaban, studded with caves, and on to the mountain fort of Kawkaban. One can climb the 1,312 feet (nearly 400 metres) up the old track in about an hour. The wonderful views of the town of Shibam and the surrounding fields compensate for the exertion.

For some years it has also been possible to use a narrow track to Kawkaban in a vehicle suited for rough terrain. You drive along Djebel Kawkaban in the direction of At Tawilah, and take a well-marked route to the right which winds its way up the mountain to Kawkaban.

An unusually impressive gate in the huge wall is the entrance to the inner city which played an important role as a refuge during wars in the Islamic history of Yemen (probably also in pre-Islamic history). Like Thula, it had been used as a fortress by the Zaidi Imams against the Turks in the last few centuries. Kawkaban was also a popular meeting-place for many famous artists and musicians.

However, in the past few decades, it has declined considerably in importance and many inhabitants have left forever, even though electricity and running water are now installed. Until some years ago, the inhabitants had no running water and relied on the use of rainwater collected in cisterns for drinking and washing.

By following a straight road through the town you come first of all to the main mosque; immediately next to it is a (now dry) large cistern. Further south is the former house of the Imam which now serves as a *funduk* and is named as such. A friendly knock and the door will open, and tea will be offered in the

He fought with the troops of the Imam—old man from Mahwit.

mafradsh. Such a visit allows one to have a view of the interior of the houses.

Djebel Kawkaban is an excellent area for a long walk of several days across the high plateau to such lovely settlements as **Hosn Bokhur** or **Beit Manein** and **Sadallah**, both situated in a beautiful wadi. From there, a number of other long walks lasting several days lead along the mountain range to At Tawilah and Al Mahwit.

The track way carries on in a southerly direction at the foot of Djebel Kawkaban. To the left is **Djebel Arus.** On the flattened peak of the mountain the remnants of an old fort can still be seen. After a few kilometres the small Wadi Na'im appears on the right, which is overlooked by the numerous houses of Kawkaban.

At Kilometre 48 the track leads through **Bab al-Adshar**, the "Gate to Wadi Adshar", and crosses the perennially green valley. The steeply descending slopes of the wadi finally join **Wadi Surdud** which itself leads into the desert region of the Tihama. Wadi Adshar is supposed to have once had 360 sources, and although several small brooks still exist, the increased use of water in the drainage area of the wadi may have led to the lowering of the water table and the drying up of the majority of these sources.

After crossing the wadi for a mile and a half (two km), the road climbs again along the other wadi bank and, once again, as a farewell, offers an unforgettable view of the entire valley.

The next settlement along this route is the village of **As Sa'ila**. A *nauba*, one of the traditional round tower houses seen frequently on the high plateaux in Yemen, is located in the centre of the village and is visible from afar. The single-storey, long buildings with their flat gable roofs which line both sides of the road are chicken farms for meat production.

The next settlement worth mentioning is **Hosn Shamat**. The settlement is characterised by a huge fort on a mas-

Smiths from Mahwit producing agricultural implements with the simplest of tools.

sive rock. The houses at the foot of the mountains and along the track are only a few years or decades old. The original settlement is on an inaccessible rock.

The road then crosses **Wadi Asnaf**. On your left, on a long stretched-out ridge of rock, lies **Bazt Qatina**. Further ahead you can already see the three striking rocky peaks which is the town of **At Tawilah**.

Beyond Wadi Asnaf lies **Wadi Salama**, with the village of **Jawanah** at its end. Shortly after this village, at the foot of the jagged mountain range, the town of At Tawilah finally appears; which can be reached after passing some other small settlements at Kilometre 75.

AT TAWILAH

The town lies at a height of 8,858 feet (2,700 metres) and has a population of 2,524 (1986 figures). At Tawilah was first mentioned in writing in a document dating from 1210 as a fortress on one of the characteristic jagged rocks.

At Tawilah, together with another fortress of probably the same age, Al Qarani, played an important strategic position in Yemen. It is not possible to ascertain today whether there was already a settlement there at the time. What is certain is that originally At Tawilah lay in the shadow of Kawkaban, which was a much older and politically more important town.

Only after the second conquest by the Turks was At Tawilah elevated to district capital in 1871–72. After taking power in 1918, Imam Yahya left the Turkish structures untouched. Not until recent years did At Tawilah, because of its location at the important Sana'a-Al Mahwit route, surpass Kawkaban in terms of inhabitants and importance.

At Tawilah has an especially beautiful suq which is full of life on the two market days, Sunday and Wednesday. For the rest of the week, only a few shops are open; but a walk through the suq is still worthwhile just to see the lovely stone arches which line both **The whole region meets in the weekly market of At Tawilah.**

sides of the street. Most of the inhabitants are traders and merchants. To the right of At Tawilah the wadi bank rises, offering a beautiful view of **Wadi La'a**. On the opposite side the mountain range of **Djebel Masar** rises.

At Tawilah is the start of the descent into **Wadi Ma'kar**. Right down in the bed of the Wadi a very lovely stone bridge has been preserved. This is where the old footpath from At Tawilah to Al Mahwit went. The track is only a few years old.

The road then leads through a wonderful terraced landscape, studded with many tiny villages which are so well adapted to the rocky surroundings that on first sight they are hardly visible. Near the settlement of Alhan you can get a spectacular view of the whole region. The rocks are mostly white limestone and are quarried by the inhabitants to build their houses.

On another high plateau the town of **Rudshum** appears to the right; it is still surrounded with an entirely intact city wall. The track then carries on through a rocky terrain, with steeply sloping valleys. At Kilometre 125 the track finally reaches Al Mahwit.

AL MAHWIT ■■■■■■■

The capital of the province of the same name is, with 5,166 inhabitants (1986 figures) the largest town in the wider region. The original core of the town is widely visible, lying on a rough rocky ledge. In the north west part of the old city the old city wall is still clearly recognisable. At a height of 7,218 feet (2,200 metres), Al Mahwit is situated lower than At Tawilah and therefore has a comparatively mild, pleasant climate. The temperature practically never drops below zero in winter.

In recent years Al Mahwit has spread rapidly, especially in the southern part of the town, and has developed into a medium-sized town which now includes **Ad Dubr**, until recently an independent settlement.

Just to the right of the main street is

Thula, built entirely of stone, is surrounded by a well-preserved town wall.

the suq – small and simply constructed compared to At Tawilah. A caravanserai, estimated to be three hundred years old, is said to have been the central collecting point for green coffee beans at the height of the coffee trade. From there, donkeys transported the coffee beans a long way into the Tihama to Bayt al-Faqih or to the harbour town of Al Mokha, and from there they were exported all over the world. The **main mosque of Al Masiya** is situated close to the suq.

A short excursion of about a mile (1.5 km) in a westerly direction takes one to the so-called "vulture rock", which is actually a steep wall of rock. In good weather, the view takes in the whole lower part of the **Wadi La'a** right into the Tihama. In the early morning there is an imposing spectacle showing the layers of fog rising along the slopes, with the clouds sometimes shifting to reveal a breathtaking view of the villages which hang onto the mountain peaks like swallows' nests.

From Al Mahwit the track winds its way to the valley and offers a grandiose view of the range of the western mountains. Thousands of terraces planted with millet cover the steep slopes, and innumerable little villages cling closely together in the rocks. In sheltered corners coffee shrubs grow in the shade of the high *tujas*, the shade trees. In the last two centuries, the coffee trade has been greatly reduced, but because of increase in demand coffee has gained growing popularity again. The coffee tree still commands the highest profits after the *qat* tree. Some banana and papaya trees are already growing up here.

At Kilometre 129 there is one final great view of Al Mahwit to the left. The gullies built into the track direct the flow of water coming from the mountains during the rainy season off the road surface and down to irrigate the terraced fields below.

At the settlement of **Arquq** the track takes a sharp left turn. After the settlement of **Al Manach**, the track goes steeply into the valley. The houses are now more flat and simpler. The huge mountain range of Djebel Hufash in the south comes closer. In this region, many small terraces have been abandoned by the inhabitants and are lying fallow, flooded and carried away by the occasional rainfall.

In the bed of **Wadi Lahima**, a plantation grows tropical fruit trees. The wadi, which is at a height of 1,968 feet (600 metres), has water all year round and a rich vegetation.

At Kilometre 145 the route crosses the riverbed and goes across a small pass into the **Wadi Qita'**. During the rainy seasons the path can only be driven on with great difficulty because of flooding. The complexion of the people around the wadi is much darker skinned than the mountain inhabitants and their dress reminds one of the Tihamis who live in the coastal plain.

The upper course of the wadi narrows and there are only a few settlements there now. The route goes across a small pass down into **Wadi Sari**, which stretches as far as **Khamis Bani Sa'd** at the tarmac road between Sana'a and Hudaydah.

To the left and right of Wadi Sari are millet and maize fields. There are also many beds with gourds which, when dried and hollowed, are used by the women to make butter. The leaves of the bamboo, which grows wild, are picked by the women as animal fodder. Hand-dug wells provide water for the fields higher up.

At Kilometre 164 the road passes the town of **Al Dschuma'a**, situated in the wadi, which was named after the weekly market day on Friday. Shortly before one reaches the tarmac road, Wadi Sari joins **Wadi Surdud** which is on the left. At Kilometre 184 it crosses Wadi Surdud and from there leads to the tarmac road. This goes to the right to **Bajil** and **Hudaydah**, and climbs to the left up Wadi Mawsana as far as **Manakha**, from where it runs on to end finally in Sana'a.

THE OLD INCENSE ROAD

The unification of the two Yemens, those once such hostile brothers, on 22 May 1990, heralded a new era for tourism. The dream of many seasoned travellers to Yemen became true: the old Incense Road is now accessible once more. What hitherto had been blocked off by prohibited zones and borders can now be visited without any great difficulty. That includes the old route into the **Wadi Hadramaut** via the ancient cities of Timna and Shabwa.

The desert route: Today there are two routes which lead from Ma'rib into the Wadi Hadramaut, which after the Wadi Ram is the largest wadi of the Arabian Peninsula. Those who enjoy travelling on dust tracks will probably opt for the direct route through the desert. First of all one travels 35 miles (57 km) along a surfaced road to the town of **Safir**.

Just beyond Ma'rib lie the obligatory oil fields as well as remains of a far more ancient source of wealth – the open-cast salt mines. After Safir, a desert road leads towards the east through the **Ramlat as Sabᶜatayn**, which means something like *Sand between the two Shebas* and probably refers to the two ancient cities of Saba and Shabwa, towards the western extremity of the Wadi Hadramaut.

The route can be covered in two days, with a night spent in the desert, provided that you carry enough petrol and have a driver who knows the area. On the second day the road reaches the table mountains which form the northern boundary of the Wadi Hadramaut, and continues towards the east following the base of the mountains until near Haynan it meets the old Hadramaut Road, surfaced with cobblestones. These roads were laid throughout the Hadramaut in the 1930s. Near **Al Qatn**, the route intersects with the important connecting road between Mukalla and Seyun.

The Timna-Shabwa route: This route, which was opened to tourists in 1991, provides a real treat for the Yemen traveller. Running from Baraquish through Ma'rib, its course is practically identical to that followed by the old Incense Road leading to the ancient cities of Timna and Shabwa. The road between Ma'rib and Harib is surfaced and work on improving the stretch going over the pass over to **Bayhan** is now underway. The route passes through a number of settlements, with a medical post at Jubat al Jadidah. In places there is intensive cultivation of the land, but despite this it hard for the visitor of today to imagine that complete ancient cities once flourished in this part of the world.

Fertile oases: "So fertile was the area around Ma'rib, that one might conceive that the whole region between Ma'rib and Hadramaut was once under cultivation", wrote Brian Doe, the former Director of Antiquities in Aden, in 1970. Since then, Satellite photography has indeed confirmed that an extensive net-

work of irrigation canals and dams once ensured the existence of the southern Arabian cities of Baraquish and Shabwa. It is estimated that the irrigation system around the Ramlat as Sab^c atayn alone covered an area of 172 square miles (445 sq km), and some 200,000 people probably lived in the cities it supplied.

Nowadays, these regions, particularly above the wadis, are among the most barren and deserted areas in the entire Yemen. The old dam at Ma'rib is only the most famous example of this ancient Arabian hydraulic engineering. A much older dam was constructed only a few miles from the Wadi Adhana at the **Jebel Balaq ash Shrq**. Studies of the sediments, including those around Baraquish and Shabwa, confirm the existence of such structures.

HARIB

For many years **Harib** was a remote border post. The region around the town was only occupied by the kingdom of Yemen at the beginning of this century,

under the Imam Yahya who subjugated the tribes of the Garui and Beni Abd. In the two restaurants in Harib one comes across dashing figures of men, often Bedouins from the still remote side valleys of the Wadi al Guba or the fringes of the Rhub al Khali. Above the town, which boasts a number of fine modern buildings testifying to a certain prosperity, are the remains of the old fortifications built to guard this strategically important route. Hans Hellfritz, the legendary Arabia traveller of the 1930s, was kept prisoner in Harib for three weeks. Harib was also a centre of indigo production, and Hellfritz reports seeing trampled squares outside the town at which the seeds of the indigo plant were threshed and the dye extracted.

Via a pass to the east, the top of which is guarded by a defiant tower, one enters the territory of the former South Yemen. Only the portraits of the "heros of 1986" remain to recall the past division of the country. But much more impressive than these four socialist heros are the mighty

Ancient inscriptions adorn Timna's southern gate.

dunes of the Ramlat as Sab^catayn, the southernmost extremity of the great Rhub al Khali desert, stretching away to the north and east.

WADI BAYHAN AND TIMNA ━━━

For anyone who could get a permit, the **Wadi Bayhan** was accessible by road from Aden or Mukalla via Al Ataq. A military airport was even built in the main centre of **Bayhan al Qasab**. Nevertheless, prior to unification only a few Europeans managed to get through to Bayhan and Timna, the ancient capital of Qataban. Coming now from the direction of Harib, the traveller reaches the Wadi Bayhan and the asphalt road at the little town of **Nugub**. Apart from the palace of the former ruler of Bayhan, Sharif Hussein al Madhi, there is nothing of particular interest to see in Nugub, although with its avenues of date palms and the proud splendour of it houses, the place does provide a taste of what is to come in the Wadi Hadramaut. The palace itself is now in a very poor state of repair and houses offices of the Ministry of Education.

The ruins of **Timna**, the ancient capital of the southern Arabian empire of Qataban, lie some distance outside Nugub, near a military post. In contrast to Ma'rib, here in Timna extensive archaeological excavations could proceed without undue difficulty thanks to the excellent relations that the British established with the local sultans of Bayhan. The work was carried out between 1950–51 under the direction of Wendell Phillips.

With the constant power struggles that took place in ancient Southern Arabia, it may seem surprising that a city such as Timna could emerge in such close proximity to the sphere of influence of the all-powerful Sabaean Empire. But around 400 BC, Qataban succeeded in establishing its independence from Saba and extending its influence as far as the sea. Timna, whose founding Phillips guesses at 800 BC, others later, was destroyed by fire sometime in the

The inhabitants of Shabwa province were once feared robbers and Bedouins.

first or second century AD. The walls excavated in 1950 have now been practically buried again by the drifting sands of the desert. So, too, has the **Main Temple** (3rd century BC), which was dedicated to the god Athar (Venus). It was in Timna that the famous stele with market regulations were found. It is still possible to see the inscriptions of the municipal laws on the south gate to the city, as well as the ancient cemetery which lies outside the city itself. Some of the finds from Timna can be seen in the National Museum in Aden as well as in a museum in Bayhan.

From the edge of the mound, there is a wonderful view over the Ramlat as Sabᶜatayn. A new asphalt road, partly still under construction, continues to the east through a fascinating desert landscape to **Al Ataq** and the oil fields of Shabwa. Interesting settlements such as **Hadjar as Sadah** or **Nisab** lie off the main route, but the detour is well worthwhile because they retain much more of their original character than Al Ataq which has been completely transformed by the oil boom. Even before reaching the town, the traveller will notice that the land has been neatly parcelled off, and it is not difficult to see why. The airport and the giant transport parks of sundry oil companies provide a clear enough indication of the developments taking place in this part of the world.

The province of Shabwa is one of the richest oil areas in Yemen, and although exploitation in recent years has been greatly hindered by the border disputes between the north and the south, the future looks very rosy indeed.

Together with the Ma'rib oil fields, which are already in full production, it is estimated that there are a total of some 2 billion barrels of crude and 20 billion cubic feet of natural gas lying under this desert. The crude oil is transported by pipeline to the southern Yemen port of Bir Ali.

The main road continues from Al Ataq via the Wadi Yashbum and the Wadi Habban to meet up with the highway

You can still come across camel caravans in the Hadramaut.

connecting Aden with Mukalla (see chapter "Aden to the Wadi Hadramaut"). The **Wadi Yashbum** is particularly worth a stop on account of its beautiful houses. Before the village of **As Said** stands the palace of the former local sultans.

SHABWA

Shabwa lies about 30 miles (50 km) due north of Al Ataq, right out in the desert, and can be reached by following a dust track. Even today, however, the route through this region, once inhabited by marauding Bedouins, is anything but easy to negotiate. Countless tracks, many marked by the brightly-coloured flags of the oil companies, have turned the area into a veritable maze which seems to lead everywhere but the ancient city of Shabwa.

Pliny the Elder reports that on their 65-day journey along the Incense Road, the first major stop for the caravans was Sobota (Shabwa). The city is said to have contained as many as 60 temples, and a tenth of the incense transported thus far was offered to the god Syn. From Qana, near the present-day port of Bir Ali, where the merchant ships landed, the route led through Shabwa and on to Timna, a journey that probably took about a week, while the continuation over the Maqlaba Pass, to Harib, Mar'ib and Yathul (Baraquish) lasted another five days. There are a number of ancient salt mines that indicate that this trading route was already well-known before it came to be used for incense.

Shabwa was the capital city of the empire of Hadramaut which became an independent kingdom after the decline of Sana'a around 400 BC. Research carried out by French archaeologists in 1985 confirms that the region around Shabwa was settled from the 6th millennium BC. One thing that continues to puzzle the experts, however, is the city's location: situated as it was at the end of the Wadi Hadramaut, Shabwa would hardly have been able control traffic through the wadi itself. Be that as it may, the city survived as the capital of the empire of Hadramaut right up until the 5th century AD.

And Shabwa can still be seen today, straddling the three hills situated at the head of the Wadi Irma. Clearly visible is the building next to the city gate which was excavated between 1976–85. The coins that were discovered here indicate that this was the **Palace of Shqr**. The basement of this monumental building is well preserved, as are the steps leading down to it. The floors above were constructed of clay bricks and timber. From the city gate the visitor will arrive directly at the **Main Temple** of the city god Syn. The staircase leading up to the temple is still intact and the sockets for the columns can also be seen.

Shabwa's survival was ensured by an expansive system of irrigation that optimised the meagre flow of the Wadi Irma. Evidence of these waterworks can be seen to the south of the city, where the layers of sediment suddenly cease.

The western opening of the Wadi Hadramaut lies 18 miles (30 km) away. Access is nowadays no longer blocked by the Bedouin, so the traveller can now enjoy what must be one of the most beautiful desert routes in the whole of the Yemen, even if it isn't all that easy to find. The area is almost deserted, and on a journey lasting several hours, the best orientation are the stark outlines of the surrounding table mountains.

At the northern fringe of the Wadi, the two pinnacles of the **Jebel al Tukhmayn**, rising like mighty chimneys, point the way, as does a single volcanic cone rising from the middle of the sand dunes. Despite its remoteness, the area is inhabited and one occasionally stumbles across a small settlement or encounters a pick-up truck on the road. Particularly fine houses and castles can be seen in the settlements occupying the tributary wadis.

The route meets the old Hadramaut road before the town of Hawra, and from there the traveller will soon reach an asphalt surface once more.

FROM ADEN TO THE WADI HADRAMAUT

Dominated by dark volcanic crags dropping down into the sea, the coast at Aden is impressive. It was described by Freya Stark in *The Coasts of Incense* (1953) "The rocks of Aden stand up like dolomites, so jagged and old... There is a feeling of gigantic and naked force about it all, and one thinks what it was when these hills were boiling out their stream of fire, hissing them out into the sea, and wonders at anything so fragile as man living on these ancient desolations."

It is a shame that the city itself does not quite match up to the beauty of its surroundings; few of the buildings possess much character, and those that do are generally in a pretty poor state of repair. If it wasn't for the airport and the National Museum, there would be little reason for spending much time in Aden. Even in the wake of unification, this situation is not likely to improve for some time. In the unification treaty, Sana'a was nominated as the country's capital. It is planned to make Aden the main economic centre, to take up where the prosperity of the colonial era left off.

When the British were here, up to 600 ships a month docked in the harbour. The port of Aden was the most important coaling station and transhipment point on the sea route between India and Great Britain. In the 19th century it became the third-largest port in the world after New York and Liverpool, a position it attained after the opening of the Suez Canal in 1869. But when the canal was closed in the Six Day War of 1967, the port's fortunes rapidly declined.

After the British withdrawal from Aden in that same year and the ensuing Marxist course of the new government, the docks lay practically idle. Aden was regarded as being too much of a risky proposition by international shipping companies. Operators were prepared to accept an extra two or three days added to voyages by diverting their custom to the ports of the Persian Gulf. But now, provided that the Yemen government can demonstrate stability and reliability to the rest of the world, then the future for the port of Aden should be a prosperous one. On 22 May 1991 Aden was declared a free trade zone.

Meanwhile, there are also plans to develop Aden's tourism potential. Venerable old hotels such as the Crescent are being restored to their former splendour, and the Aden Hotel, which stood empty for so so long, has been taken over by the Swiss Mövenpick concern. It can now claim to be the best run hotel in the entire country.

In contrast to medieval Sana'a, Aden has, despite all the effects of Socialism, remained an essentially cosmopolitan city. The shades of the colonial era still linger here, and the influences from Africa and India are unmistakeable. During the time of the Empire, until 1937, Aden was attached to the Bombay Presidency.

In the district of **Tawahi**, next to the market hall and the suq, is the **Military Museum**, once regarded as an absolute must on any tour of the city. Perhaps more rewarding, however, is the nearby **National Museum**, which contains some impressive exhibits from the ancient Arabian cultures. Also well-worth seeing is the expansive **Park of Tanks** in Tawahi. It is thought that even in ancient times these tanks were used to store the rain that periodically fell on Aden. The precipitation from the entire hill on which Aden stands was fed into the tanks via a series of channels, basins and overflows.

Estimates of the total storage capacity vary from between 45 and 100 million litres. There is a plaque to the memory of Sir Lambert, who in 1854 had the derelict system cleaned and restored. Today the system is used to irrigate the wonderful tropical park that surrounds the entrance – there is not enough water for it to serve any other purpose.

Preceding pages: Men in the suq in Crater. **Left**, woman in traditional Hadramaut costume.

Nearby, the **Mosque of Say'id Abdullah al-Aidras**, who is considered the patron saint of Aden, is also well-worth a visit. Erected in 1859, the building stands on the remains of the an earlier edifice dating from the 14th century. It is Aden's main mosque. Also in the Tawahi district, at **Steamers Point**, are the old Crescent and Rock hotels. It is not clear for how long the Serra beer from the Saudi Arabian peninsula's only brewery will continue to flow in these establishments. Sales of alcohol were legalised in the south, and the brewery was constructed with the help of the former GDR.

Another attraction near the main post office is the house of the famous French poet Arthur Rimbaud (*Les Illuminations*) who first arrived in Aden in 1880, having turned his back on literature at the tender age of 19. He travelled through the east as a trader, gun-runner, soldier and explorer. "That Rimbaud should have endured it… is a real tribute to the horrors of Aden," wrote Vita Sackville-West in her *Passenger to Teheran* (1926). The French provided the funds for the building's restoration.

Those in search of the Oriental atmosphere should head for the suq in **Crater**, where the fragrances of the East mingle with the sounds of Arabian music emanating from the loudspeakers. Crater is the oldest of Aden's seven districts. The bay of Crater with the outlying peninsula of Sirra was, until the middle of the 19th century, the city's original harbour. The **Bohra Bazaar** gets its name from the Bohras, an Ismaili sect, whose adherents can be seen as they make their pilgrimage to the small town of Kahil in the Harraz Mountains. Today it is still possible to see Christian churches in Aden, although they might now be used as a fire station or library.

For those who have enough time on their hands, an excursion to the **Gold Mohur Bay** with its excellent swimming is to be recommended. The bay gets its name from the *mohur*, a former gold coin of India and Persia. A steel net

The district of Tawahi in Aden.

protects the beach from the attentions of predatory sharks.

To Dhalla and Ta'izz: The drive from Aden to Ta'izz takes a good two hours. The route passes through the suburbs of Sheich Othman and Dar Saad and on to **Lahij** some 18 miles (30 km) north of the city. Known today as Al Mansura, between 1947 and 1950 this was the collection point for Jews emigrating to Israel in the "Flying Carpet" operation. Until 1976, Lahij was the seat of the Sultans to whom the Aden Peninsula also originally belonged. During the Socialist era the palace of the Abdalli Sultans was converted into an agricultural institute.

The route continues on to **Dhalla**. The area is intensively cultivated and produces an abundance of fruit, much of which finds its way to the markets in Lahij. The **Radfan Mountains**, through which the road passes, were for a long time used for South Yemen's strictly controlled cultivation of the natural stimulant qat. In October 1963, **Habilain** was the scene of the first military action of the *National Liberation Front* against the British. The road continues towards Ta'izz via the town of Kersch and joins the main Sana'a – Ta'izz road between Ta'izz and Al Janad.

To Lawdar and Mukalla: A further route through to the north is via the town of **Lawdar**. From here it is now possible to continue via Mukairas to Al Bayda at the other side of the old border, and thence directly to Sana'a. Or one can turn to the east, to the **Wadi Habban**.

The journey to Lawdar first involves following the coast from Aden as far as Shuqrah. The new coast road between Aden and Mukalla was built with the help of the Chinese and was completed at the end of the 1970s. Until the middle of the 20th century travellers from Aden could reach Mukalla only by ship, as the old land route was controlled by hostile Bedouins. Covering a distance of 385 miles (620 km), the road passes through fascinating countryside. On the left is the strange planet landscape of the desert

Time for a chat.

and on the right is the sea. The two often merge as great tongues of wandering dune reach almost to the coast and the sand is blown across the road.

After first driving along a coast of broad, lonely beaches, the traveller will come to the **Abyan Delta**, a region whose rich cultivation and tropical palm trees and papaya plantations demonstrate just how fertile the Yemen can be, provided of course that water is available. As is the case near Dhalla, the visitor will be impressed by the enormous efforts of former South Yemen to convert this desert into productive agricultural land.

Not only corn and millet is grown here, but there are also vast expanses of tobacco and cotton fields. **Al Kod** is the centre of cotton cultivation. These agricultural oases, created with the help of development aid from countries of the former Eastern Bloc, represent advances in farming that in the north of the country are matched only by the ubiquitous qat plantations.

A little farther along the coast, **Zinjibar** today displays little evidence of the glories of days gone by when it was a sultanate city. At **Shuqrah** the main road turns inland and climbs in several steps through a bizarre lunar volcanic landscape to arrive at the plateau of Lawdar. Yemen is dotted with signs of the volcanic activity resulting from the relatively recent drift of the Saudi Arabian peninsula. It was only 15 million years ago that it started moving away from Africa, creating the Red Sea and the Gulf of Aden, and the process is still continuing. Typical features include the craters, often filled with deep turquoise water, that can be found along the south coast as well as in Hammam Damt in the North.

In **Lawdar** the residences of the Abdalli Sultans still stand sentinel to the left of the main road. But when one considers how closely these residences are packed together and in what poor state of repair they are now in, it becomes clear that not all princes of old

Mukalla's main landmark is the Hosn al Ghuazi.

can possibly have lived quite such romantic conditions as those depicted in the *Tales from the Arabian Nights*.

From Lawdar, the road turns to the east and through the mountains until just before Habban the view opens out over a dreamy landscape dominated by table mountains rising out of the plains. Before Habban the road forks off to **Atak** via the **Wadi Yashbum** with the settlements of As Said, As Sufall and **Yashbum**. There are many who hold that the Wadi Yashbum presents one of the most beautiful landscapes of southern Arabia.

HABBAN

Impressive multi-storey clay-brick houses stand before the mountain ramparts ranging above the town. In times gone by **Habban** was a very prosperous place indeed, largely on account of the sizeable contingent of Jews that lived here and engaged themselves in the art of silversmithing. This fact explains the splendour and size of the houses. Habban

was the centre of the Jewish community in southern Yemen. As is the case with the succeeding settlements in the Wadi Habban, the corner parapets of the houses are mounted with goat antlers and above the door lintels are decorations of cowrie shells which were used to summon magical powers. On many of the houses it is still possible to see the original carved wooden windows with a miniature door set into them for opening. Thus it was possible to have a least some draught to combat the stifling heat.

Habban was not only a Jewish centre; it was also a an important commercial and industrial town of a former sultanate, and afterwards of the province of Shabwa. As is the case with so many such small towns, its importance has now declined and after the departure of the Jews, in recent years increasing numbers of Yemenites have also left. The repeated failure of the monsoon rains and the resultant lack of water for irrigation in the wadis has contributed to the general decline. The streets and houses

The beach below the crow cliffs is a popular place for camping.

of Habban are now but a shadow of their former selves, even if the place might look quite splendid from a distance.

A similar fate has befallen **Azzan** to the east, with its wonderful houses and palm gardens. Azzan was once the seat of the Wahidi Sultans.

For those interested in archaeology, there is the ruined city of **Mayfa'at** which lies to the south of Azzan, at the southern exit of the wadi as it meets the coastal sand dunes. The city area is surrounded by mighty walls, but the most impressive feature is the main gate with its inscriptions. Mayfa'at lay on the Incense Road as it made its way from Qana to Shabwa or Timna. It was once the capital of the southern region of the kingdom of Hadramaut. As is the case with all ancient cities of southern Arabia, here, too, is evidence of an ancient irrigation system; some distance up the wadi from Mayfa'at are the remains of an old channel that was used to divert water to irrigate the fields in the lower part of the city. Again with

Mayfa'at, which reached its heyday in the 3rd century BC, it is difficult to imagine that here, in such a hostile hostile environment, there was once a flourishing city. The city's demise came with the conquest of the "fortress of crows" city of Qana by the Himyarites.

A short distance to the south of Mayfa'at, lying nestled in the desolate sand dunes, shortly before the coast, the oasis of **Ain Ba Ma'bad** provides for welcome relaxation under the shade of its palm trees.

BIR ALI

Soon the white sand dunes disappear and the scenery is dominated by black lava. Especially fascinating are the huge wandering dunes and drifts of sand that conceal the lava in places to create a landscape full of contrast. We have arrived back at the coast at **Bir Ali**, today a town which retains none of its historical importance, although lying as it does at the end of the pipeline from the Shabwa oil fields, its future as an oil

Musicians at a wedding.

terminus and loading port seems ensured. It is impossible to miss the mighty "crow cliffs", the **Hosn al-Ghurab**. There are two beautiful beaches beneath the cliffs, but swimming demands a great deal of caution, as these are shark-infested waters.

It was below these cliffs that Brian Doe, Director of Antiquities in Aden, discovered the ancient port of Qana, where the incense from Dofar was landed and transferred onto camel caravans. The visitor is recommended to climb up the hill to the the old fortress. The foundation walls are still there, as are remains of the defensive towers and tanks. It is from above that one gets the best view of the outline of the old city and a part of the old port.

The cliff top also provides for a magnificent view of the sea and the offshore islands which are of volcanic origin. The remains of fish and crabs on the rock ledges have been left there by the crows that gave the cliffs their name.

Immediately after Bir Ali, it is well-worth climbing up to the volcanic crater to the right of the road. The lake in the middle is of a deep turquoise hue. The remainder of the journey along the coast to Mukalla is impressive as the road winds its way between the mountains on the left and the sea on the right. Shortly before Mukalla, to the left, there are dazzling snow-white mounds of freshly-burnt lime which is traditionally fired in huge furnaces with large quantities of palm wood.

MUKALLA

Hemmed in by mountains that reach all the way to the sea, the port city of Mukalla has always been short of space. And so, beyond the creation of new outlying suburbs, it was decided to raise the seafront in order to provide more building space. The consequence of this decision is that new developments now partly obscure the view of the unique harbour front of elegant old merchants' houses, nestling against their backdrop of mountains.

The tomb of Ahmed Bin Isa near Seyun.

Until well into this century, Mukalla could only be approached from the sea. As the second most important port in southern Yemen, it has developed both as the gateway to Hadramaut and as a vital link between Yemen and India. Just as in Aden, there are clear traces of influences from the subcontinent, both in the mix of peoples that live here as well as in the architecture.

Hellfritz mentions that on his arrival in Mukalla, his friend the Sultan was away on his estate in Hyderabad in India. The Quaiti dynasty to which he belonged was related to the nizams who ruled Hyderabad from 1713 to 1950. Mukalla is also the capital of the province of Hadramaut and today it can also be reached by air; the airport is located at **Riyan** along the coast to the east.

It is well worth taking a stroll through the old town along the main street which runs parallel to the sea. Of particular note are the masterfully carved doorways, particularly on the houses in the narrow side streets. The former **Sultans**

Palace is now a museum which gives an insight into the lifestyle of the erstwhile rulers. Along with the obligatory old photographs and weapons collections, a few valuable finds from the ancient trading cities are also on display. There is a fine view of the harbour front from the balcony.

When in the old city, the visitor should definitely venture into one of the small eating establishments down by the harbour and sample some of the excellent freshly-caught fried fish. One simply selects one or two pieces, orders rice and chilli to go with with it, and a Yemen delicacy is ready for eating. During Ramadan, when people fast during the day, a wonderful night market takes place in Mukalla.

On the road leading out of the city in the direction of Hadramaut, rising above the usual pandemonium and chaos of car workshops and the like, is Mukalla's main landmark, the **Hosn al Ghuazi**. Built atop a bizarre lava cliff, this is the city's old customs and guard house.

A short distance beyond Mukalla is the fishing port of **As Shihr**. Already well known in antiquity, the town can look back on a glorious past. Despite its somewhat decrepit condition, it still maintains a lively atmosphere. The handloom workshops, which still produce the coveted cloth for *futah* (the sarongs of the men), are well worth a visit. Not far away is the idyllic village of **Bada** with its thermal springs.

One of the most idyllic spots in the whole region is **Ghail Bawazir**, situated a short distance inland from the coast. A walk through the centre, with its many carved doorways, is an absolute delight. The real centre of attraction, however, is the **Summer Palace** of the Mukalla sultans, which stands in the middle of a beautiful tropical park. Amongst many other crops, the best tobacco in the country is cultivated in the vicinity.

The coast of Yemen continues for a further 300 miles (500 km) until the Oman border. But at the present time

Women wear their typical straw hats for working in the fields.

these regions are not accessible to tourists. In the past, the hostile political relationship between Yemen and Oman as well as the restrictive tourism policies of the former South Yemen kept these areas firmly out of bounds. But now the two countries seem to be on better terms and in a few years time it may well be possible to continue right along the coast to Salalah in Oman.

HADRAMAUT

Turning inland from Mukalla, the road follows the deep gorge of the **Wadi Huweirah**, gaining some 1,000 metres in height until from the top of the impressive **Jol Mountains**, the traveller is rewarded with a superb view over the coastal plain. On account of the clouds coming in from the sea, the southern flanks of the Jol receive enough moisture to allow shrub vegetation to thrive. This is in stark contrast to the landscape beyond where the dearth of precipitation allows for nothing more than a bleak stony desert. A number of valleys intersect the plateau, and amazingly these provide havens for a number of small settlements.

The asphalt road is today the quickest route into the inner Hadramaut. But there are also a number of tracks which the locals use. One such turns inland before Mukalla along the Wadi Hadjar and into the Wadi Amd to **Hawra**, a town that can also be reached via the Wadi Doan.

Continuing the bleak journey northwards from the Jol Mountains, the monotony of the journey is finally broken as the road bends round into a tributary valley of the Hadramaut, the **Wadi Amd**. It is hemmed in on both sides by the typical high vertical cliffs of the table mountains, and the valley floor is carpeted with picturesque palm groves and dotted with little clay-brick settlements. The shrine of **Mashad Ali** lies directly on the route. Once a year this settlement, which appears dilapidated and ruined, comes alive for the pilgrims' festival. Markets are set up and the place

A river oasis between Tarim and Aynat in the Hadramaut.

is a bustle. The mosque and the tomb of Ali with its beautiful wood carvings are well worth closer inspection.

Not far from Mashad Ali those interested in archaeology will be attracted by **Raybun**, a collection of clay mounds from which Russian archaeologists have unearthed a host of finds which are displayed in their own special section of the museum in the sultan's palace in Seyun.

Continuing to follow the Wadi Amd and then the **Wadi al Gabar**, the traveller will soon find himself in the little town of **Hadjarein**, which rises up the mountainside to the left of the road. Having strolled through the narrow alleyways, one arrives at the top of the town for a magnificent view over the valley, with the bizarre eroded crags of table mountains rising up on either side. The name Hadjarein means "the two cliffs". Hadjarein could be described as the southern Yemen counterpart to Al Hajjarah in the Harraz Mountains. A steep path, which is by no means easy to

negotiate, leads up the table mountain above the village. From here, over to the right, one gets a good view of the confluence of the Wadi al Gabar with the Wadi Doan. Going around the fertile oasis in an anti-clockwise direction are the settlements of **Na Hawla**, **Goureika**, **Seila** down on the river and, behind, **Muneidara** of which it is only possible to see the tallest houses.

A difficult track leads along the river bed of the Wadi Doan back towards Mukalla. In the Wadi Doan, the little town of **Sif** provides for a real taste of Yemen as it once was, perhaps more so than anywhere in the Wadi Hadramaut or the Wadi Habban.

With a bit of luck, the traveller to the Hadramaut region will come across a bee-keeper who will sell him some honey. In Yemen honey is traditionally used for medicinal purposes rather than sustenance. Bee-keeping in Hadramaut can look back on a long and proud tradition, and here, since time immemorial, a kind of wandering bee-keeping

An important place of pilgrimage: the shrine in Mashad Ali.

306

has been practised. Once the acacia blossoms have been exhausted in one area, the bee-keeper simply packs everything up, beehives and all, and moves on.

The amounts produced are very small, but the quality is quite excellent. And the prices are quite horrendous; in the shops a litre of the cheapest variety costs around £50.

Back on the main road, **Huraydah** in the Wadi Amd is well worth a visit. Here, apart from the usual simple clay-brick houses, there a number of splendid villas belonging to wealthy citizens who earned their money in India or Indonesia. Generations of people from the Wadi Hadramaut or the Wadi Doan emigrated to these countries and made their fortunes in business. Many married and had families and only returned to their homeland later in life. It is not uncommon to see aged Hadrami folk in Indonesian costume, for instance at the As Salam hotel in Seyun.

Near Huraydah lie the ruins of **Madabum**. Unfortunately, the remains have either been buried by wind-driven sands or unscrupulous collectors have pilfered the site. Only the plans and descriptions of the 1937 excavations can provide any information about this ancient moon god shrine from the 5th century BC.

The inner Hadramaut: The main road now begins to pass through an intensely cultivated area. The town of **Al Qatn** contains a number of impressive buildings, which, however, are hardly visited. We have now arrived at the inner Hadramaut. A common feature along the road are the groves of date palms. The dates in the Hadramaut are among the best of their kind to be found anywhere. And on both sides of the road, the traveller will also see women wearing traditional costume working in the glowing green alfalfa fields. Dressed in black, their headgear is normally a tall pointed straw hat, the *madhalla*.

The millet, maize and alfalfa are transported to the towns on donkey carts. By the side of the road stand *sikaia*, well-

An irrigation channel in the Wadi Doan.

houses, built by wealthy Hadramis to provide refreshment for travellers. There are also the *wali*, the shrines of saints, which are usually whitewashed.

SHIBAM

There is some justification to Hans Hellfritz' comparing the clay towers of **Shibam** to the skyscrapers of Manhattan. Here, the houses are up to eight storeys high, and just like in Manhattan, they stand densely clustered together, only separated by narrow alleyways.

Because the living quarters occupy the top floors, these are commonly linked directly with those of the neighbouring houses to facilitate communication and a good neighbourly atmosphere, without the need for the occupants to descend the stairs and climb back up again. The town is completely self-contained and looks to the approaching traveller like a mighty fortress rising out of the valley floor.

According to the experts, the settlement, which can be considered as the successor to Shabwa, dates back to the 2nd century AD, although few of the houses standing today are any more than about 300 years old. Despite occasional claims to the contrary, photographers are advised that the best time of day for taking pictures of Shibam is at sunrise.

Shibam today gives a good impression of what many of the early southern Arabian cities must have looked like. It isn't only in name that Shibam and Shabwa are similar: research in Shabwa suggests that the 60 "temples" described by Pliny were in fact tall houses of the kind seen in Shibam today. This leads us to the conclusion that the first of these towers, which became so typical of the settlements in the deserts and mountains of southern Arabia, were probably constructed at the beginning of the 5th century BC.

As was always the case, Shibam has only one real entrance, namely through the city gate. And just inside this gate on the left, there are two little shops which

Ibex were considered an especially sacred animal in Yemen.

sell some of the rare old everyday items that are normally so difficult to obtain in the country. Together with Sana'a, Shibam's future preservation is now ensured by UNESCO, whose headquarters is situated in a building across the square to the right, easily recognisable by the sentries standing guard outside.

SEYUN

The capital of the Wadi Hadramaut is **Seyun**. Its centre is dominated by the mighty **Sultan's Palace**, which is slightly raised above the level of the marketplace and the suq which stand before it. Seyun, too, has a long history dating back to the pre-Islamic era. Provided it is open, visitors will be impressed by a visit to the **Museum**, which is located in the palace. It is divided into three departments: historical, folkloric and a special section where finds from Raybun (see above) are on display.

Some particularly beautiful features of the palace are the carved doors and the ornate roof terraces which provide an excellent view over the broad expanse of the city. But while the dazzling white palace might look impressive from the outside, the interior space of the building is less spectacular, consisting of countless rather plain-looking rooms. Built entirely of clay brick, the palace was the seat of the Kathiri sultans whose ancestors came from Sana'a in the 15th century to settle down in the Hadramaut. The last Sultan of Seyun ruled here until the end of the 1960s.

Highly recommended is a stroll through the old city with its mosques, cemeteries and houses with exquisite architectural details. The thirsty visitor will doubtless wish to relax in one of the many tea shops – good places for meeting the locals.

To the side of the Sultan's Palace, behind a rather insignificant looking iron door, is where building materials are traded. And here is one of those rare opportunities to procure items of handicraft, pottery, old utensils and the like. The noble **As Salam Hotel** with its

expansive grounds and pool is located some distance from the centre.

No sooner has one left Seyun in the direction of Tarim than the glowing white domes of the **Tomb of Ahmed Bin Isa** come into view situated on a mound to the right of the road. The shrine is an important centre of pilgrimage. Ahmed Bin Isa is said to have come from Basra in Iraq more than 1,000 years ago to convert the inhabitants to the true faith. He is considered to be the father of all sayyids in the Hadramaut. He was a direct descendant of Ali, the son-in-law of the Prophet, and his son Imam Hussain. It was after a pilgrimage to Mecca that he set out from Mashad Ali to convert the Hadramaut to the doctrine of the sunna.

A female saint, a *sheicha*, is also buried below the Ahmed Bin Isa shrine, making the site an important centre of pilgrimage for women; the lower shrine is only open to women, whereas the main mosque and shrine can be visited by all.

Bedouin from Shabwa province.

The road forks at **Al Ghuraf**. To the right it leads into the **Wadi Adim** and to the old route to Mukalla. Going left, the main road continues into the eastern, lower reaches of the Wadi Hadramaut. From here the main wadi becomes known as the **Wadi Masilah**, "flowing water", and it flows directly into the Arabian Sea.

TARIM

This city is the spiritual centre of the country and has a large number of mosques and libraries; it is said that there were once as many mosques as there are days in the Islamic year: 354. With a bit of luck, the visitor may get shown some fine examples of the calligraphic masterpieces contained in the **Al-Kaf Library**.

The symbol of Tarim is the minaret of the **Al Mihdhar Mosque**. Whether or not the visitor is allowed into the building will depend on the prevailing attitude of the authorities. Because it gets extremely narrow towards the top, the minaret itself can only be climbed by small groups at a time in "one-way traffic". While the mosque is older, the minaret was only constructed at the beginning of the 20th century.

The strange style of the edifice reflects the development of Tarim as a whole. Since the beginning of the last century, many of its citizens have spent time in Southeast Asia, particularly in Indonesia, where they achieved great wealth as traders. And it was this wealth that enabled them to come back and finance the many fine houses in the area surrounding the Mihdhar mosque. The often highly ornate baroque forms reflect the contact that the patrons had with other cultures and their efforts to introduce new styles to their homeland.

Sadly, many of these palatial residences are no longer kept up these days; they are being allowed to decay by their owners who spend most of their time either abroad or in Sana'a.

A particularly restful break can be enjoyed at the **Al Qubba Summer Pal-**ace, which is situated in a pleasant park on the outskirts of town. Here one can relax on carpets under the shady trees at the edge of the pool and enjoy the luxury of having one's tea served from a samovar. At the present point in time, only the two hotels at Seyun and Tarim are open to travellers, and these are largely booked out by travel operators.

Continuing the journey to the east, the traveller arrives at **Aynat**. The cemetery here, dominated as it is by nine huge domed tombs, is well worth seeing. The tombstones carry elaborate inscriptions, quite a rarity in the Islamic world. The building opposite the cemetery is also worth a closer look; the outer wall is decorated with a row of ibex horns. Ibex are now extinct in the Yemen, but in ancient times they were considered an especially sacred animal. They are depicted on the frescos at Ma'rib and other towns, as well as on the cliff paintings in the Wadi Dhar. The protruding corners of the clay houses are not a structural feature but symbolise the "horns" of the houses and, just like the ibex horns, are said to ward off misfortune.

On a small mound to the right of the main road is the old **Abu Bakr Mosque**, another centre of pilgrimage. At the other side of the river, which peters out after a few miles, is the village of **Bur** with its gushing spring.

Qabr Huth is the mosque of the tomb of the prophet Huth. He was the father of Qahtan the father of all Yemenites. It is the largest shrine in the whole of the Hadramaut and once a year the deserted place comes alive as pilgrims throng here from far and wide. Huth is mentioned in the 46th sura of the Holy Koran, wanting to convert the members of the Ad tribe to the true faith. But the tribesmen pursued Huth and wanted to kill him, whereupon a cliff opened up and saved him from his enemies. The crack can still be seen in the mosque of Qabr Huth. The Ad tribe received their due punishment, then "who else should die but the people of the transgressors".

Right, the minaret of the mosque of Tarim. Following page, detail of a glass window.

310

TRAVEL TIPS

GETTING THERE

BY AIR

A number of international airlines, in addition to the Yemeni airline Yemenia, fly to Sana'a. The most important ones, apart from Yemenia, are KLM, Lufthansa, Air Egypt, and Indian Airlines. Most flights from Europe are via Paris with Air France, or via Addis Ababa with Ethiopian Airlines, or via Moscow with Aeroflot or with a combined ticket via Sana'a or Aden with Yemenia or Alyemda airlines.

BY SEA

Although there is no direct passenger service by boat to Yemen, it is sometimes possible to get a cargo boat from Djibouti to Yemen. Most of the ships dock at either Aden or Hudayah. While much of the shipping for the northern part of Yemen was traditionally concentrated at Hudayah, it is now certain that Aden, particularly since it was declared a free trade zone, will become the leading port in the new Republic of Yemen.

BY ROAD

The only overland possibility of entering Yemen is via Saudi Arabia. While this is without problems for Yemenis and those holding Arabic passports, travellers from Europe and the United States often encounter considerable difficulties.

TRAVEL ESSENTIALS

VISAS & PASSPORTS

The unification of the two Yemens has made things much easier for visitors. Nearly all areas of the country are now accessible. Southern Yemen, to which access was once so restricted, can now be freely explored.

Travellers to the Republic of Yemen require a passport that is valid for at least three months and which does not have an entry stamp for Israel or South Africa. The visa is valid for three months and can be extended, if necessary, in Sana'a. The processing of visa applications is relatively quick and uncomplicated. An application must be submitted in triplicate and with three passport photos to the relevant consulate or embassy.

UNIFICATION

With the proclamation of the Republic of Yemen on 22 May 1990, a united state was created out of the former Yemen Arab Republic and the People's Democratic Republic of Yemen. The terms "North" and "South" Yemen are therefore no longer valid, and indeed the people of Yemen no longer like to hear them. The capital of the Republic of Yemen is Sana'a. The port of Aden will be developed as the major commercial centre.

The new flag consists of horizontal black, white and red stripes. The black at the top represents the dark days of the Imamate, the white is for the native soil and the red at the bottom stands for those who died in the battle for freedom and independence.

At least until the elections in 1992, the former president of the Yemen Arab Republic, Ali Abdullah Saleh, remains the top man in the new republic. Al Attas from the former South Yemen is prime minister. In the wake of unification a broad spectrum of political parties has emerged, and these will all take part in the elections at the end of 1992. Meanwhile, the People's Parliamentary Assembly in Sana'a carries out its function actively and democratically. The debates are covered live on TV.

MONEY MATTERS

There are exchange bureaus in the arrival halls in both Aden and Sana'a. The rates in the banks and hotels are well below those offered by the money

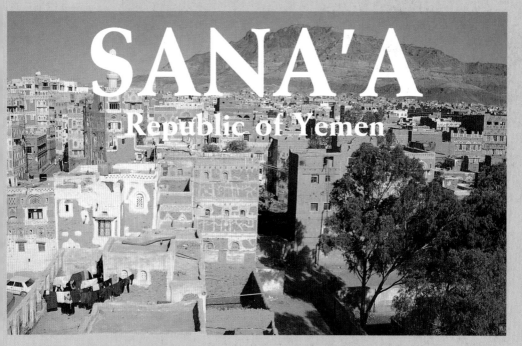

SANA'A
Republic of Yemen

In the lush and majestic land of the Queen of Sheba...

Yemen. Site of one of the world's oldest civilizations. An enchanting country whose beauty culminates at Sana'a, the capital city ... rightly called the 'Pearl of Arabia'.

Here lies the Taj Sheba Hotel ... bringing all the comfort and convenience which the tourist and the businessman could wish for.

Rooms and Suites: 200 rooms and suites: relaxed living in a restful setting.
Bilquis: the Coffee Shop.
Golden Peacock: The restaurant of-

fering European elegance with Oriental opulence. Serves Continental and Oriental food.
Abu Nawas: The Banquet Room. Perfect for conferences, banquets, receptions and parties. Equipped with comprehensive conference facilities.
The Health Club: With the only outdoor Jacuzzi Whirlpool in the Middle East. And besides other facilities, a heated swimming pool.
Yemen. You'll appreciate it best when you stay at Taj Sheba.

TAJ ✿ SHEBA HOTEL

Gracious hospitality in the heart of the city

RESERVATIONS

Reservations can be made through your travel agent or travel consultant or directly through:

USA New York 1-800-458-8825 FRANCE Numero Vert 19.05.90.83.38
U.K. Toll free: 0800 282 699 • CANADA: 1 800 825 4683 • HONG KONG: Tel: 52550058 • Australia 008-252-355
• JAPAN Toll free: 0120-394489 • GERMANY (130 Service) 01 30 2428

• Utell International Worldwide

• Taj Sheba Hotel, P.O. Box 773/ Ali Abdolmoghni Street, Sana'à, Republic of Yemen.
Tel: 272372 Fax: 274129 Telex: 2551 SHEBA YE, 2561 SHEBA YE.

✦ Taj International Hotels

changers in the suq. The black market is officially tolerated, and normally no action is taken against the changers, despite the fact that it reduces the state bank's hard currency revenues. Before changing, however, visitors should definitely inform themselves of prevailing government policy.

For tour groups, the tour operators in Yemen usually organise exchange matters on arrival. The rate usually lies somewhere between the official and the black market rate.

At the time of writing, there are still two currencies in Yemen, the Rial in the north and the Dinar in the south. Both are valid in the whole country and can be freely exchanged, although the rate is constantly changing. There are plans for a new currency – which will be either the Rial or the Dirham.

Traveller's cheques and credit cards are accepted in the major hotels in Sana'a, Ta'izz and Aden. In the suq you can often buy your silver and other items with credit card or cheques. But it is still wise to make sure you have enough ready cash.

HEALTH

There are no particular immunisation requirements for entry. It is necessary to have a yellow fever injection if one has been in an infected area in the previous six days. Malaria pills and a hepatitis injection (e.g. gamma-globulin) are advisable.

One should not underestimate the effect of the altitude and the strong sun in Yemen; slow acclimatisation and a protective sun lotion will help.

As in many countries, the rule for any raw fruit, vegetables and salad is: peel it, cook it, or leave it alone. This rule should also be observed in the restaurants. The drinking water is not always of the best quality; in some places – for instance, in Shahara – it's occasionally taken from cisterns. It is advisable to purify the water with sterilising tablets or a filter. Even simpler is buying the bottled mineral water which is available in sufficient quantities and is of good quality. Tea and packed fruit juices, lemonade and coca cola can be drunk without qualms.

We strongly advise against any bathing in ponds or wadis because of the prevalence of bilharzia in Yemen.

WHAT TO WEAR

Light cotton clothes are appropriate to the climate in Yemen, particularly for the Tihama and the area around Ma'rib. But it's best to also pack some warmer clothes, light jumpers or jackets. Sometimes the temperature in the mountains can drop to zero.

Travelling off the few main tarmac roads is usually very dusty, and a scarf to protect your mouth is useful. A sun hat will keep the sun at bay.

Yemen is a strictly Islamic country. Men and women in shorts, or uncovered arms and thin T-shirts for women offend the sensitivity of Yemenis. Although Western female visitors are not expected to wear the sharshaf, tourists are nevertheless expected not to offend the country's morals with shameless dress (defined more strictly in the Arab world).

CUSTOMS

The usual customs regulations apply. Tourists are permitted to import one litre of alcohol. Video cassettes will be checked at the airport, film and video equipment will be stamped in the passport.

Newspapers and journals will be closely checked at the customs post for pornographic material (again according to strict Arabic codes). Any nude pictures – whether in a book or magazine – will, at best, just be torn out.

The customs and entry procedures in Sana'a are lengthy and chaotic. Each piece of luggage has to be marked with chalk by the customs officials. You should make sure that all luggage – including hand luggage – has been marked.

ALCOHOL

Since unification, there has been certain amount of confusion concerning the consumption of liquor in Yemen. In the south, the sale of liquor was allowed, and in Aden there is still the Serra Brewery, whose beer can be purchased quite normally in the hotels in Aden and the Hadramaut. There is even a duty-free shop in Aden which sells all kinds of liquor for hard currency.

However, the strictly Moslem north is now bringing pressure to bear on the south. In Sana'a, alcohol can be purchased only at the bars of the Sheraton and Hadda Ramadah Hotels. Basically, the visitor should remember that drinking alcohol in public is not the done thing and should be avoided.

Getting Acquainted

GEOGRAPHY

Total area: 205,355 sq. miles (531,869 sq. km)
Capital city: Sana'a
Commercial capital: Aden

Population (1988): 11 million
In the major cities: Sana'a   500,000
Aden   400,000
Ta'izz   178,000
Hudaydah   155,000
Population density (per sq. mile): 47

TIME ZONES

Yemen time is three hours ahead of Greenwich Mean Time. Otherwise, the only comment on time and time-keeping in Yemen is that it plays a subordinate role. Appointments or arrangements for meetings tend to be made roughly for the morning or the afternoon, without fixing a precise hour.

CLIMATE

Yemen has basically three climatic zones:
- Tihama, the humid and hot coastal strip
- The mountainous region, with moderate, partly cool climate
- The desert area around Ma'rib and the Wadi Hadramaut with dry, hot desert climate

In Tihama the temperatures rise to above 40°C (104°F) during the hot summer months. Added to this is an unbearable humidity, so that a visit is not advised. The summer monsoon brings devastating downpours. In the winter months, the temperature goes up to 30°C (86°F) and even at night it does not fall below 20°C (68°F).

In the mountain region there are steep temperature differences of as much as 20°C. In the winter months especially, the temperatures can reach close to zero when there is a strong wind. Strong rain during the small monsoon (March/April) and the summer monsoon (July–September) makes walks and drives away from the tarmac roads almost impossible. Sometimes the rain will come as far as the edge of the Rhub al Khali. Heavy rain causes sudden flood spates in the Wadis – which often makes a crossing in a jeep at Al Jawf, for instance, impossible.

The climate in the desert area around Ma'rib and in the Hadramaut is dry and hot. During the rainy season especially, the rivers from the mountain region run underground in the sand desert. After heavy rainfalls, the Wadi al Jawf is a bursting river which covers large areas of its estuary in mud.

During the rainy season in March/April and June to September, a visit to Yemen, with certain restrictions, is possible.

CULTURE & CUSTOMS

Yemen is a strict Islamic country very conscious of its traditions. Culture and customs are today still guided by this tradition.

Most noticeable for a foreigner is undoubtedly the daily use of the natural stimulant *qat*. It determines the entire day, and even the traveller is not immune from its effects. The best recommendation is that, while not chewing it oneself, it is best to adjust to this habit. To try and persuade a Yemeni to give up *qat*, to postpone taking it or to reduce it, would certainly be a wasted effort.

The Yemenis have a concept of time which is completely alien to a Western visitor. The fact that there are no clocks anywhere in public places indicates that one won't get very far with our Western notions. The day is not divided into hours and minutes, but into mornings, lunchtimes, and evenings. Arrangements for meetings such as "around 2pm in the hotel lobby" mean in effect sometime between lunch and dinner. Most wrist-watches work by Arabic not European time.

Eating manners in Yemen are clear: the left hand is considered unclean and taboo, one eats only with the right hand. The left can be used for breaking off bread or meat pieces. One washes one's hands before and after a meal. No cutlery is used except in the hotels.

A foreigner or friend is often given the best pieces of meat at a meal. It would be an insult to the host to refuse these. If one is really full-up, one gets up saying *"all hamdulli'lah"*, goes to the tap and washes one's hands. If one is seated on the floor while eating, one doesn't show the soles of one's feet to the person opposite.

Dress should conform to the moral sensitivities of the Yemenis. Shorts for men are just as ridiculous as wearing the country's traditional clothes. While European women don't have to wear a veil, they should keep their body covered and possibly wear a scarf.

Exchanging intimacies in public is seen as indecent. It is permitted, however, to walk around the streets hand in hand.

MOSQUES

Especially in the southern part of the country, mosques are frequently open to "non-believers". However, access is totally dependent on the prevail-

Yemenia

MORE THA

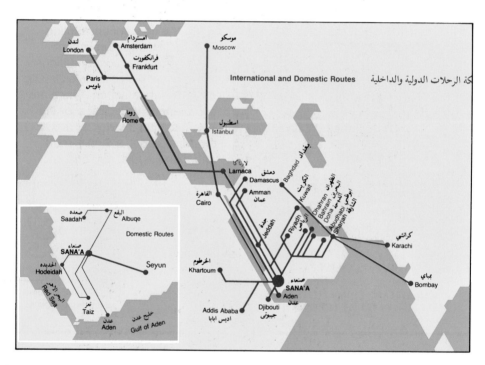

International and Domestic Routes — كة الرحلات الدولية والداخلية

NEW YORK (London)
Yemen Airways
554 Fifth Avenue
Suite 1004-A
New York N.Y. 10017
Tel: (212) 286-0660

LONDON (U.K.)
52 Strattonstreet/Mayfair
Place
London W1
Tel: (01) 4917186

STOCKHOLM (Sweden)
Rudbecksgatan 37
S-70211/Örebro-Sweden
Tel: 139033

BRUSSELS (Belgium)
Rue de Champs de Mars 13
1050 Brussels/Belgium
Tel: 511610

ATHENS (Greece)
9, Patission St.
Athens 10431
Tel: 5245-912

MOSCOW (U.S.S.R.)
A/P Sheremetyevo
Room 646
Tel: 5789081

COLOMBO (Sri Lanka)
Interlink House
37 Queen Street
Colombo - 1 (Sri Lanka)
Tel: 35899

AMSTERDAM
(Netherlands)
Yemenia
Leidsestraat 74
1017 PD Amsterdam
Tel: 220494

HONG KONG
Tung Ming Building
40 Des Voeux Road
Tel: 251365

KUALA LUMPUR (Malays
1st Floor Wisma Golden City
75 Jalan Bukit Bintang
55100 Kuala Lumpur
Tel: 2415637

MANILA (Philippines)
11 Valero Corner - Sedeno St
Salcedo Village Makati Metro
Manila
Tel: 817-1631818-7866

SINGAPORE (Singapore)
06-09, 6th Floor
Ocean Building
10, Collyer Quay
Singapore, 0104
Tel: 5330681

اليمنية

CHOICE

ing attitude of the religious authorities. The visitor can never be absolutely sure that he will be allowed inside. The general climate has changed in recent years due to the increasing fundamentalist tendencies in the country.

Before entering a mosque, shoes should be removed and left outside. Women should wear a head-scarf. Arms and legs should be covered – shorts are definitely not the correct attire. Friday is a special day of worship and for that reason it is better to choose other days for visiting. In general, try to avoid visiting during prayer times.

THE ISLAMIC CALENDAR

The Islamic calendar is purely a lunar calendar – the 12 months begin each time when one can see the first narrow strip of the new moon in the evening dusk (though there are also other definitions).

A lunar year has around 354½ days; a lunar month 29 or 30 days. The lunar month is easy to observe, but extremely impractical. The solar year, according to which the seasons and the animals, light and plants, sowing and harvesting, and festivals are planned, has around 365¼ days – that is, 11 days more than the lunar year. Therefore, the oldest calendar of the Arabs, as that of the other peoples with Semitic languages, must have been a solar calendar – the meaning of Arab names of many months makes this obvious.

Since during Muhammed's time the art of keeping correct calendars by augmenting the lunar year through accurate intercalary months (in order to harmonise it with the solar year) had been forgotten, Muhammed ordered the use of a strict lunar calendar whose months (because of the 11 days' difference mentioned) passed through all the seasons of the (Christian) solar year in the course of 32½ years.

It is for this reason that the time of Ramadan, the Muslim month of fasting, when night becomes day, is at a different time each year. In Yemen particularly, where the street lanterns cast the life and bustle in an unreal light, it is the most picturesque period.

The same is true for the the two main festivals of the Islamic year, the sacrificial festival *Id al-Adha*, also called "Great Festival", *Id al-kabir*, and the Festival of ending the fasting at the end of Ramadan, *Id al-fitr*, also called "Small Festival" or *Id al-saghir*. The Festival of ending the fasting begins on the first day of the month Shauwal (and lasts a few days); the Hadj Festival begins on the 10th Dhu al-Hijja.

THE ISLAMIC MONTHS

Muharram	30 days
Safar	29 days
Rabi'al-auwal	30 days
Rabi' al-thani	29 days
Jumada al-ula	30 days
Jumada al-thania	29 days
Rajab	30 days
Sha'ban	29 days
Ramadan	30 days
Shauwal	29 days
Dhu al-Qa'da	30 days
Dhu al-Hijja	29 days

In the coming years, the first day of Ramadan will be on the following days:
1. Ramadan 1412 H = 5 March 1992
1. Ramadan 1413 H = 24 February 1993
1. Ramadan 1414 H = 12 February 1994
1. Ramadan 1415 H = 1 February 1995

These dates can shift by one day depending on the method of calculation. The small *Id* is always 30 days after the 1. Ramadan, the great *Id* 99 days after the 1. Ramadan.

HOLIDAYS

Most holidays are geared to the Islamic calendar. Official holidays in Yemen are:
• 1st day of the Month of Muharram
• 12th day of the month of Rabi' al-auwal, the birthday of the Holy Prophet.
• 22 May – National Unity Day
• 26 September – Day of the Revolution
• 14 October – National Holiday
• 1 January – New Year
• 1 May – Labour Day

BUSINESS HOURS

Public offices are closed on Thursday afternoon and Friday – which is the equivalent of our weekend. Offices and government departments are open from 8am to 2pm, banks from 8am to noon, the post office from 8am to noon and again from 4pm to 8pm.

Despite Friday being the day of rest, many shops are open on that day, especially in the suqs. During important public holidays, all shops are usually closed in the mornings.

ELECTRICITY

The voltage in the big towns is mostly 220V. In the smaller towns generators provide electricity. This can result in a lowering of voltage; in particular at night there is no electricity in many towns. If you depend on sockets, you should get all available adaptors before the trip.

COMMUNICATIONS

MEDIA

The radio stations broadcast from 6am to 10am and 1pm to midnight. There has been radio in Yemen since 1956. All programmes are broadcast in Arabic.

Television was introduced in 1975. The programmes are screened from 4pm to midnight, and on Fridays from 9am to 1pm. All programmes are in Arabic. Many productions from friendly Arab states, e.g. series from Egypt, are shown. There is an English language news review at 7.30pm.

POSTAL SERVICES

The post offices are open Saturday to Thursday from 8am to noon, and 4pm to 8pm.

The postal services were extended with German help; consequently most letter boxes and post bags come from the Federal Republic.

Post is not delivered in Yemen; most Yemenis have a PO Box. The main post office in Sana'a is at At-Tahrir Square; Aden, in the Tawahi district.

As with the currency, unification has also created anomalies in the postal service. All the old stamps must be used first, and so there is a colourful mixture of stamps from the two former republics. The layman may have difficulty in knowing how much they are now worth; one simply has to trust the clerk.

TELEPHONE & TELEX

Cable and Wireless provides an international telephone service in Sana'a. International calls can be made for 150 Rials without problems to nearly all countries with phone cards which have at least 80 units. Whether this will remain so after the transfer of the services into Yemeni hands is questionable.

Telex and telegrams can also be sent from here.

The central telephone office is located in Az-Zubayri Street, opposite the Chinese embassy.

The national telephone network is also now fully operational, and faxes can also be sent.

The code for Yemen is: **967**

Sana'a	02
Hudaydah	03
Ta'izz	04
Aden	0911
Sa'dah	051
Hajjah	07

NEWSPAPERS

Great advances have been made in recent years. The press has become more free and varied. Published in English in Yemen are:

The Middle East Times – Yemen Edition (monthly)
The Yemen Times (weekly)
Arab News

These and other well-known internationally available publications can be purchased in most hotel shops.

EMERGENCIES

MEDICAL SERVICES

Many foreign doctors give excellent treatment in many Yemeni hospitals and first aid posts, since the Yemeni health system is still very dependent on foreign assistance.

SANA'A

Al-Jumhuri (Republic) General Hospital
Bab Shau'b. Tel: 222238/091.
Al-Askari (Military) General Hospital
Bab al-Balqua. Tel: 72724.
Al-Thawra (Revolution) General Hospital
Bab al-Salam. Tel: 246971-5.
Kuwait General Hospital
Bir al-Shai'f. Tel: 73280.

TA'IZZ

Al-Jumhuri (Republic) General Hospital
Al-Mustafa Street. Tel: 1450.
Al-Thawra (Revolution) General Hospital
Al-Mustafa Street. Tel: 210842-4.
Al-Askari (Military) General Hospital
Al-Mustafa Street.

HUDAYDAH

Shahid al' Ulfi
Al-Mustafa Street.
Al-Thawra (Revolution) General Hospital
Corniche Street. Tel: 25217-9.

SA'DAH

Al-Salaam Hospital

The Beauty of Yemen
with

BAZARA TRAVEL & TOURISM

SANAA AL-ZUBAIRY STREET
P.O. BOX 2616
TELEPHONE: 205925 205865 206965
TELEX: 2598 NDASAD
TELEFAX: 00967 1 209568

IBB

Nasir Hospital
Tel: 402583

JIBLAH

American Hospital

HAJJAH

Al-Jumhuri (Republic) General Hospital
Hawra. Tel: 40252.

RADA'A

Al-Thawra (Revolution) General Hospital

The embassies keep lists of doctors who can speak particular foreign languages. If a serious illness occurs it is best to fly back home if possible.

GETTING AROUND

AIRPORT TRANSFER

The price of a taxi from Sana'a airport to the town centre is 180 Rial.

PUBLIC TRANSPORT

A large proportion of public transport is by taxi and collective taxi. Collective taxis, mostly Japanese minibuses, travel within the towns of Sana'a, Ta'izz and Hudaydah along specific routes and stop at designated stops which, however, are not immediately obvious to foreigners.

If you take a private taxi, it cannot be assumed that the taxi driver knows the route or the destination. In many cases you will need to give directions or have the address written in Arabic on a piece of paper.

The collective taxis also travel between the larger towns. They are mostly Peugeot or Toyota landcruisers. Each route can be recognised by the colour of the stripes on the side of the taxi:

Sana'a – Hudaydah	blue
Sana'a – Al Mahwit	blue
Sana'a – Ta'izz	green
Sana'a – Sa'dah	brown
Sana'a – Ma'rib	yellow
Ta'izz – Aden	green
Ta'izz – Hudaydah	red
Ta'izz – At Turbah	red
Hudaydah – Sana'a	blue
Hudaydah – Ta'izz	red
Hudaydah – Jizan	red

The taxis wait till they are fully occupied and then drive off. The fare depends on the distance and bargaining skills. Travelling in these collective taxis is sometimes hazardous because the drivers can get overtired.

There is also a public bus service which covers the main connections. The busses usually go twice a day – in the mornings and afternoons.

From Sana'a (Bab al-Yemen) to Ta'izz, Hudaydah, Al Beidha, Sa'dah.

From Ta'izz (Hawdh al-Ashraf) to Sana'a, At Turbah, Al Mokha, Hudaydah.

From Hudaydah (Al Hay al-Tijari) to Ta'izz, Sana'a, Jizan (Saudi Arabia).

Tickets for the long-distance buses are bought before departure from the GCOT office located at the bus station.

INTERNAL FLIGHTS

Yemenia airline flies from **Sana'a** to the following destinations several times a week, if not daily: **Ta'izz, Hudaydah, Ma'rib, Al Jawf, Sa'dah, Albuqe, Aden, Riyan** and **Seyun**.

WHERE TO STAY

HOTELS

There is no abundance of hotels of international standard to be found in Yemen. The big chains)Sheraton, Sheba and Ramada) have hotels in Sana'a; Mövenpick has one in Aden. During the busy season one often has difficulty finding rooms.

Apart from the few large and a number of smaller hotels with modest to basic standards the guest houses, *funduks*, offer lodgings to travellers. The five-star rating conforms only to internal Yemeni standards.

SANA'A

Sheraton ☆☆☆☆☆
Dahr Himjar, PO Box 2467. Tel: 237500-3, telex: 2222.

Taj Sheba ☆☆☆☆☆
Ali Abdul Moghni Street, PO Box 773. Tel: 272372, telex: 2561.
Haddah Ramadah ☆☆☆☆
Haddah Street, PO Box 999. Tel: 215214/5, telex: 2227.
Ar Rawdah Palace ☆☆☆
Ar Rawdah, PO Box 533. Tel: 340226/7, telex: 2498.
Dar al Hamd ☆☆☆
Al Hay al-Izaya, PO Box 2187. Tel: 74864/5, telex: 2270.
Al Mukha ☆☆
Ali Abdul Moghni Street, PO Box 533. Tel: 72242, telex 2298.
Al Ikhwa ☆☆
Bin Dhi Yazin Street (behind the Taj Sheba), PO Box 344. Tel: 74026, telex: 2350.
Al Iskandar ☆
Rep. Palace Street, PO Box 4466. Tel: 72330.
Shahara ☆
Ali Abdul Moghni Street, PO Box 1446. Tel: 78502.
Al Anwar ☆
Ali Abdul Moghni Street, PO Box 530. Tel: 72457.
Al Kayam ☆
Al-Qasr Street, PO Box 1117. Tel: 75272.

Since 1990, another hotel for travellers has opened up in the old city. It is the Al Gasmy Palace, a simple but comfortable establishment. From the roof there is a wonderful view over the old city.
Al Gasmy Palace
Harat Al gasmy. Tel: 273816, telex 2595.

TA'IZZ

Mareb ☆☆☆
Djebel al-Dabua, PO Box 5285. Tel: 210350, telex: 8848.
Al Ikhwa ☆☆☆
Djebel al-Dabua, PO Box 4413. Tel: 210364/5, telex: 8839.
Plaza ☆☆
26 September Street, PO Box 4166. Tel: 220224.
Al Janad ☆☆
Midan al-Myama, PO Box 6866. Tel: 210529.
De luxe ☆
Jamal Street, PO Box 4476. Tel: 226251/2.

MA'RIB

Bilqis Hotel ☆☆☆☆
Tel: (063)2666-2371-9.
Ard al-Janeten
PO Box 2309. Tel: (063)2306.

HUDAYDAH

Ambassador ☆☆☆
Sana'a Street, PO Box 3491. Tel: 231247/50, telex: 5626.

Bristol ☆☆☆
Sana'a Street, PO Box 2405. Tel: 239197, telex: 5617.
Al Ikhwa ☆☆
Sana'a Street, PO Box 3389. Tel: 76195.
Al Buri ☆☆☆
Sana'a Street, PO Box 3712. Tel: 75852.

HAJJAH

Hajjah Tourist Hotel ☆
Tel: 220285.

SA'DAH

Rachban ☆
Al Mamoon ☆☆☆
Tel: 2203.

ADEN

Aden Hotel ☆☆☆☆☆
Khourmaksar, PO Box 6111. Tel: 32070, fax: 32947, telex: 2319.
Gold Mohur ☆☆☆
Al Tawahi. Tel: 24171, telex: 2312.
Crescent ☆☆
Al Tawahi. Tel: 23417, telex: 2275.
Chalets ☆☆
Khourmaksar. Tel: 31301, telex: 2330.

SEYUN

As Salam Hotel ☆☆☆
Tel: 2208.

MUKALLA

Al Shab ☆☆
Tel: 2345.

Many small towns only have *funduks* to stay in. The hotels and *funduks* located in converted Imam Palaces in Thula, Ar Rawdah, Rada' and, in Sana'a, the Dar al-Hamd are particularly beautiful.

There are no camp sites in Yemen. There are several places to sleep near Al Khawkha on the beach which are run by locals. Sleeping in the open, for instance on while hiking, usually doesn't present any problems. It would be best, though, to ask advice from a local companion about the best places.

The Smiling Face of Yemen
AL MAMOON GROUP

AL-MAMOON INT'L TOURISM AGENCY

TOURIST SERVICES, NORTH AND SOUTH YEMEN

Group tours 2-25 days; Daily Tours
Hotel Reservations, Guide speaking either
English, French, German or Italian

SPECIALISTS FOR INDIVIDUAL TOURS
Tailored made programmes
Illustrated Catalogue Available

H.O.
Zubeiry Street
SANA'A – REPUBLIC OF YEMEN
P.O. Box 10127
Tel: 967-1-74349
Telex: 2919 MOON YE
Fax: 240 984

SAM CITY HOTEL, SANA'A

*** Stars
In City Center
72 Rooms
Restaurant
Hall for wedding Ceremonies
and reception parties
Tel: 76254-5/270752/275168
Telex: 2919 MOON YE
Fax: 275 435

AL-MAMOON HOTEL
SAADA *** Stars

• 45 Rooms
• **Coffeeshop & Restaurant**
Tel: 051- 2203/2459

ABU NAWAS RESTAURANT
Sana'a, City Center
* Arabic, European &
typical Yemeni food
* Special farewell dinner party
for groups
Tel: 205 899

AL-MAMOON RENT A CAR

4WD cars, private cars, buses
With or without drivers
Tel: 242008-256273

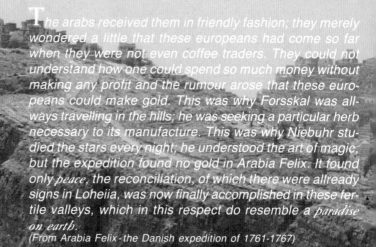

The arabs received them in friendly fashion; they merely wondered a little that these europeans had come so far when they were not even coffee traders. They could not understand how one could spend so much money without making any profit and the rumour arose that these europeans could make gold. This was why Forsskal was allways travelling in the hills; he was seeking a particular herb necessary to its manufacture. This was why Niebuhr studied the stars every night; he understood the art of magic, but the expedition found no gold in Arabia Felix. It found only *peace*, the reconciliation, of which there were allready signs in Loheiia, was now finally accomplished in these fertile valleys, which in this respect do resemble a *paradise on earth*.

(From Arabia Felix - the Danish expedition of 1761-1767)

FOOD DIGEST

WHERE AND WHAT TO EAT

Culinary delights are hard to come by in Yemen. Lunch is taken quickly so that one can get on to more important things such as *qat*. Since *qat* also diminishes the appetite, many Yemenis don't have any dinner.

The national dish in Yemen is probably *selter*, a steaming hot, bubbling concoction with a gravy. Another dish, which is eaten at every meal, is called *chops*, which is a delicacy when it is served fresh from the oven. When it's half a day old, however, it rather resembles an old tough rag. *Shafut*, a cold dish made from sour milk with various spices, is refreshing. Meat, mostly mutton, is only served on special occasions. You can, however, find *digag*, chicken, being grilled at the entrance to each restaurant.

We cannot give special recommendations for any restaurants apart from the hotels Sheraton, Taj-Sheba, Ramada and Dar al-Hamd.

DRINKING NOTES

Qishr and *bun* are very popular drinks. The first is a drink made from roasted coffee husks prepared with cardamom and other spices. *Bun* is coffee prepared in the traditional Arab manner. Mineral water, which can be bought everywhere, is of particularly good quality.

THINGS TO DO

COUNTRY

If you want to get to know the country better and get away from Sana'a, it is a good idea to find a local tour organiser. Hire knowledgeable local drivers who can show you the towns and places which are difficult to reach by public transport.

What makes independent travelling so difficult is the dearth of suitable accommodation. In the main season, particularly around Christmas, the hotels that would be suitable are hopelessly overbooked by tour operators. So the problem is often not so much getting there than finding a place to sleep when you've arrived.

SANA'A

Yemen Tourism Company, PO Box 1526. Tel: 240372.
Yata, PO Box 1153. Tel: 224236/77, fax: 251597, telex: 2326.
Qahwash Travel and Tourism, PO Box 1255. Tel: 240909.
Universal Travel and Tourism, PO Box 1047. Tel: 275028.
Al Mamoon Travel and Tourism, PO Box 10127. Tel: 79261.
ABM Tours, PO Box 10420. Tel: 270856/7, fax: 274106, telex 3253.
Marib Travel and Tourism, PO Box 161. Tel: 272432/5/6, fax: 274199, telex: 2243.

Rent-a-car:
Al Mamoon. Tel: 242008.
Haddah Car Hire. Tel: 240237.

ADEN

Arabia Felix Tourist, PO Box 6233, PDRY. Telex 2319.
Yemen Tourism Corporation, PO Box 1419, PDRY. Telex: 2348

CULTURE PLUS

MUSEUMS

The National Museum and the Military Museum in Sana'a are very close to At-Tahrir Square. In Ta'izz, the museum in the old Imam's Palace and one in the Salah Palace are worth visiting. There is also a small museum in the town by Yarim Zafar.

In Aden, the National Museum and Military Museum are both in the district of Tawahi. There is also a small museum in the Sultan's Palace in Seyun, although its opening hours are pretty irregular. And in Mukalla, there is a small museum attached to the Sultan's Palace that can be visited in the morning.

GALLERIES

The only art gallery in Sana'a at the moment is the **No.1 Gallery** of probably the best-known Yemeni modern artist, Foad al-Futah. It is situated in the Samsarat Abu Nawas, a large caravanserai restored with Norwegian financial aid. A number of other artists also have their studios here. The National Museum has a small exhibition of contemporary paintings on the first floor.

EVENTS

Cultural life in terms of theatres etc. is limited to events at the foreign embassies in Sana'a. The various programmes can be found out from them. There are a number of cinemas in Sana'a, which show only Arab soap operas.

SPORTS

The big hotels Sheba and Sheraton in Sana'a, and the Aden Hotel in Aden each have a fitness club with sauna, whirlpool, swimming pool and fitness centre; the Sheraton and the Aden Hotel have tennis courts.

PHOTOGRAPHY

A strong warning: don't take photos of women or girls without their permission, otherwise it could provoke unpleasant situations – fights, police intervention, confiscation of the camera. There are enough other lovely sights to photograph in Yemen.

Films, particularly Kodacolor and Ektachrome films are available in almost all photographic shops in Sana'a. The processing labs are not recommended, since they tend not to be very careful (example, scratched negatives).

Film and video cameras are marked in the passport; sometimes video cassettes will be checked at the airport.

USEFUL ADDRESSES

EMBASSIES IN SANA'A

Algeria, Ring Road al-Safiya al-Ghabiya, Haddah, PO Box 509. Tel: 247755-6.
China, Zubayri Street, PO Box 482. Tel: 275337.
Czechoslovakia, Satia South West. Tel: 247946.
Federal Republic of Germany, Haddah Road (opposite the Haddah Cinema Complex), PO Box 4. Tel: 216756-7.
France, Gamal Abdul Nasser Street, PO Box 1286. Tel: 275995.
Great Britain, Haddah Road, PO Box 1267. Tel: 215629-30.
India, Zubayri Street, PO Box 1154. Tel: 241980.
Italy, Gamal Abdul Nasser Street, PO Box 489. Tel: 73409/78849.
Japan, Al-Safiya al Gharbiya, Ring Road, PO Box 817. Tel: 207356.
Kuwait, Haddah Road, PO Box 17036. Tel: 216317.
Netherlands, Chancery: Near Haddah Road by the Kuwaiti Real State Building, PO Box 463. Tel: 215626-28.
Oman, Haddah Road, PO Box 105. Tel: 208933/4.
Saudi Arabia, Haddah Road, PO Box 1184. Tel: 240429-31.
CIS, 26 September Road, PO Box 1087. Tel: 78272.
United Arab Emirate, Haddah Road, PO Box 2250. Tel: 248777/8.
United States of America, 26 September Road, Al-Halali Building, PO Box 1088. Tel: 238842/52.

EMBASSIES OF THE REPUBLIC OF YEMEN ABROAD

Czechoslovakia, Washingtonova 17, Prague 1. Tel: (2) 222411.
Federal Republic of Germany, 5300 Bonn, Adenauer Allee 77. Tel: (0228) 376851-4.
France, 75007 Paris, 21, Avenue Charles Floquet. Tel: (1) 43 06 66 22.
Great Britain, 41 South Street, London Wl. Tel: (71) 4914003/629, 9905-8.
India, New Delhi, B-55 Pashami Marg, Vassant, Vihar. Tel: (11) 674742-3
Italy, 00161 Roma, Via Verona 3. Tel: (6) 4270281, 4270811.
Japan, 38, Kowa Building Room 807, 12-24, Nishi-Azabu-4-Chome, Minato-Ku, Tokyo. Tel: 499-7151-2

Netherlands, 2414 GC The Hague, Noordeinde 41
Tel: (070) 653936-7.
Oman, Muscat, 16, Alqarm-Villa 52. Tel: 696966.
Saudi Arabia, Jeddah, 84, al-Burace Street, Mecca
Road, PO Box 2793. Tel: (2) 6873934; Riyadh,
South of Oroba Street. Tel: (1) 4642077
CIS, Moscow, 2 Neopalimovskii Per 6.
Tel: (95) 2461814.
Switzerland, Geneva, 19, Chemin deu Jonc, 1216
Cointrin, Geneva. Tel: (22) 284921-3.
United States of America, New York, 747 Third
Avenue 8th Floor. Tel: (212) 355-3355; Washing-
ton, 600 New Hampshire Avenue, NW, Suite 840.
Tel: (202) 965-4760.

ART/PHOTO CREDITS

INDEX

A